★ A CIA ★
ANALYST'S GUIDE
TO SPOTTING
FAKE
NEWS

TRUE OR FALSE

CINDY L. OTIS

FEIWEL and FRIENDS
New York

A FEIWEL AND FRIENDS BOOK
An imprint of Macmillan Publishing Group, LLC
120 Broadway, New York, NY 10271

Photos on p. 14 by Daniel Csorfoly, p. 21 by Peter Heeling, Wikimedia Commons. Images
on pp. 25, 31, 67, 68, 224 Wikimedia Commons. Images on pp. 39, 50, 54, 71 Library of
Congress. Images on pp. 247-249 courtesy of the author, edited by Raphael Geroni.
Screenshots of Shelly LaMonica, Holly West, Tasman Kekai social media pages used with
permission.

Our books may be purchased in bulk for promotional, educational, or business use. Please
contact your local bookseller or the Macmillan Corporate and
Premium Sales Department at (800) 221-7945 ext. 5442 or by email at
MacmillanSpecialMarkets@macmillan.com.

Library of Congress Cataloging-in-Publication Data
Names: Otis, Cindy L., author.
Title: True or false : a CIA analyst's guide to spotting fake news / Cindy L. Otis.
Description: First edition. | New York : Feiwel & Friends, 2020. | Includes bibliographical
references. | Audience: Ages 13–18 | Audience: Grades 10–12 | Summary: "A YA Nonfiction
book about the history of Fake News and tips for how to spot it"—Provided by publisher.
Identifiers: LCCN 2019036127 | ISBN 9781250239495 (hardcover)
Subjects: LCSH: Fake news—Juvenile literature. | Fake news—United States—
Juvenile literature. | Media literacy—Juvenile literature.
Classification: LCC PN4784.F27 O85 2010 | DDC 070.4/3—dc23
LC record available at https://lccn.loc.gov/2019036127

Book design by RAPHAEL GERONI
Feiwel and Friends logo designed by FILOMENA TUOSTO

FIRST EDITION, 2020

1 3 5 7 9 10 8 6 4 2

fiercereads.com

To Mom and Dad,

who are my favorite part about life.

And to my mentor and friend, Wade Jacoby,

who taught me it is always worth it

to ask why.

Table of Contents

PART II: HOW WE FIGHT BACK!

Introduction

I was twenty-three years old the first time I walked through the doors of the Central Intelligence Agency's headquarters in McLean, Virginia. The lobby at the main entrance reminded me a little of a museum. It had gray-and-white-checkered floors, rows of thick pillars, high ceilings, and in the center of the floor the giant granite CIA seal of an eagle, shield, and sixteen-pointed star. All I had been told was that a point of contact from the office I was going to work in would meet me in the lobby. I wasn't given a name or any kind of physical description of said person. At the time, the lack of details had felt deliciously spy-like. But it became instantly terrifying the moment I arrived and found absolutely no one waiting for me at the entrance.

I had expected the lobby to be full of people rushing about doing important things, but it was utterly silent and completely empty, except for a guard at a small desk. A million doubts swam through my mind, and I froze in front of the seal. *Am I really supposed to be here? What if I got the date wrong or went to the wrong entrance? What if no one is coming for me, because they've changed their mind about hiring me, and this is their way of letting me know?*

I took a shaky breath to work up the courage to approach the guard.

"Hi, uh, someone is supposed to meet me here at nine o'clock, but I don't know their name or where they're coming from, but I was told someone would be here and this is my first time here . . ." The words tumbled out in an embarrassing rush, my voice at a squeaky pitch I wasn't sure it had ever reached before.

"Do you have a phone number for them? I can call them," he said. His hand reached for the phone.

"Oh gosh, no, I don't." The situation was feeling more hopeless by the second.

The guard smiled. "No problem. You can just wait here for them. Feel free to look around in the meantime, if you want."

I felt myself relax a little. If he wasn't worried that no one had arrived to collect me yet, I guessed I shouldn't be either. It was the CIA, after all. Perhaps no one knew anyone's names.

I had wanted to work for the CIA almost my whole life. I had finally made it, but couldn't quite believe it now that I was actually here. It hit me then that I would never again have a first day at the CIA, so I decided to take the guard's advice and wander a bit. On the right side of the room, there was a wall of stars chiseled into the marble, one for each CIA officer who had lost their life in the service of their country. On the left, a fourteen-foot-tall bronze statue of the man largely considered to be the founding father of the CIA, William "Wild Bill" Donovan, loomed over the lobby. I crossed the room and stood transfixed, staring up at the man I'd only ever read about in history books. Next to him, there was a single star on the wall to honor all the people who'd died while serving under the CIA's predecessor, the Office of Strategic Services.

I was about to head back to the seal to wait when something caught the corner of my eye. It was a sentence, high up on a wall of white marble, carved in large capital letters:

AND YE SHALL KNOW THE TRUTH AND
THE TRUTH SHALL MAKE YOU FREE.
JOHN VIII–XXXII

I recognized the Bible verse, but something felt different about reading it again at the CIA, though I wasn't quite sure why. I was too busy processing the words to notice a person approaching until she was standing next to me.

"Hi, you must be Cindy," the woman said.

She introduced herself and I shook her hand, perhaps, in my relief, a little more enthusiastically than I normally would have. For a moment, my eyes flickered back to the verse on the wall. The woman followed my gaze.

"It's our motto, and it guides our work here every day," she explained before waving for me to follow her.

As we passed through the lobby together, I couldn't help it. "This place is so cool," I breathed.

The corners of her mouth turned up in a small smile. "Yes, I suppose it is."

I would like to be able to tell you my job there as an intelligence analyst was like being the American version of James Bond, if only because it sounds really exciting. Hollywood's depiction of the spy life involves a lot of blowing things up and daring fistfights with villains on top of moving vehicles. My job was not like that. But still, it was, as I had predicted that first day, "so cool," because the heart of the job was important—I was discovering the truth.

As an intelligence analyst at the CIA, I was responsible for keeping senior American government officials informed about current, fast-moving events happening all around the world. I looked at things like wars in other countries, terrorist attacks, and what policies foreign governments were making that might affect the US. To do this, I had to comb through information, or intelligence, that constantly poured in from many kinds of sources every single day. Some of that intelligence was from "human assets" in other countries (people the CIA has recruited to collect information) or from satellite imagery or electronically gathered information, like intercepted emails and phone calls.

But some of our biggest sources of information came from things anyone could find online, like news reports, academic studies, and even social media. Maybe that comes as a surprise, but think about it—people put their whole lives on the internet. Foreign politicians have social media accounts where they post about what they are doing or where they are going, governments publish reports about their work, and investigative journalists constantly publish breaking news stories about events all over the world faster than most intelligence collection platforms can pick up and process the information.

With all that information available to analysts, collecting intelligence is a little like fishing sometimes. We cast our line into the water and hope that eventually we will feel a tug at the end of it. That tug might be an actual fish—that is certainly what you're hoping to catch—but in some cases it might turn out to be a plastic bag, or maybe it's a tin can someone intentionally dropped into the water that found its way onto our hook. All this garbage makes it difficult for analysts to figure out what is real and what isn't.

So, what's the garbage we pull out of the water? Some of it is lies and deceptions from a government trying to hide what it is really doing, or false information that governments, groups, or individuals put out to try to influence people's opinions. Some of it is news that has been intentionally sensationalized in an effort to attract more readers, but that has lost some of its accuracy in the process. Other times it is a joke or a prank a person or group is trying to pass off as true. If I had to put all these pieces of information garbage under one umbrella term, it would be this: fake news.

This is a term you have probably heard a lot in the last few years, but it's not a new phenomenon. Fake news has gone by many different names in the past. Yellow journalism, propaganda, junk news, tabloid journalism, disinformation, and hoaxes can all be considered a part of fake news. All these terms have the same basic definition at their core: an attempt to deliberately spread inaccurate or false information in order to mislead others, presenting it in a way that makes people likely to believe it to be true.[1]

Let me be really clear right up front about something. Fake news is not the actual news media. Fake news does not include reporters working hard to bring you accurate information each day. Fake news is not when media outlets report something you disagree with. It also is not when they report something that ends up being wrong. News is gathered by journalists, and journalists are human. Their job is thankless and hard, and sometimes they get it wrong. The difference between that and fake news is their intent. Legitimate media is trying to inform you. Fake news is trying to deceive you.

Now, if collecting intelligence is like fishing, then being an intelligence analyst is kind of like trying to put together a puzzle with whatever you fished out of the water, garbage (or fake news) included. Analysts have to weigh all the information we receive to figure out what, if any of it, is reliable and accurate. That's why we are trained from the first day on the job to look at information critically. Analysts can't afford to be wrong when national security is at stake.

They also can't let their opinions, political views, or personal biases influence their analysis. In fact, the CIA headquarters is not even in Washington, DC, where most of the major government agencies have offices. It is quite intentionally set in a forest on the other side of the river in Virginia, miles away from Congress, the White House, and other political officials. The idea when construction began on the building in the late 1950s was that the CIA needed to be able to do its work in an unbiased way without the influence of politicians trying to push for a certain outcome, and that meant keeping the two worlds physically separate.

What does any of this have to do with me? you might be asking. *I'm not protecting national security.* You might not have access to super TOP SECRET classified intelligence like a CIA analyst does, but you're constantly learning new information and having to decide what you think about it. You probably spend a lot of time online, right? You watch videos on YouTube or follow your family and friends on social media. Maybe your aunt likes to post a lot of news articles about politics. Your friend might really be into memes. Maybe you like to skim through websites like BuzzFeed. And then there's school. You constantly have to look up stuff online for homework, papers, and tests. Your teachers always tell you to cite your sources in your papers, and there's so much stuff to sift through. If you stopped to think about it, you'd realize you're basically standing under a showerhead of information all day, every day. It doesn't stop, and it's a lot.

With so much material being thrown at you, it can be difficult to know what is true and what is false. Through this book, I'm going to give you the same knowledge and tools I learned as an analyst so that you too can avoid becoming a victim of fake news. I hope to show you how to think critically about what you observe, how to ask questions, and ways to better analyze what you are reading and seeing. Because the truth is: Fake news isn't going away, and in fact it's only going to get worse. It is up to all of us to make sure we are each doing our part to fight it.

By the end of this, you will be able to spot fake news like a CIA analyst. Next stop: McLean, Virginia!

PART I

THE HISTORY OF FAKE NEWS

In times of universal deceit,
telling the truth will be a
revolutionary act.

—GEORGE ORWELL (Maybe)*

*This quote is widely attributed to Orwell, however
it never appears in any of his writings.

SECTION 1

Fake News Has Been Around a Lot Longer Than You Think

CHAPTER 1

THE IMPACT OF
FAKE NEWS

I**T WAS ALMOST FOUR A.M. AND STILL DARK**
out when two men on their way to work in the local markets
found a woman lying unconscious in the street between a warehouse and a row of houses in London's East End. There was only one
oil lamp lit nearby, so they could not see the blood pooling under her.
She might have been drunk and simply passed out, they thought. It
would certainly not be the first time that had happened in the neighborhood known as Whitechapel. After all, it was August 31, 1888, and
that part of London was filled with brothels, crime, overcrowding, and
drunks.[1] But something did not look quite right about this woman,
so the men hurried off to find a policeman. They had no idea they
had just stumbled upon the work of one of the most notorious serial
killers in the world.

The policeman on duty, Constable John Neil, had witnessed his
fair share of grisly crimes, so when he got to the scene, he could tell
right away—the woman had been murdered. This was not the first

murder to hit the area, not even close. Women in the East End were often targets of violent crimes, and the police already had more ongoing investigations than they could manage. But this victim had been murdered in a way that shocked and horrified the police and local residents alike. The PG-13 version is that the killer slit the woman's throat and mutilated her body, mostly by cutting out her internal organs like he was conducting some kind of nasty science experiment. It was the work of a monster.

The unfortunate woman, the police discovered, was forty-three-year-old Mary Ann Nichols, or "Polly" to those who knew her. Polly was an alcoholic and had had a hard time keeping a job. She had been living on and off the streets since separating from her husband years before. In her desperation to afford a place to stay, she had turned to prostitution. It had not been hard for the police to identify Polly, but tracking down her killer was another matter.

Constable Neil had patrolled the very same area where Polly had been found just a few minutes before the men stumbled upon her body. How had he not heard the inevitable scream or at least come across the killer mid-butchery? The police were baffled. With how quickly he had committed his crime, it almost seemed like the killer was a phantom.

Meanwhile, wild rumors quickly spread across London by word of mouth and in newspapers. Local residents came forward in droves to tell the police what they knew about the crime, which was not much, and they all seemed to have different accounts. One local said they had seen a deranged-looking man with a knife in the area the same day as the murder. Another said they had seen Polly talking to a man with a foreign accent on the street earlier in the day. But these tips all led the police to dead ends.

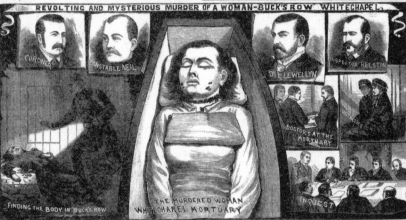

The front page of the *Illustrated Police News* on September 8, 1888, depicting the death of Mary Ann "Polly" Nichols[2]

Eight days after Polly's murder, the killer struck again less than half a mile away from the original crime scene. The new victim, forty-seven-year-old Annie Chapman, was found mutilated like Polly was, but at the back of a boarding house. Chapman had a similar story of drinking heavily and turning to prostitution to pay for her room and board. It was official: London had a serial killer on its hands, and he had a target. The newspapers, meanwhile, had their next big story—a shadowy demon on the hunt for his next victim.[3]

The gruesome tales of the killer's butchery and his poor victims did not just grip all of England; they created a frenzy all over the world. "London lies today under the spell of a great terror. A nameless reprobate—half beast, half man—is at large, who is daily gratifying his murderous instincts on the most miserable and defenceless of classes of the community," the *Star* newspaper reported after Chapman's murder. Fathers and husbands refused to let their wives, daughters, and sisters out after dark. The police increased their patrols in Whitechapel to look for the murderer. People lined up to buy newspapers to read about new developments in the police investigation and the grisly details of the latest murder. The newspapers did not hold back any of the details and often included faceless, frightening sketches of the mass murderer, which haunted people's dreams, even though no one had actually ever seen him. The more graphic their articles were, the more newspapers they sold, and that meant that profits soared. Readers simply could not get enough of any of it.

Some regional newspapers even started printing special short bulletins to keep readers up to date with the latest information. But these newspapers quickly ran into a problem. The more they wrote, the less new information they had to report. They tried to get the police to tell them more about their investigation. When that did not work, some journalists came up with a solution: fake news.

Many people said that the murders were too gruesome for an Englishman to have committed. There was a significant undercurrent of racism across Europe, and London was a hotbed of anti-Semitism and anti-immigration sentiment. Local sex workers told investigators that there was a Jewish immigrant from Poland nicknamed "Leather Apron." They said he kept several knives in his shop that could have easily done the job, and that he frequently walked around the East End threatening to "rip open" and murder them if they did not give him money. Another woman claimed to have seen Chapman with a man before she was murdered, and said he had a "foreign appearance," even though she admitted she'd only seen him from the back. But the theories gained the attention of the police, and they turned their attention to the immigrant community.

Soon many newspapers were reporting that this man had "Jewish features" and even drew racist caricatures of the supposed killer.[4] A piece of leather had been found at the scene of Annie Chapman's murder, and the *Star* seized on it and reported that the killer was the Jewish bootmaker, without any evidence other than the fact that the man wore a leather apron for his work, as most bootmakers did back then. The police arrested the man, but released him shortly afterward, as he had airtight alibis during the murders.[5]

Meanwhile, letters poured into newspapers and police stations from all over the country with tips, advice, and speculation. Some were from people who genuinely thought they could help with the investigation. Some letter writers claimed that they had spotted the infamous killer lurking in the shadows all over London, or that their neighbors were a bit sketchy and might be worth investigating.

25. Sept. 1888.

Dear Boss

     I keep on hearing the police have caught me. but they wont fix me just yet. I have laughed when they look so clever and talk about being on the right track. That joke about Leather apron gave me real fits. I am down on whores and I shant quit ripping them till I do get buckled. Grand work the last job was. I gave the lady no time to squeal How can they catch me now. I love my work and want to start again. You will soon hear of me with my funny little games. I saved some of the proper red stuff in a ginger beer bottle over the last job to write with but it went thick like glue and I cant use it. Red ink is fit enough I hope ha. ha. The next job I do I shall clip the ladys ears off and send to the police officers just for jolly wouldnt you. Keep this letter back till I do a bit more work. then give it out straight My knife's so nice and sharp I want to get to work right away if I get a chance. Good luck.

yours truly

Jack the Ripper

Dont mind me giving the trade nam

wasnt good enough to post this before I got all the red ink off my hands curse it No luck yet. They say I'm a doctor now ha ha

Others shared their theories that the killer seemed to have some tragic history with his mother that had led him to seek revenge, since both his victims were women. Some thought the killer had to be a surgeon or a doctor of some kind, because of the way he liked to disembowel his victims. The newspapers reported it all equally, rumors and speculation as much as actual facts, and without distinguishing between them.[6] Reporters even joined in on the guessing game, printing sketches of known police suspects.

But in late September, a different kind of letter was delivered to the Central News Agency in London, and it was written in bloodred ink. "Dear Boss," the letter, postmarked September 25, read. "I keep on hearing the police have caught me but they won't fix me just yet.... Grand work the last job was. I gave the lady no time to squeal. How can they catch me now. I love my work and want to start again." The author of the letter promised the police he would be striking again soon and that they would know it was him because he planned to cut his next victim's ears off. A little killer calling card, if you will. The letter was signed "Jack the Ripper."[7] Now the killer had a name.

The newspaper almost discounted the letter as a hoax, but something about this one seemed different to the reporters. And they were right. They delivered the letter to the police the same day that Jack the Ripper struck again, this time killing two women within an hour of each other. He kept his promise to take an ear.

The rumor mill began again. Some locals reported seeing a fair-haired man with the second woman before her death, and soon after, a bloody apron was found in front of an apartment building near the area. There was graffiti on the wall behind the apron that mentioned Jews. Graffiti was common on buildings back then, as it is now, but without knowing when the writing had been made, who actually did it, or if it was at all tied to the murder, newspapers and their readers latched onto the idea that it was written by the killer himself. They were certain then that the killer was Jewish.[9] The rise in anti-Semitism spurred on by the newspaper coverage led to anti-Semitic demonstrations in London and violence against the Jewish community.

Between August and November, a period dubbed the Autumn of Terror, Jack the Ripper killed at least five women in all. But even after the killings stopped, some reporters continued connecting murders to Jack the Ripper, even years later and even when the method of killing did not quite fit his particular style of butchery. It was a way to keep the intrigue going. As a result, his tale cast a shadow over London for a long time.[10]

Jack the Ripper was never caught. Over time, more than one hundred people have been listed as possible suspects, including the police investigators working on the case, a Russian doctor who worked in a London maternity ward, and even the son of England's own Queen Victoria. For a decade after, London police and the media received more than a thousand letters claiming to be from Jack the Ripper. Each time there was a letter, it became front-page news and public speculation began all over again on Jack the Ripper's identity. Most of the letters are believed to be fakes, and here's the real kicker: It was discovered many years later that some of them had actually been written by a journalist from the Central News Agency, the same news organization that received the first letter from Jack the Ripper, trying to make a splash on what would have otherwise been a slow news day.[11]

Today, Jack the Ripper still occasionally appears in newspapers, as hobby investigators, forensic scientists, and historians try to piece together one of the world's most notorious unsolved murder mysteries. It is worth spending a bit more time dissecting (yes, I went there) the impact the news media had in fanning global hysteria and racism, and ultimately how those things helped create Jack the Ripper's lasting legacy. Even though the media had a responsibility to report on topics of interest to the public, it is clear from the ways newspapers manipulated the facts in their stories, spun up conspiracy theories, and built on existing anti-Semitism that their main concern was making money.[12] They reported every rumor the same way they reported facts, without telling the readers what was speculation and what was known to be true. In that day, reporters did not have the same journalistic standards that they have now, and sensationalism sold papers. Things like verifying claims before publishing a story were not considered necessary.

Historians mostly agree that one person was responsible for the five murders between August and November 1888, but the sheer amount of fake news, hoaxes, and contradictory media reports from the time period has made it impossible to know who else might have been his victim. As a result, to this day we do not know for sure how many people he killed.

But, more importantly, these false reports had a more immediate impact on the situation. They may have distracted the police from pursuing credible leads. When the media turned to point the blame at the Jewish community, so too did the police, even when it was clear there was no evidence the killer was Jewish. Fake news could very well be one of the reasons why he was never caught and his identity remains a mystery to this day.

As we often see today, the hotter an issue is—whether it is a topic or an event—the more people talk about it and newspapers write about it. Everyone wants in on the conversation. But that can make it difficult to find the truth amid all the noise. The spiral of fake news around Jack the Ripper was not a rare incident, nor was it the first. Fake news has been a problem a lot longer than that. So, to really understand how widespread fake news is, we have to go back to the very beginning. Okay, not the *very* beginning—we don't need to go as far back as the first ancient cave paintings found in France and Spain. But almost.

CHAPTER 2

THE BEGINNING OF FAKE NEWS

RAMSES II, THE YOUNG PHARAOH OF EGYPT, looked out from his chariot over a sea of his enemies. More than 2,500 horse-drawn chariots surrounded him, three soldiers in every one. Just moments before, the Hittite army had launched a surprise attack on his camp, and Ramses had watched with a sinking heart as his own troops ran away, leaving their commander in chief to face death alone.

It was 1274 BCE, and Ramses had learned weeks before that the Hittites were planning to invade the city of Kadesh, an important trading route near what is now modern Syria. He had quickly called up his army and set about to claim Kadesh for himself. After all, as a descendant of the gods, he was responsible for protecting his people. Ramses had spent years fighting the Hittites and other empires for control over the Near East, and the pharaoh was known far and wide for his many victories and his military prowess. But now, with the Hittites ready to pulverize him, things looked pretty hopeless, and he wondered if rushing to Kadesh had been a good idea after all.

Feeling his courage falter, Ramses raised his head to the sky and asked the gods if they were really going to just stand by and watch him get slaughtered:

> *Father Ammon, where are you?*
> *Shall a sire forget his son?*
> *Is there anything without your knowledge I have done?*
> *From the judgments of your mouth when have I gone?*
> *Have I e'er transgressed your word?*
> *Disobeyed, or broke a vow?*
> *Is it right, who rules in Egypt, Egypt's lord,*
> *Should e'er before the foreign peoples bow,*
> *Or own their rod?*[1]

As he spoke, the pharaoh could feel the power of Ra, the sun god, and Baal, the thunder god, flow through him. Ramses knew one thing then—he could not let Kadesh fall to his enemies. He raised his spear in his left hand and his sword in his right, and, with a loud cry, drove his chariot straight through the middle of the Hittites. The Hittite soldiers were stunned as they watched the mighty pharaoh transform into a god before their very eyes. They dropped their spears and bows and were dashed into pieces under the feet of his horses.

Ramses returned home having single-handedly destroyed the Hittite army and claiming rightful ownership of Kadesh.[2] He had the story of his great victory carved onto his royal monuments and temples all over Egypt so his bravery could be properly immortalized.[3] But temples did not exactly travel easily, and *all* his subjects deserved to hear the tale, so he had a poem about the battle, called the Poem of Pentaur, written on thick papyrus. He then dispatched royal messengers to every town and village in the empire with a copy of the poem in order to spread the story of his courage and strength.[4]

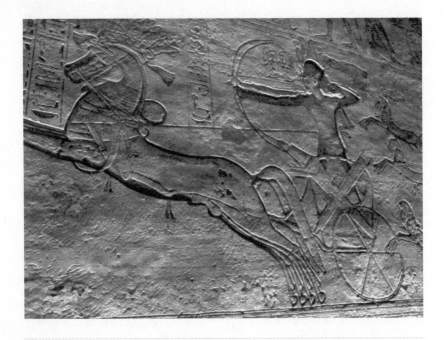

Relief of Ramses II at the Battle of Kadesh in the Great Temple of Abu Simbel in modern-day Egypt

For hundreds of years afterward, historians believed that the battle between Ramses and the Hittites occurred more or less the way the poem described (without the whole transforming-into-a-god thing, of course, but including the Egyptian victory). It was the only record they had to go on. That is, until they discovered more than a hundred private letters Ramses II and his Hittite counterpart, Hattusili III, sent each other after the pharaoh's supposed victory.[5] If we were to translate one of the letters Hattusili III wrote to Ramses about the battle into 2020 English, he basically asked: "Dude, why do you keep lying about what went down in Kadesh?"

Here is what really happened. When Ramses II heard the Hittites were on the move, he left for Kadesh with twenty thousand soldiers. They were slow moving, and Ramses was anxious to get to the fight. On the way, the pharaoh's soldiers captured two local tribesmen and brought them in front of Ramses. The tribesmen flattered and praised the young pharaoh and told him the Hittite army was still hundreds of miles away from Kadesh. They reassured him it would be an easy victory for him. Emboldened by the information, Ramses II broke off from the rest of his army and headed for Kadesh to take the city. He brought only a small force with him for his protection—he thought he was in for the kind of easy victory that involves being the first one there and claiming it. Little did he know, the men Ramses thought were tribesmen were actually Hittite spies who had purposefully gotten caught so they could feed him false intelligence.

When Ramses and his small contingent arrived, they found that the Hittite army was already there, chariots and all. The Poem of Pentaur was right on one count—most of Ramses's soldiers were not with him that day. But that was a result of his own overconfidence. The young pharaoh and his men probably would have been slaughtered if the Egyptian army had not swooped in and saved them at the last minute. Still, the Egyptians had to retreat without taking over Kadesh. Ramses II got out of the fight alive, but the battle was hardly a victory for the Egyptians, and there were huge casualties on both sides.[6] Later, Ramses and Hattusili III signed what is believed to be the world's first peace treaty, even though the pharaoh continued to claim victory.

Ramses's self-promoting fake news story is not all that out of the ordinary. Much of the ancient history we study today was written, or at least dictated, by the same people who were in power, so they controlled what got recorded and how their histories were told. But the ruler isn't always the person with the power to spin the story. Centuries later, Roman Emperor Justinian found that out the hard way, or at least his ghost did.

THE DEMONIC RULERS OF CONSTANTINOPLE

JUSTINIAN MAY HAVE BEEN BORN INTO A PEASANT family in 482 CE, but he sure was lucky with his extended family—his uncle Justin was the Eastern Roman emperor. Justin adopted Justinian and brought him to Constantinople (now called Istanbul) to receive an education in order to replace him someday. As his uncle aged, Justinian took on more and more responsibilities, until he was practically already running the empire, and he loved every moment of it. Justinian had a vision for the empire and was singularly focused on making it come true. That is, until he met Theodora in 522 CE.

Theodora had lived on and off the streets before winding up working as a courtesan in a burlesque theater.[7] Theodora was a relatively small woman with eyes that stopped Justinian in his tracks. She was about twenty years younger than him and beautiful. But there was something else he sensed about her—a natural intelligence and strong will that would make her a perfect partner for a future emperor. Justinian was smitten. As a courtesan, Theodora was from an entirely different social class (the lowest one, in fact), and legally, they were not allowed to marry. But there are perks to being in charge. Theodora became his mistress, and eventually Justinian changed the law so they could get married.

In 527 CE, Justinian and Theodora became the Holy Roman emperor and empress. They ran the empire like true partners. Justinian's goal as emperor was to restore the greatness of the Roman Empire by taking back the western part of it (including what would become Italy, England, France, Spain, and parts of Northern Africa), which had been lost to rival empires in previous years. That meant launching new wars. Lots and lots of wars. Theodora, on the other hand, thought they should focus on matters closer to home in the east. But she still supported Justinian through all his military campaigns. At the same time, Justinian worked to completely overhaul the empire's legal system and created rights to protect women and children from crimes. He also became increasingly religious throughout his reign and was an active participant in theological discussions about the future of Christianity. Justinian worked so hard that he came to be known as "the emperor who never sleeps."[8]

But Justinian and Theodora's rule was not exactly a smooth ride. For starters, the aristocracy constantly whispered, quietly and not so quietly, about Theodora. Most people did not believe someone of her low-born class deserved to be an empress. They also thought that she was too outspoken for a woman. There were a couple of attempts by Justinian's rivals to take his throne from him, and violent riots in 532 CE burned down half of Constantinople and led to tens of thousands of deaths. In 541 CE, Justinian contracted the plague when the disease swept through the empire. He survived, but the pandemic killed a quarter of the population. Okay, so his reign was not smooth *at all*.

So much happened during Justinian's rule that he appointed the scholar Procopius of Caesarea to be the court historian and document it all. Procopius wrote eight books about the Roman Empire and

Justinian's wars in Africa, Persia, and Italy. Procopius often traveled with the Roman military to give firsthand accounts of the battles and to write about military leaders, kind of like the war correspondents who report news from the front lines on the news today. In one of his earlier books, Procopius wrote admiringly of Theodora when she gave an impassioned speech to buck up Justinian's courage during the violent riots of 532 CE. Justinian wanted to flee Constantinople, but Theodora convinced him to stay and defend his rule, which he ended up doing successfully.

But several years after Justinian died, Procopius wrote a different kind of book. It was a lengthy treatise called *The Secret History*. This book painted a very different picture of Justinian and Theodora from any of his other histories.[9] In fact, it reads a lot like a tabloid magazine. His view of Justinian was mixed. On the one hand, Procopius said he had a "tranquil" manner and that he was approachable, willing to have long conversations with anyone from any class. On the other hand, Procopius said that Justinian and Theodora had secretly plotted to ruin the empire. Sections of Procopius's treatise include such subheadings as "How Justinian Killed a Trillion People" and "Proving That Justinian and Theodora Were Actually Fiends in Human Form." In one part, Procopius said that Justinian was literally half demon:

> *It is said that Justinian's own mother told some of her close friends that he was not the son of her husband Sabbatius or of any man at all. For when she was about to conceive she was visited by a demon, who was invisible but gave her a distinct impression that he was really there with her like a man in bodily contact with a woman. Then he vanished like a dream.*

Some of those who were in the Emperor's company late at
night, conversing with him (evidently in the Palace)—
men of the highest possible character—thought that they
saw a strange demonic form in his place. One of them
declared that he more than once rose suddenly from the
imperial throne and walked round and round the room;
for he was not in the habit of remaining seated for long.
And Justinian's head would momentarily disappear,
while the rest of his body seemed to continue making
these long circuits.[10]

Now that would be a trick, right? Procopius continued, saying
that Justinian had contained so much supernatural evil that he had
caused plagues, earthquakes, and other natural disasters wherever
he went.

As for Theodora, Procopius did not hold back, taking the same
approach trolls on the internet today often take against their female
targets. He went after her morality and her looks, claiming she'd
slept with everyone in and out of the royal court and had had one
of her many lovers killed to hide their affair. If anyone did anything
to upset her, Procopius said, Theodora would make up fake charges
against them, handpick a jury to make sure they were condemned,
and then confiscate their property for herself.

There is a saying that "history is written by the victors." (The
quote is attributed to many different people, from former British
prime minister Winston Churchill to author George Orwell. Although
that too is fake news. No one really knows who said it.) But these two
cases show that is not really true.

For Ramses II, history was written by the loser of the battle who
happened to be the ruler at the time. Is it any wonder that he wanted
to make himself look good by embellishing or flat-out lying about

his success? When we look at information, it is important to think about whether there is motivation behind it. For example, Ramses did not only lie about how the battle turned out. He also lied about how he won—with the power of the gods. A pharaoh's rule was safest when his people believed he had the support of the gods, so it was in his best interest to convince his people that the gods were at his beck and call, ready to transfer their power to him when he needed it.

In the case of Justinian, at the end of the day the emperor was not the one telling the story of his rule. It was the historian who had the power. He was able to tarnish Justinian's reputation with fake news after Justinian was not around anymore to correct the record. Procopius's books are still the most comprehensive source of information historians have about the wars and Justinian's rule. But since his accounts of the time vary so wildly across his books, it is difficult for historians to figure out what really happened.[11] Some historians believe that Procopius wrote *The Secret History* to distance himself from the former emperor because the new emperor did not care for Justinian. Others think that he never intended to publish it—that it was a private rage diary, if you will. If we read his book knowing that he wrote it to try to minimize his connection to Justinian, we would probably assume not much in it is accurate. But if Procopius wrote it for himself without any other agenda, it starts to seem more credible.

History might not always be written by the victors, but the quote's larger point holds, no matter who actually said it. That is, we should always think about who is writing what and why. Fake news, at least, is usually written by people who have a motivation for doing so.

THE TALKING FAKE NEWS STATUES OF ROME. In Rome in the 1500s anonymous written messages started being posted on an ancient Roman statue. The messages included poems, stories, and true and fake criticisms of the monarchy, the aristocracy, and the Catholic Church.[12] It was like an early form of a neighborhood bulletin board or a WhatsApp message group. Locals started calling the statue Pasquino after a man by the same name who some historians believe worked as a tailor at the Vatican. He

would pick up the latest gossip and information about Catholic Church leaders and royals, and then return home to tell his friends and neighbors about it. The statue named after him became a similar source of information, except with handwritten anonymous messages. Romans started the tradition of collecting the best messages and compiling them into a book. Over the years, messages started appearing on other statues throughout Rome. It is a tradition that continues to this day.

The Pasquino statue in Rome

THE PRINTING PRESS

THE ABILITY TO PASS ALONG FAKE NEWS BACK in the day of Ramses II and Emperor Justinian was limited because people had few ways to send or receive communication. Most people then could not read or write. Stories and information, whether they were true or false, depended on individuals spreading them by word of mouth. News was often passed along by traders traveling between towns. But without widespread written communication and transportation options, there were serious geographical limitations to sharing things.

Few inventions changed the world like the invention of the printing press.[13] As cities grew and universities were established over the centuries, there was such a big demand for access to books that the natural solution was a machine that could mass produce them. It led to the birth of journalism, to economic growth, and to a boom in literacy rates, education, and, yes—fake news.[14]

Before the printing press, each book was handwritten and usually ornately illustrated, making every page one of a kind. Some books, like the Bible, could take a monk over a year to copy by hand, and there was no guarantee that they would do it without making mistakes or changing up the language just for fun. More and more monasteries and workshops were established throughout the Middle Ages to keep up with the demand for books and make them more affordable. But as a result of the labor that went into copying them, books were often still too expensive for the lower socioeconomic classes.[15]

A goldsmith named Johannes Gutenberg always gets the credit for inventing the printing press, but the first versions actually started to appear in China. The first known printed book was *The Diamond Sutra*, a Buddhist text, in 868 CE. These first presses invented in China required the printers to carve the letters of each page out before applying ink and pressing the paper onto it. It was okay if you wanted to print thousands of copies of a single page, but it was much harder and more time-consuming if you had multiple pages or different books.

It was not until approximately 1450 that Gutenberg's printing presses started cropping up in Europe. Gutenberg's press was the first in Europe to use what is called movable type: metal molds of each individual letter in the alphabet. Someone had to lay out every single letter in every single word by hand, but unlike the original printing presses, you could change the letters around. The printer would then press ink onto the letters. The Gutenberg press was a screw press in which the user set the sheet of paper on a thin board over the type and then lowered the sheet down until it pressed against the inked letters. Once they had a page set up, printers could make as many copies as they wanted until they ran out of paper and ink. It definitely beat waiting for monks to write down each line.

The printing press allowed people to produce books, pamphlets, and other printed materials in mass quantities, and all in one standard format. The very first book Gutenberg printed was the Bible in 1452. He printed 180 copies, and each one had 1,300 pages. In just fifty years after the Gutenberg printing press was invented, there were over a thousand presses in Europe and about five hundred thousand printed books.[16] (With the impact Gutenberg's press had on the world, it hardly seems fair that he died just a few years after inventing it, completely broke.) Some historians estimate that before the printing press, fewer than 25 percent of adults in Europe could read, but by the mid-1600s that rate had doubled, as more people had access to literature.

Before the printing press, the monarchy, the wealthy, and the church largely controlled what information people had and what was made public knowledge. (Spoiler alert: They were big fans of censorship.) But the printing press changed all that. It was like opening a floodgate, allowing new thoughts, ideas, and information to pour out to anyone, anywhere. With the invention of the printing press, reading and information became much more open to the common people, and that gave many people something they had never had before—a voice. And, as it turned out, people had a lot to say.

CHAPTER 3

FAKE NEWS
AND THE FRENCH
MONARCHY

I N 1610, KING HENRY IV OF FRANCE WAS ASSAS-
sinated. His son, Louis XIII, was only nine years old at the time,
so his mom, Marie de Médicis, became the regent of France.
Her job was to run the country until the young king was ready to
rule. But, over the years, Marie came to like having so much power,
and when Louis XIII was old enough to take his place on the throne,
she refused to step down.

To justify her decision to the people of France, Marie decided
she needed to spread some fake news. So she started the rumor
her son was "simple" and "too feeble" to rule.[1] The problem was,
Marie was easily manipulated by the people around her, including
her longtime friend's husband, Concino Concini, who Marie made
her chief adviser. The French nobles, whose support Marie needed
to keep her job, hated Concini, and they staged a revolt to protest

An oil painting of Marie de Médicis with her son Louis XIII,
painted by Charles Martin in 1603

Marie's regency. In 1617, when Louis was just sixteen years old, he
gathered his supporters, exiled his mother to a château in the middle of nowhere in France, had Concini killed, and took his rightful
place on the throne.

The château was not exactly a prison, but Marie itched to return to the excitement of court life in Paris, and more importantly, to get her position as regent back. After two years of isolation in the château, Marie staged a daring escape by climbing down a ladder and hiding out in a fortress in western France. From there, she launched a war of words against her son, printing pamphlets to convince people that Louis was immature and weak, and that France would be better under her rule.

PRINTED BOOKS WERE STILL QUITE EXPENSIVE TO PRINT AND TO BUY, SO PRINTED PAMPHLETS BECAME POPULAR. Pamphlets were printed on both sides of a single piece of large paper and then folded several times, making them anywhere from three to sixteen pages long, and sometimes longer. Thousands could be printed and circulated in just a few days.[2] They were also relatively cheap to print, making them a good way to spread information to the masses. This also meant that people could spread and amplify fake news to a degree they had never been able to before. People printed everything on pamphlets: opinions, criticisms, conspiracy theories, rumors, and wild stories and exaggerations. It was kind of like when blogs were really popular in the early 2000s— everyone had one and the internet was full of people's opinions and thoughts. Monarchies often used pamphlets to spread information about new laws and royal decrees. Thousands of pamphlets were printed each year. People went from having rulers restrict information to being absolutely inundated with it, even outside the major cities.[3] The problem was that people had no way to verify what was being circulated.

Marie's pamphlets did not always criticize her son directly. Often she went after him by targeting his best friend and main adviser, the Duke of Luynes. The duke was greedy, her pamphlets claimed, and he had brainwashed Louis into letting him run the country into ruin. Her pamphlets blamed the duke for everything going wrong in France, even after he was killed in a military campaign against the Protestants in 1621. Marie said Luynes was the reason she had been exiled and that he was keeping her—a devoted and loving mother—from her son. Her pamphlets made a compelling case, because the nobility of the French court were very jealous of anyone who had the king's attention. When the king started to show a preference for one person, the court instantly rushed to hate them.

Another part of Marie's strategy in her war of words against her son was that she had many of her letters to important nobles printed into pamphlets and distributed to the public. In them, Marie made her case for why she would be a better ruler. More importantly, she tugged on the readers' heartstrings by claiming she was the victim of her son's cruelty. Printing what was supposed to be private correspondence between France's most important people made readers believe her words even more. When Marie was able to start rallying troops and supporters to her side, she published yet more pamphlets saying it was simply her duty to protect her beloved country from evil forces. (Translation: This giant army I'm amassing to take power? Nothing to see here!)

Louis, understandably, hated Marie's pamphlets. He wrote to her saying so in a letter in 1619: "You could tell me what you think in a private interview without publishing it for the whole kingdom to read."[4] But he also had no intention of letting Marie near his court, so he responded with his own pamphlets. In fact, Louis published more than double the number of pamphlets Marie had—the equivalent of shouting over someone else to drown out their words. He took the tried-and-true approach used for many years before him of painting any powerful woman as both dangerous and incompetent.[5] His pamphlets called Marie an irrational, confused woman who was being manipulated by her selfish advisers, who preyed on her own mental weakness. He said she had abandoned her role as mother to pursue her selfish interests and asked, in his pamphlets, how she could be so cruel as to try to fight him. Louis also used the pamphlets to create an image of himself as a young and noble warrior king fighting for his God-given right to rule. Talk about family drama.

In all, Marie and Louis had about 3,300 pamphlets printed between the two of them during what is sometimes called "the war between mother and son." It was a massive number when you consider that the general population mostly still could not read.[6] In the end, Louis XIII's pamphlets were more persuasive, and Marie's supporters started switching sides. When their armies met on the battlefield in 1620, Marie lost. She eventually gave up her attempts to become regent and went back to live at the court in Paris.

The pamphlet wars between Marie and Louis XIII show us that fake news is most effective when it is written with certain audiences in mind. People are more likely to accept information that they already agree with. Louis's arguments were successful because they reinforced what many nobles already thought of Marie. The French court had always been suspicious of foreigners, and Marie was originally from Italy, so it was not difficult to paint her as an inappropriately power-hungry foreigner. His pamphlets also played to the gender stereotypes of the time—women as emotional, feeble creatures, and men as warriors. It was a winning message with the nobles, who were mostly men.[7]

THE OTHER MARIE

MARIE ANTOINETTE MARRIED THE HEIR TO THE
French throne, Louis-Auguste, in 1770 when she was just four-
teen years old. She was the youngest daughter of Empress Maria
Theresa of Austria and the Holy Roman emperor, Francis I, and her
marriage was meant to cement the alliance between France and
Austria. Louis-Auguste, who was fifteen years old at the time, was
not exactly the knight in shining armor Marie had hoped for. He was
awkward and quiet. He was also obsessed with hunting, an activity
Marie Antoinette hated, and was terrible at dancing, which Marie
Antoinette loved. Louis-Auguste was not supposed to be the heir
to the throne, but his older brother, who was more that knight-in-
shining-armor type Marie Antoinette had imagined, had died. Still,
he seemed nice enough to Marie Antoinette, and that was often the
most a female noble could hope for when her parents picked out her
future husband for her, sight unseen.

Court life overwhelmed Marie Antoinette. She did not speak or
write French very well, and her family back home expected her to act
as a sort of ambassador for Austria in France. It put her in an awkward position, because any time she mentioned her home country,
the French royal court criticized her as being some kind of spy. The
court at the palace of Versailles, just west of Paris, hated outsiders,
and they were immediately suspicious of Marie Antoinette. Many
nobles had been against forming an alliance with Austria to begin
with. After all, France had gotten dragged into and ultimately lost
an expensive seven-year-long war (1756–1763) against the Prussians
and the British thanks to that alliance. The court was also much

more rigid and had more rules and customs than Marie Antoinette was used to—dictating how she did her hair, what she wore, and how she ate—and the court whispered about her every time she got something wrong.[8] But it was not only the scrutiny of the French court she had to deal with.

By the time Marie Antoinette arrived, small pamphlets or books called *libelles* had flourished in France for more than a century. You can probably get the gist of what these were by the English translation of the word: offensive works.[9] *Libelles* mostly attacked public figures and other prominent individuals, but they especially went after the French monarchy and the aristocracy. *Libelles* were often written as short stories, essays, cartoons, or plays. They were also a popular source of fake news, and by the late 1700s, the cities of France were awash with them. As someone seen as an outsider, Marie Antoinette quickly became a target for the *libelles*.[10]

The monarchies of Europe did not care for the surge in complaints through the *libelles*, especially not from the common people, and passed laws throughout the continent to ban the printing of any criticism against them—whether or not the criticism was true. In France, they required press owners to get licenses from the government before printing anything, which meant they could deny or revoke licenses for anyone seen as unsupportive of the monarchy. They also jailed and executed people who printed things illegally. With the restrictions on printing in France, most *libelles* were written outside the country and then smuggled into France.[11]

Before Marie Antoinette had left for France, her mother had given her these last words of advice: "Do so much good to the French people that they can say that I have sent them an angel." Between the court and the *libelles*, Marie Antoinette felt like she was failing from the start.

ami cheri, mets ta main fur mon cœur
et dans tes fens fais en paffer l'ardeur

Marie and Louis-Auguste were just eighteen and nineteen years old in 1774 when Louis-Auguste's grandfather, Louis XV, died suddenly and they became queen and king of France. The only way for a ruler to secure his place on the French throne was to provide a male heir as soon as possible to make sure that the family line would continue. But for eight long years, Marie Antoinette and Louis-Auguste remained childless. The *libelles* were full of theories about why. Some said it was because Louis-Auguste was impotent. One asked, "Can the king do it? Can't the king do it?"[12] Others claimed that Marie Antoinette was not sleeping with Louis-Auguste because she was too busy having multiple affairs with other people, including with her own brother-in-law. Other *libelles* said that she was secretly gay and wanted nothing to do with Louis-Auguste. Many of the *libelles* included pornographic illustrations of Marie Antoinette's supposed affairs and group orgies.[13]

The truth was, Marie Antoinette desperately wanted children. Her mother wrote to her regularly telling her that she was putting herself in danger the longer she was not pregnant. The actual problem was . . . well, Marie Antoinette and Louis-Auguste did not really know what they were doing in the child-making department. After a few years, Marie Antoinette's brother came to France to investigate why there was no heir yet. After talking separately to Marie Antoinette and Louis-Auguste, he wrote back to Maria Theresa that the problem was that they were "a couple of complete blunderers."[14] Marie Antoinette eventually had four children, but when one of them died of tuberculosis, a *libelles* series called the *Essays* accused her of having poisoned him.[15]

Under so much pressure, Marie Antoinette turned to the two things she loved the most: fashion and gambling. She wore expensive feathers in her hair, and massive wigs sometimes as tall as three feet.

She had a dressmaker come to Versailles twice a week to design new and expensive dresses for her. What she did not fully understand at the time was that she had become queen of a country that was on the brink of a financial crisis.

The former king, Louis-Auguste's father, had spent all of France's money on fighting alongside Austria for seven years and on paying for his extravagant lifestyle at Versailles. And the new king and queen were not good with money either. Louis-Auguste took the throne when the American Revolution was underway, and he believed in the American quest for independence from the British. Despite his country's debt, he sent the Americans money, troops, and aid for years, and he paid for it by taxing the peasants (the aristocracy were exempt from having to pay taxes) and going into more debt.

Then, even though they had the palace at Versailles, Louis-Auguste had an opulent château built for his wife so she would have a private place of her own. The *libelles* started blaming Marie Antoinette for all the country's financial troubles. They called her *Madame Déficit*, claiming that she had single-handedly bankrupted France and that she was everything wrong with the monarchy. They also said she was sending millions of assignat, France's currency then, to her family in Austria.[16] When the cost of flour and bread skyrocketed in France, the *libelles* blamed it on Marie Antoinette's lavish spending, which led to violent riots in Paris's streets.

It was reported that when Marie Antoinette heard that the people of Paris could not afford bread, she simply shrugged and then joked, "Let them eat cake!" (*"Qu'ils mangent de la brioche!"*) But that too was fake news.

It was almost as though her mom, Maria Theresa, could see the writing on the wall. She wrote often to Marie Antoinette to try to persuade her to scale back her spending, citing the public unrest it was causing in Paris.

Marie could not understand why the *libelles* targeted her so much. Sure, she loved expensive things, but she also sent a lot of money to charities and genuinely cared about helping the poor, especially children. She was known to make her carriage driver stop to assist people who needed help along the road, and to send money to families when she heard they had experienced an illness or a death. But in Paris and all across France, her charitable acts were simply not enough.

Taxes and bad weather ruined farms all over the country, leading to bread prices that got so high in 1788 that the poor could no longer afford to eat. In a time known as the Great Fear, a new rumor spread all throughout France that the lack of food was a plot by the monarchy to starve the population. The people had had enough. Peasants and townspeople around the country rose up against the aristocracy. By 1789, a full-on revolution had begun in France. Rioters overran the Bastille, an important storage site for the monarchy's weapons.[17] The people were sick of living in poverty without getting a say in the government. That meant they needed to end the absolute rule of the monarchy and the control of the aristocracy over their lives.

The royal family realized they were in danger and tried to escape, but they were caught and arrested, including the children. Louis-Auguste was charged with treason and beheaded in 1793. Marie Antoinette was put on trial and ultimately executed nine months after her husband. Demonstrating just how much fake news had influenced Marie Antoinette's reputation, many of the things she was charged with, like infidelity, were the claims made in the *libelles*.

Libelles did not create the French Revolution, but they certainly stoked the flame of anger against the monarchy. Where did all the ideas for these fake stories come from? A lot of the stories were simply gossip. People who wrote for *libelles* would often hang around public places in Paris or coffeehouses in London to listen for juicy conversations they could write about. But most of the stories were just made up.[18]

One of the key reasons the *libelles* were so effective was that the monarchy did not tell the French public much about the royal family or the court. Reporters were not allowed at Versailles, and the government did not believe it needed to be transparent with the common people. There was so little information about the monarchy that *libelles* filled that space, and people believed them because: What else did they have to compare it to? Like a lot of the fake news we encounter today, these *libelles* often promised to tell the reader the real truth—to give the inside scoop on what was happening at Versailles that they could not get anywhere else.

The common people already disliked the excess wealth of the monarchy. And who could blame them? The attacks on Marie Antoinette in the *libelles* gave people an explanation for their poverty and a focus for their anger—a corrupt French monarchy. Even today, fake news is often not meant to change our minds completely. Instead, it simply tries to make us even more set in our views by telling us exactly what we want to hear.

ANOTHER POPULAR VEHICLE FOR FAKE NEWS IN FRANCE WAS A NEWS SHEET CALLED A *CANARD*. *Canard* is the French word for "duck," but it also came to mean "an unfounded rumor or story." Canards made up sensational stories: One famously reported in 1780 that a monster—imaginary, of course—had been found and captured in Chile.[19]

THE FIRST NEWSPAPERS

LESS THAN A HUNDRED YEARS AFTER THE printing press came to Europe, people began writing reports about one-time events. They were called "news books." Can you guess what "news books" became? That's right. Newspapers. The first actual newspapers that were printed regularly were created in 1605 in Europe. Newspapers were different from other printed materials, like pamphlets, in that they were published regularly. Soon after newspapers were created, they started cropping up in all major cities in Europe and in the American colonies.

Fake news hit America before the country even gained independence from Britain in 1776. The first newspaper, *Publick Occurrences*, was published in the American colonies in 1690, but it was shut down after only one edition when it claimed the king of France was sleeping with his daughter-in-law. Surprisingly, it was actually agents of the British monarchy who killed the paper. Britain and France might have been on-and-off-again enemies throughout history, but they believed that criticism from the common people against any monarchy threatened the order of the whole world.[20]

By 1775, at least thirty-seven different newspapers were being published in the colonies.[21] But they were still quite different from the hefty newspapers we are used to today. Politicians and public figures owned most of them, which meant they were basically full of partisan attacks against opposing political parties and rivals, rather than actual news reports. And since paper was still expensive, until the nineteenth century newspapers were also short and mostly read by the wealthy elite, who had the money to buy them. In America before the 1830s, a paper cost around six cents—about ten percent of the average person's paycheck—which meant that the working class could not afford them.[22] They were also kind of boring for anyone not involved in politics, with articles written by people trying to show how smart and witty they were, rather than to make them easily understandable and interesting to a wide range of readers.

The people considered to be the founders of the United States had a love-hate relationship with fake news. On the one hand, they knew the importance of keeping public opinion on their side no matter what as they built their new country, and they found fake news a handy way to do so. At the same time, many of the founders found it very annoying when anyone else used fake news against them or the eventual American government, even as they ensured the freedom of speech and the press by including them as rights in the First Amendment to the Constitution.

The primary architect of the Constitution, James Madison, once wrote that "public opinion sets bounds to every government, and is the real sovereign in every free one." So the founders took a page from the Europeans and waged their own pamphlet and newspaper wars to fight against their enemies—mostly the British and one another.

CHAPTER 4

FAKE NEWS AND AMERICA'S FOUNDERS

I N 1777, BENJAMIN FRANKLIN WAS WORKING on a very special project. He had only just arrived in France as the ambassador from the American colonies, but he immediately put together a printing press he could run himself in Paris.

Franklin got a thrill out of putting the press together and finding different fonts to use. As a hobby inventor, he loved learning how things worked and pulling apart pieces to re-form them into something different, like turning a key and a kite into a lightning rod. But the most exciting part of the press for Franklin was knowing just how powerful his words could be in changing public opinion on the topics that he cared about most, which was exactly what he intended to do to help the war effort from France.

By then, the American Revolution had been raging for twelve months, and Franklin was focused on keeping France as an ally in the war against the British. But there was another big problem. The thirteen colonies that would become the United States were exhausted and morale was low. They needed more troops if they were ever going to have a chance at gaining independence. Franklin was certain that with his press, he could do more than just print official government documents, like he was supposed to as ambassador. He could help turn the tide of the war. [1]

This was not Franklin's first foray into the world of newspaper publishing. In fact, he had made a fortune as the publisher of the *Pennsylvania Gazette* newspaper out of Philadelphia. There he had learned that a well-placed political cartoon, like his most famous—a snake cut into pieces to represent the colonies under the ominous heading JOIN, OR DIE—or, yes, even a fake news story, could have a big impact. [2]

Political cartoon published by Benjamin Franklin in the *Pennsylvania Gazette*, May 9, 1754

Printing presses had been critical for people like Franklin, George Washington, and Alexander Hamilton in building support and sustaining momentum for the revolution in the first place, so it is no wonder Franklin turned to them again in Paris. By 1782, Franklin believed he was very near to convincing the British to sign a peace treaty with the colonies. He could feel an independent America just within reach, but he needed to do something to tip the scales so that Britain would finally give up. So he turned to fake news.[3] Franklin's press was fully functioning by then, and with it he printed a paper styled as a supplement to the very real *Boston Independent Chronicle*, using the same design and font. He worked hard to make it look like a real newspaper page.

BRITAIN KNEW HOW POWERFUL THE PRINTED WORD COULD BE AND TRIED TO QUASH IT IN 1765 BY PASSING THE STAMP ACT. The act taxed printers for each page they printed and still more for every advertisement they published. Any paper or book printed in a foreign language was taxed even more. Even a person who wanted to become a printer's apprentice had to pay a tax. The British taxed the printers so much that some were forced to shut down, which was the whole point.[4]

Each edition of a newspaper had a number printed on it, so Franklin made sure to print the corresponding number on his fake supplement. His paper was one big page, with one article on each side and advertisements and notices scattered throughout, such as a notice about a missing horse in Salem, Massachusetts. He also wrote the articles under pseudonyms so they looked like they were written by real journalists, and so no one could trace them back to him. When his paper was ready, he sent it to his friends in the colonies and in England so that it would arrive around the same time the *Boston Independent Chronicle* would be published. He hoped his friends would get his articles published in other newspapers, too. If he could turn British public opinion against the war on the colonies, Franklin thought, America might just have a chance.

Franklin knew from past experience that shocking stories of violence grabbed the public's attention the most, so most of his articles tapped into the deep-seated racism of the era. One of his first articles was about the British and Native American tribes working together. Some tribes did actually work with the British, because they wanted to stop the colonists from taking their land, but many tribes stayed neutral, and some even joined the side of the colonists. Franklin, though, made up stories about tribes committing attacks against colonists. According to one article, American troops had found packages of money and goods bound for the king. Among the bags were found the scalps of hundreds of men, women, and children murdered by the Seneca tribe and a letter addressed to the king offering the scalps as a token of loyalty and friendship. To make it convincing, he printed a fake letter, claiming to be from a New England militia officer to his commanding officer, reporting on the supposed scalping, saying that King George had hired the Seneca tribe to attack people, and warning about the importance of an independent America. He included graphic details and listed all the people who had been killed. The letter also included the transcript of a speech a Native American chief supposedly gave upon sending the scalps to "the great King, that he may regard them and be refreshed; and that he may see our faithfulness in destroying his Enemies."

Franklin sent the supplement to his friends, including future president John Adams, hinting in a letter he attached that the stories were not real. Soon enough, several colonial newspapers and British papers reprinted his made-up story. It didn't stop there. His fake news story was also published years later in at least twenty-seven newspapers before the next war between the United States and Great Britain, the War of 1812. [5]

PRESIDENTIAL FAKE NEWS BATTLES

THE FOUNDERS DID NOT JUST USE FAKE NEWS during wartime. They also used it to fight their political battles. Thomas Jefferson was desperate to become president after the American Revolution, but there was a long line of other men who wanted the same thing. They were all eagerly awaiting the day George Washington would decide to step down. Then Jefferson had an idea that he thought might help him skip to the front of that line. When he was still the secretary of state, he secretly hired a newspaper editor, Philip Freneau, to set up a newspaper called the *National Gazette*. Although Jefferson officially gave Freneau a job at the State Department, which is where Freneau got his paycheck, he really worked for Jefferson's newspaper. Jefferson never wrote for the paper himself, at least not under his own name. But he did not have to, since Freneau published whatever Jefferson wanted. Jefferson used the *National Gazette* to attack then-president George Washington by calling him America's new tyrant king. Jefferson also went after the man he saw as his main competition for the job of president: Alexander Hamilton, who was the secretary of the treasury. Jefferson worked with James Madison to get subscribers for the newspaper, and Madison even wrote articles for it, both under pen names and his own.[6] One article published in the *National Gazette* had the headline THE FUNERAL OF GEORGE WASHINGTON AND JAMES WILSON with an illustration of an emperor-like Washington being put on a guillotine.[7]

The other thing Jefferson used the paper for was to promote the Democratic-Republican Party he had founded, and, of course, himself as the next natural leader. Jefferson gave Freneau secret intelligence to publish about issues he was working on as secretary of state to help build public support for his positions and his work. Jefferson also saw an opportunity to get the public on board with his becoming president by using the *National Gazette* to promote the fact that he had written the Declaration of Independence. It was not exactly a lie: Jefferson had taken the lead in writing the document. But he had written it as part of a group of men who had worked together. Jefferson's claim of sole authorship rubbed many of the founders the wrong way, especially John Adams, who had been part of the original group. "Jefferson ran away with all the stage effect . . . all the glory of it," Adams complained years later. But Adams got a bit of payback—when Washington finally stepped down, it was Adams, not Jefferson, who became president in 1797.

For his part, Hamilton saw right through the *National Gazette* and Jefferson's ties to it. He wrote an essay in 1792 calling out Freneau and, by extension, Jefferson. As a fan of the musical *Hamilton*, I like to read this quote as a rap:

[Freneau] is the faithful and devoted servant of the head
of a party, from whose hand he receives the boon. The
whole complexion of his paper is an exact copy of the
politics of his employer foreign and domestic, and exhibits
a decisive internal evidence of the influence of that
patronage under which he acts. . . .

. . . Is it possible that Mr. Jefferson, the head of a principal
department of the Government can be the Patron of
a Paper, the evident object of which is to decry the
Government and its measures?[8]

In other words: Why is a government official trying to destroy the very government he works for with fake news? It was a good question. Maybe Hamilton saw through Jefferson's fake newspaper so easily because of his own closely held secret—Hamilton was paying a different newspaper to print what he wanted, too![9]

Jefferson became John Adams's vice president, even though the two were from different political parties. (That's how it worked back then: The runner-up became the winner's VP.) But Jefferson still had not given up his goal of becoming president, nor was he done using fake news to help him get the job. Jefferson ran against John Adams during the presidential election of 1800. They both relied heavily on fake news to go after each other in what was one of the most malicious political campaigns in American history. Adams said Jefferson was an atheist and a coward. Newspapers run by Adams's political party, the Federalists, claimed Jefferson was soft on crime. If he became president, they warned, "Murder, robbery, rape, adultery, and incest will be openly taught and practiced, the air will be rent with the cries of the distressed, the soil will be soaked with blood and the nation black with crimes."[10]

Jefferson fired back with his own personal attacks.[11] He used toxic gender stereotypes of the era to claim Adams was not man enough to lead and claimed that Adams was neither male nor female. Repeating his past strategy against George Washington, Jefferson also depicted John Adams as a wannabe American king and tyrant. His supporters spread a story that Adams planned to arrange for one of his sons to marry a daughter of King George III, a deal that would have essentially put America back under British rule if George Washington had not stopped Adams just in time. Jefferson also hired a journalist, James Callender, to get his fake news out for him so he did not have to get his own hands dirty. Jefferson's efforts worked—he won the presidency and booted Adams out of the White House. As a result of the contentious race, Jefferson and Adams, who had actually been close friends up until this point, did not speak for twelve years after the election.[12]

JEFFERSON ALSO USED JAMES CALLENDER TO BREAK THE NEWS THAT ALEXANDER HAMILTON HAD HAD AN AFFAIR WITH MARIA REYNOLDS, A MARRIED WOMAN.[13] IN 1800, CALLENDER WAS SENTENCED TO NINE MONTHS IN JAIL FOR PRINTING "FALSE, SCANDALOUS, AND MALICIOUS WRITING" AGAINST THEN-PRESIDENT ADAMS. From jail, Callender continued to write articles supporting Jefferson for president. In return for what he thought was quite loyal service, Callender asked Jefferson for a paid government job when he was released from jail.[14] When Jefferson refused, Callender published a series of articles on Jefferson's biggest secret—he had children with Sally Hemings, a black woman he kept as a slave.

With how ferociously the founders used fake news and how fiercely they defended the right to free speech and a free press, it is perhaps a bit ironic that they complained a lot about newspapers. As president, John Adams signed a series of laws in 1798 called the Alien and Sedition Acts, which allowed the government to fine or imprison people who had any part in "false, scandalous, and malicious writing" about the government. The laws expired at the end of Adams's presidency, but in those three years alone, federal courts prosecuted at least twenty-six people who were publicly critical of the Adams administration.[15] The laws were highly unpopular with the public, however. Most historians agree it was one of the major reasons Adams lost his reelection campaign.

Jefferson, too, though a firm believer in the free press, did not always care for the consequences when they affected him personally. In 1807, he said, "Nothing can now be believed which is seen in a newspaper" and that "the man who never looks into a newspaper is better informed than he who reads them."[16]

The fake news battles in America's early years show us the importance of knowing not just what motivation the author of a story may have for telling it, but who else might be behind the story, whether it is another person, a government, or a partisan organization. Jefferson could have just used his own statements to get out fake news about his opponents and to push his own agenda, but it was much more effective when it came through the *National Gazette*—which seemed like a legitimate newspaper—in a way that did not link to him directly. People might have been skeptical about things Jefferson or Adams said about each other—the two men were campaigning for the same office, after all, and had obvious agendas—but they took more seriously information that was reported by others, even if they knew that most newspapers were partisan. If it had been public knowledge that Jefferson, for example, paid the editor of the *National Gazette*, or had hired someone to spread the rumor that Adams wanted war with France, those stories probably would have been discredited.

Perhaps more importantly, the stories of the founders show us that people have long used false information during the course of political campaigning and elections to try to influence public opinion on issues and candidates. That means it is especially important for us to pay attention to things billed as political news to make sure we are receiving accurate information from reliable sources.

CHAPTER 5

FAKE NEWS TAKES ON SCIENCE

EDGAR ALLAN POE WAS USED TO BEING broke. He had been orphaned at just two years old when his father abandoned his family and his actress mother died. In 1827, when he was eighteen years old, he joined the army because, if nothing else, it meant a stable paycheck. But a few years later, just a short time after starting as a cadet at West Point, he was dismissed for bad behavior. The truth was, Poe's heart just was not in the army. He desperately wanted to be a writer and had even published his book *Tamerlane and Other Poems* while he was in the military, though not many people bought copies.[1] It was tough to make a living as a writer. America's economy had tanked, which hit the publishing industry hard. So after the army, Poe also worked as a clerk and wrote for newspapers and literary magazines.

In the 1830s, a different kind of newspaper started to emerge in larger cities in America—one known as the penny press. These shorter newspapers were geared toward the working class, both in content and cost (just one cent, hence the name). They were printed daily and on cheaper paper than regular newspapers. These newspapers became a way to give people information and entertainment all in one place. They reported on current events, but also included short stories and poetry, jokes, satire, and illustrations. The stories were also shorter and about things that affected the working-class reader, including human-interest articles, gripping crime stories, and discussions of labor issues.

> POE WAS REPORTEDLY PAID ABOUT NINE DOLLARS—
> APPROXIMATELY THREE HUNDRED DOLLARS TODAY—
> FOR HIS FAMOUS POEM "THE RAVEN," PUBLISHED IN 1845.[2]

One of the ways penny-press papers attracted readers was by printing sensational stories and hoaxes right alongside the real news. This new direction was perfectly suited to Poe, who liked the idea of elaborate literary hoaxes. In 1844, Poe wrote a story for *The Sun*, the biggest penny press in New York City, about a European balloonist who crossed the Atlantic Ocean in only seventy-five hours in a kind of hot-air balloon. *The Sun* presented Poe's story as if it were real news. The first hot-air balloon was launched in 1783, but no balloon had ever come close to the one Poe described in his article.[3] With commercial airlines still decades away from being invented, readers latched onto his story.

The article included a lot of details about how the balloon worked and even a drawing of it, so it seemed very convincing. Readers were thrilled by the possibility that such fast international travel might be possible. Poe also included long chunks of text from the very real account of a hot-air ballooner who flew from England to Germany in 1836.[4] A fake news story is always much more believable when there are enough true details to sound like the writer knows what they are talking about, and when it also happens to confirm something we want to hear. Sadly, the story was not true, and *The Sun* printed a retraction two days after it was published. But by then, it had already been picked up and reported by other papers.

Daguerreotype of Edgar Allan Poe taken by W. S. Hartshorn in 1848

In 1838, Poe published a book called *The Narrative of Arthur Gordon Pym of Nantucket*. It was a harrowing ocean-adventure story about a boy who stows away on a whaling ship that is quickly over-taken by an onboard mutiny. The book starts with a preface sup-posedly written by Arthur Gordon Pym himself, who says he was nervous about writing the book because he did not think anyone would believe his story. Made-up Pym says he only agreed to do so after his editor, Edgar Allan Poe (aka the actual author), promised to publish it as fiction. True to his style, Poe wove real accounts from actual explorers, as well as his own personal experiences on the high seas, right into the otherwise completely fictional story. To confuse readers even more, Poe's publisher sold the book as an authentic travel journal. But there were too many inaccuracies in the book, and reviewers saw right past Poe's hoax. One said the book was "an impudent attempt at humbugging the public."[5] *The Narrative of Arthur Gordon Pym of Nantucket* was the first and last novel Poe ever wrote.

EVEN POE'S MYSTERIOUS DEATH WAS PLAGUED BY FAKE NEWS. In 1849, he was found dazedly wandering the streets of Baltimore, Maryland, wearing someone else's clothes. He died just a few days later. His literary rival Rufus Griswold wrote his obituary in the *New-York Daily Tribune* and filled it with false information to make Poe sound like he had no morals, saying "few will be grieved" by Poe's death.[6] Different accounts of his death over time have blamed it on everything from rabies to alcoholism to a broken heart.

Historians and literary critics still debate whether Poe's writings were intentional hoaxes, or if he was just a genius at satire. The truth is probably somewhere in the middle. In his eyes, life was one big hoax anyway. He believed not only that people were naturally gullible, but that they always lived in a state of deception because of the simple fact that no human could possibly know everything. Hoaxes were good reminders that people were vulnerable.[7] Vulnerability was not a bad thing to Poe. Life, he thought, was best when people viewed it with "the half-closed eye" that blurred the lines between fiction and reality.

THE DIFFERENCE BETWEEN SATIRE AND FAKE NEWS.
There is a big difference, and it is important to be able to identify each one. Satire has been around almost as long as fake news. It is a form of calling out or exposing political or social issues, usually using humor and irony. Satire often includes real, factual information at its base, but it usually adds fake elements or exaggerations to poke fun at reality. It also often impersonates real news as a parody. While fake news is meant to deceive people, satire does not try to pass itself off as real news. However, people can still be fooled by satire if they do not understand that what they are reading or hearing is not real news. Examples of modern satire are *The Onion*, the Borowitz Report, and *The Daily Show*. It is important to remember that satire is not real news, though it may discuss real events. In a Pew Research Center survey in 2014, 12 percent of participants said they got their news from *The Daily Show*, a show that, yes, raises important issues, but is ultimately meant to make people laugh.[8] If what you are reading just sounds too outlandish to be true, it might be satire, but the best way to find out for sure is to do a quick online search about the publication.

LUNAR CREATURES AND A DOOMED EARTH

POE'S BALLOON STORY WAS NOT THE FIRST ARTI-
cle to put *The Sun* in hot water with the public. In 1835, the newspaper had published a series of articles supposedly reprinted from
Edinburgh Journal of Science that claimed there was a civilization of
aliens and fantastical creatures on the moon.[9] The articles documented the findings of a well-known and respected astronomer of
the era, Sir John Herschel. Herschel had actually published articles
about an expedition he had taken to the Cape of Good Hope in South
Africa to catalog the stars he could see from the southern hemisphere
with a powerful new telescope. It was on that expedition, *The Sun*'s
fake articles said, that Herschel discovered life on the moon. They
claimed he had found nine kinds of mammals on the moon through
his telescope. But mammals no one had ever heard of, like a horned
bear and blue goats. There were also winged men who looked like
bats and fluttered around collecting fruit amid the moon's surface
of craters and giant purple amethysts.

Of course, Herschel never said such things, and the whole story
sounds ridiculous now (and, okay, it is). But think about what it was like
back in 1835. The world did not know very much yet about the moon
or space. No one had even landed on the moon. The telescopes they
had could not see very far, and most working-class and middle-class
people, who were the main readers of the paper, had never even gotten
close to a telescope, let alone looked through one.[10] They had no clue
how far one could see.

An illustration that appeared in *The Sun*'s series, 1835

The article was written to sound extremely scientific, and readers did not know that the quotes from the astronomer were made up. They simply saw that a well-known expert they could trust had been quoted, and they took what he said as fact. No one had ever been to the moon, so why would they question an expert astronomer with a high-tech telescope? There was no way to verify the information or even to call out the story once people learned it was false since they didn't have social media, the internet, or TV. The *Edinburgh Journal of Science* was real, but had shut down years before, a fact that the average American would not have known.

Readers were enthralled with the story, and newspapers in Europe printed it. It even fooled a group of scientists from Yale University who traveled to New York to meet with *The Sun*'s staff because they wanted to read over the original articles.[11] Even though

The Sun eventually admitted that the whole story was a hoax (after a rival newspaper ran a story saying so, of course), the story did what it was intended to do—it sold newspapers. Between 1834 and 1836, the *Sun's* circulation increased from five thousand to over nineteen thousand copies, eventually making it the most widely read newspaper in the world.[12] Edgar Allan Poe even weighed in on how much the story fooled people, saying, "Not one person in ten discredited it . . . A grave professor of mathematics in a Virginian college told me seriously that he had *no doubt* of the truth of the whole affair!"[13]

As for the very real Herschel, he was understandably upset to be used in a hoax. He complained in letters to family members later that people from all over the world had written to him about his supposed finding because they had not yet found out the whole thing was a hoax. A year later, when newspapers were still printing *The Sun's* article as real news, Herschel had had enough. Worried about the harm that repeating the story over and over again was doing, he wrote a letter to a French newspaper disavowing all knowledge of the "discoveries."

> *I consider the precedent a bad one that the absurdity of a story should ensure its freedom from contradiction when universally repeated in so many quarters and in such a variety of forms. Dr. Johnson Indeed [sic] used to say that there was nothing, however absurd or impossible which if seriously told a man every morning at breakfast for 365 days he would not end in believing—and it was a maxim of Napoleon that the most effective figure in Rhetoric is Repetition.[14]*

It was not always newspapers trying to fool their readers. Sometimes the readers fooled the newspapers! In 1874, the *Wichita*

City Eagle printed a letter from a man named J. B. Legendre who said that a friend of his, an American living in Florence, Italy, had learned at a scientific meeting that the respected Italian astronomer Giovanni Donati had discovered that the telegraph, which had been invented earlier in the century, was causing the Earth to move closer to the sun. The telegraph cables' magnetism, combined with gravity, pulled on the Earth. As a result, Europe was going to become tropical during the next twelve years, and then the entire Earth would become uninhabitable. Eventually, it would collide with the sun and explode, the astronomer had concluded.[15]

According to Legendre, Donati had tried to warn governments across Europe about the Earth's impending destruction, but no one would listen. In a last-ditch effort to save the world, he'd gathered several of his colleagues, chartered a boat, and broken one of the cables in the ocean to try to stop the Earth from moving. But the cable had been repaired, and Donati died in 1873 from "nervous excitement or fright," the letter said, because of the enormity of his discovery.[16]

A collision between the Earth and the sun? Impending doom? The letter was too juicy not to print! Soon newspapers all over the country were writing about the prediction, even printing the full text of Legendre's letter so readers could see it for themselves. Many of the newspapers that ran the story added their view that it all sounded absurd or made up, but they still printed it.

In truth, two whole things were correct in the story: There was an astronomer named Giovanni Donati, and he did die in 1873. That was it.

Fake news can be dangerous to spread, even when it includes a caveat that it's been proven not to be true. Spreading the story legitimizes it to a degree by saying it is something worth talking about. It also sows doubt into our heads about things we otherwise know are true. Of course the hoax did not stop the world from using the telegraph, nor did it prevent the invention of even-faster communication systems in the future. But it may very well have convinced some folks that getting news faster was not worth the possible destruction of the world.

Many of the fake news stories of the eighteenth and nineteenth centuries were about science. Fields like astronomy, chemistry, and physics were relatively new. Scientists were rapidly making new discoveries, but the general population was pretty uninformed about it all. That made them easy to fool.

When we read what we think is news, it is important to look at who or what is being cited as evidence. In the case of the Great Moon Hoax, the article quoted a well-known astronomer. Or so the writer made readers believe. Since fake news is meant to deceive people into thinking something is true, one of the ways to do it is by making it look like the news comes from real experts. At the time, people could not go online to verify what Donati had said or look up what other astronomers might be saying about it, but nowadays we can. If the news is reporting something like creepy creatures might be living on the moon based on one person's claim, it is absolutely worth it to make sure that person actually said what they're quoted as having said.

THE IMPACT OF THE TELEGRAPH ON FAKE NEWS

SAMUEL MORSE WAS A PAINTER BY TRADE, BUT he also liked to invent things for fun. In 1825, he traveled to Washington, DC, to paint a portrait of the Marquis de Lafayette. It was a big opportunity for Morse. But in the middle of the job, he received a letter saying that his wife had become gravely ill after having their third child. Morse left everything and raced back to his home in New Haven, Connecticut. But it was too late. By the time the letter reached Morse and he traveled home, his wife had already died and been buried. Morse was grief-stricken by the loss.[17] If only he had had the chance to say goodbye. That was when an idea occurred to him—there simply had to be a faster way to send important messages, especially when it was a matter of life and death. A little over ten years later, in 1838, Morse was demonstrating his new invention: the telegraph.

The telegraph worked by sending electrical signals through wires connecting telegraph stations. It was an early form of text messaging. But messages were sent using what became known as Morse code—a series of combinations of dots and dashes that represent the letters of the English alphabet and numbers.[18]

It is hard for us to understand how revolutionary the telegraph really was, because today we can send an email or a text to anyone anywhere at the click of a button, or video-chat people on the other side of the world as if they were with us in person. But at the time it brought the world closer together in a way it had never been before. Back then, the ability to send messages almost instantly was such an amazing feat that people first thought the creation of the telegraph was fake news itself.

> SAMUEL MORSE SENT THE VERY FIRST TELEGRAM ON MAY 24, 1844, FROM WASHINGTON, DC, TO BALTIMORE, MARYLAND. It said: "What hath God wrought!"[19]

The invention of the telegraph rocked the newspaper world, too. By 1858, a telegraph cable had been laid across the floor of the Atlantic Ocean, connecting the United States and Europe. Soon after, telegraph stations were all over the world.[20] Until then, newspapers had been almost entirely focused on local issues. Covering world events was still pretty rare, but when newspapers did, it was usually about events that had happened weeks before, because it took so long for information to travel through the mail. But with the telegraph, newspapers were able to station reporters all over the world who could send news almost instantly instead of taking weeks through letters in the mail. An article in *Harper's Monthly Magazine* in 1925 described the phenomenon perfectly, saying:

> Not so long ago something might have occurred in Washington so portentous as momentarily to shake public confidence in our institutions without causing a ripple of excitement a thousand miles from the capital. By the time the news reached Chicago, Washington would have regained its mental equilibrium. So as the news wave rolled slowly on, district after district might be convulsed, but never the whole country at once. But not now. There is no chance to "break the news gently." It explodes with a bang and its echoes are heard in

The process of sending a telegram also had an interesting effect on how news was gathered and reported. It took so long to tap out the code for each individual letter and number (and the longer the message was, the more it cost) that people had to send news in short factual bursts. For newspapers, there simply was not time to tap out the personal opinions and commentary that reporters usually mixed into their news articles.

With so much news being flung across the world, in 1848 four newspapers decided to pool resources to report the news. Eventually, the group named itself the Associated Press. The AP collected all the news and sent it to a variety of publications to use in their coverage. Each publication had different reporting interests, political leanings, and kinds of readers, so the AP's reporting had to be factual, neutral, and without any opinions or analysis attached.[22]

Instantaneous communication created a different problem for newspaper publishers. While information could travel across the world in a matter of seconds, it still took a lot longer for reporters to verify the information they received. But people now expected them to report on the latest news, not what happened four weeks ago. Newspapers also competed with one another for sales, which put pressure on reporters to be the ones to publish the latest breaking news.

Fake news pushers took advantage of this situation to try to get newspapers to publish rumors and false information as real news. For example, for years after the *Titanic* sank in 1912, the AP regularly received rumors over the telegraph claiming that other ships, all over the world, had hit icebergs, making reporters scurry to verify each and every report.[23] This put media outlets in a difficult position. If the AP and other newspapers could not verify the information they received before their publishing deadline, some editors could be tempted to report it anyway so their papers would not lose out on a big scoop. But if they reported it and it was not true, the newspaper could lose

MORSE CODE ALPHABET

A	●—	N	—●
B	—●●●	O	———
C	—●—●	P	●——●
D	—●●	Q	——●—
E	●	R	●—●
F	●●—●	S	●●●
G	——●	T	—
H	●●●●	U	●●—
I	●●	V	●●●—
J	●———	W	●——
K	—●—	X	—●●—
L	●—●●	Y	—●——
M	——	Z	——●●
1	●————	6	—●●●●
2	●●———	7	——●●●
3	●●●——	8	———●●
4	●●●●—	9	————●
5	●●●●●	0	—————

Yellow Journalism,
Propaganda, and
Disinformation, Oh My!

CHAPTER 6

YELLOW
JOURNALISM

I N 1895, THIRTY-TWO-YEAR-OLD WILLIAM
Randolph Hearst bought the New York *Journal* newspaper,
with a little financial help from his parents. Hearst came from
a wealthy family whose dad had made millions from mining. Hearst
had had a troubled past and had even gotten expelled from Harvard
for his wild behavior. But for several years, he had been running
the San Francisco *Examiner*. His father had won the newspaper as
payment for a gambling debt and had given it to the younger Hearst,
hoping it would force him to settle down. And Hearst had risen to
the occasion, turning the paper into the most successful paper in
the area—much to the relief of his parents.

Hearst had a big dream: He wanted to dominate America's newspaper business. But Hearst knew he would never achieve his dream
if he did not own a successful paper in New York City. The problem
was, his *New York Journal* was not the only game in town.[1]

Twelve years earlier, Joseph Pulitzer had bought the biggest newspaper in New York, the *New York World*. Pulitzer's background could not have been more different from Hearst's. While Hearst had inherited his fortune, Pulitzer had immigrated from Hungary when he was seventeen and spent much of his early adult years homeless, penniless, and scrounging for jobs. He taught himself English by reading books in a public library in St. Louis, Missouri, and was eventually hired as a reporter. Working sixteen-hour days, Pulitzer soon rose to the top and built one of the most successful newspapers in St. Louis before acquiring the New York *World*.

Hearst and Pulitzer quickly engaged in a fierce battle, each determined to make sure his New York paper was the most successful. To do this, they filled their papers with dramatic headlines, flashy fonts, a lot of eye-catching cartoons and illustrations, and scary or exciting stories—some true and some totally false.

As they were trying to outdo each other, the Cuban people had long been fighting to become their own country and launched a final battle for independence from Spain in 1895. Hearst and Pulitzer both knew from experience that nothing could sell newspapers like a war, and each man decided that this was the perfect opportunity to best his rival by convincing the American public that the US needed to intervene in Cuba. Hearst had an artist stationed in Cuba to draw eye-catching illustrations of the revolution for the newspaper to print. One historian wrote that Hearst wanted "readers to look at page one and say, 'Gee whiz,' to turn to page two and exclaim, 'Holy Moses,' and then at page three, shout 'God Almighty!'"[2]

Hearst and Pulitzer began filling their newspapers with articles about Spanish atrocities against the Cuban resistance. Much of it was true. The Spanish military used brutal tactics, such as destroying whole villages and farms, and executing rebels in public. But even though the reality was already horrific, many of the stories they published were embellished, or made up completely.[3] Some of these stories were based on information journalists got from Cuban exiles who supported the revolution. The newspapers printed stories about Spanish troops holding Cubans in concentration camps or murdering men, women, and children and leaving them in giant piles on the side of the road.[4] For the most part, the journalists writing about the revolution did not try to confirm the information they received before writing articles and handing them in for publication. They did not need to—editors often exaggerated the stories even further after journalists submitted them, because the articles were supposed to stir up public support for a war.

IN 1901, ONE OF HEARST'S REPORTERS, JAMES CREELMAN, WROTE A BOOK CLAIMING THAT AT ONE POINT, THE ARTIST SENT A TELEGRAM TO HEARST COMPLAINING THAT HE WAS BORED AND ASKING TO BE BROUGHT BACK TO THE US. "Everything is quiet. There is no trouble. There will be no war," the telegram allegedly said. Hearst famously responded: "Please remain. You furnish the pictures and I'll furnish the war." The story of their interaction spread rapidly as evidence of Hearst's plot to sell papers with a war, and the anecdote still appears in books and journals about this time period. However, no telegrams were ever found and historians believe he made the whole thing up.[5]

One story that especially gripped *New York Journal* readers centered on the experiences of a young Cuban woman who was taken into custody while traveling on an American ship, the *Olivette*, bound for New York City. Spanish officials suspected her of delivering letters to Cuban rebel leaders in the city and took her to a room to be searched. That much did happen. But she was searched by women. Instead of reporting that, Hearst did a series of articles about how the Spanish were sexually abusing women, saying that a bunch of male Spanish soldiers had strip-searched the woman, and showing an exploitative drawing of her naked. REFINED YOUNG WOMEN STRIPPED AND SEARCHED BY BRUTAL SPANIARDS WHILE UNDER OUR FLAG ON THE *OLIVETTE*, part of a headline read.[6]

Repetition is key to getting people to believe fake news, so Hearst and Pulitzer published articles constantly, tailoring their news coverage to what readers in different parts of the country would care about most. In their view, readers in the American Midwest were not as moved by stories about violence, so newspapers there pivoted to talking about how Cuban independence was vital to America's economic prosperity, and discussing the importance of trade with Cuba. Midwestern readers were much more supportive of a war if it would protect US interests.

Their big break came when a US Navy battleship, the USS *Maine*, mysteriously blew up off the coast of Havana, Cuba, in February 1898. At the time, no one knew what had happened to it, but an investigation almost a century later discovered that the explosion had come from within the ship. More than two hundred fifty sailors died. Hearst published an article afterward with the headline THE WAR SHIP *MAINE* WAS SPLIT IN TWO BY AN ENEMY'S SECRET INFERNAL MACHINE, claiming the Spanish had sunk the ship.

$50,000 REWARD.—WHO DESTROYED THE MAINE?—$50,000 REWARD.

EDITION FOR GREATER NEW YORK

NEW YORK JOURNAL
AND ADVERTISER.

NO. 5,572. ———NEW YORK, THURSDAY, FEBRUARY 17, 1898.—10 PAGES. PRICE ONE CENT

DESTRUCTION OF THE WAR SHIP MAINE WAS THE WORK OF AN ENEMY

$50,000!
$50,000 REWARD!
For the Detection of the
Perpetrator of
the Maine Outrage!

Assistant Secretary Roosevelt Convinced the Explosion of the War Ship Was Not an Accident.

The Journal Offers $50,000 Reward for the
Conviction of the Criminals Who Sent
258 American Sailors to Their Death.
Naval Officers Unanimous That
the Ship Was Destroyed
on Purpose.

$50,000!
$50,000 REWARD!
For the Detection of the
Perpetrator of
the Maine Outrage!

NAVAL OFFICERS THINK THE MAINE WAS DESTROYED BY A SPANISH MINE.

Hidden Mine or a Sunken Torpedo Believed to Have Been the Weapon Used Against the American Man-of-War—Officers
and Men Tell Thrilling Stories of Being Blown Into the Air Amid a Mass of Shattered Steel and Exploding
Shells—Survivors Brought to Key West Scout the Idea of Accident—Spanish Officials Protest Too Much—Our Cabinet Orders a Searching Inquiry—Journal Sends
Divers to Havana to Report Upon the Condition of the Wreck.

The sinking of the USS *Maine* covered the front page of William Randolph
Hearst's *New York Journal* on February 17, 1898, with the headline
DESTRUCTION OF THE WAR SHIP MAINE WAS THE WORK OF AN ENEMY.

The public was incensed and demanded that America respond.[7] Meanwhile, Hearst's *New York Journal* became the first paper in the US to sell one million copies in a single day—the day after the sinking of the USS *Maine*.[8]

Hearst even manufactured public support for the war. THE WHOLE COUNTRY THRILLS WITH WAR FEVER, one of his headlines read after the sinking of the *Maine*. It was a kind of peer-pressure nudge to reluctant Americans that they should get on board, since everyone else apparently was already.[9]

In April of that year, Hearst and Pulitzer got their war. The US involvement in the battle for Cuban independence, known as the Spanish-American War, only lasted ten weeks before Spain surrendered. For the United States it cost $250 million (almost $8 billion today) and three thousand lives. In return, Spain ceded control of Puerto Rico, Guam, and the Philippines to the United States.[10] Cuba did not gain its independence from the United States until 1902.

More than sixty thousand Spanish soldiers were killed over the course of their three-year battle with Cuba. The exact number of Cuban deaths is not known, but by 1899, it was estimated that half of Cuban wives were widows.[11]

Hearst and Pulitzer did not *make* the United States go to war, but they certainly helped influence public opinion. As this case shows, fake news is most successful when it plays on people's emotions. Strong emotions can make people overlook factual inaccuracies, things that do not sound quite right, and things that would ordinarily be red flags.

"The Yellow Kid's New Phonograph Clock" by Richard F. Outcault, published in the *New York Journal* on February 14, 1897

HEARST'S AND PULITZER'S SENSATIONAL AND EXAGGERATED FAKE-NEWS CAMPAIGN WAS SO BAD IN THE RUN-UP TO THE WAR THAT A NEW TERM (A PREDECESSOR TO FAKE NEWS) WAS CREATED FOR IT: YELLOW JOURNALISM. No one knows the exact origin of the term, but some historians believe it has to do with a comic called *Hogan's Alley* first published in Pulitzer's *New York World* each Sunday. The comic strip was about a bald child who wore yellow pajamas and was known as the Yellow Kid. When Hearst paid the cartoonist to come work for him and *his* newspaper instead, Pulitzer had a new cartoonist continue the comic strip for the *World*. So, for a while, New York had two Yellow Kids competing with each other in Hearst's and Pulitzer's newspapers, just like the publishers competed against each other.[12]

BACKLASH AGAINST YELLOW JOURNALISM

THE PRACTICE OF YELLOW JOURNALISM LED to a much-needed public backlash against sensationalized journalism. In fact, the first consistent use of the term *fake news* began in America in the 1880s and 1890s, when sensational news was in its heyday.[13] People became desperate for more objective news. They did not want to be tricked or fooled anymore; they simply wanted the news. At the end of the 1800s and beginning of the 1900s, some respectable media outlets decided they were going to fight back against fake news. They recognized that its spread had made the public distrust news altogether.

This sparked a rise in more objective journalism and better journalistic standards, which did important things like separating news from opinion and only printing information reporters could corroborate. American newspapers also started hiring reporters to cover local stories, like city and state politics, to try to build trust between reporters and communities. After how it handled the Spanish-American War, Pulitzer's *New York World* also set up the Bureau of Accuracy and Fair Play in 1913 and told readers to send them examples any time they found false information in their newspaper so they could investigate it. Other newspapers put pledges of accurate reporting right on their newspapers, like the *St. Paul Globe*, which printed this at the top of the front page for most of the month of May in 1898: THE GLOBE'S MOTTO: LIVE NEWS, LATEST NEWS, RELIABLE NEWS—NO FAKE WAR NEWS. Tennessee's *Polk County Republican* printed a warning for anyone submitting articles, saying, "All communications to receive attention, must have the writer's name to it. This is our only protection against 'fake' news and the rule will not be broken under any

Header of the *St. Paul Globe* newspaper on May 8, 1898, proclaims,
"No Fake War News."

Perhaps the biggest impact of all was that larger newspapers began hiring what we now call fact-checkers to review the accuracy of what they wrote. By the 1920s, it was common to have a person or group within a newspaper whose job it was to look for accuracy.[15] This meant writers had to provide the sources of their information—and ones that could be verified by the fact-checkers. This helped ensure that reporters did not intentionally or unintentionally get things wrong, or that if a reporter could not verify a statement, they said so in their articles.

A small portion of a larger illustration by Frederick Burr Opper published in an 1894 issue of *Puck* magazine that depicts a Pulitzer-like newspaper owner watching money roll in from the publication of fake and sensational news.[16]

CHAPTER 7

FAKE NEWS AT WAR

JUST A FEW DECADES AFTER THE SPANISH-
American War, the Nazi regime in Germany ran one of the
most successful fake news campaigns in history. In 1933,
Adolf Hitler became chancellor of Germany, at a time when the coun-
try was still struggling financially and politically after losing World
War I fifteen years earlier. Hitler promised that he and his Nationalist
Party (the Nazis) would not just fix Germany's problems, but also
make the country the leader of Europe.[1]

At the core of his plan, Hitler believed Germany needed to get rid
of anyone who was not part of what he considered the "master race."
He began a systematic genocide. Ultimately, the Nazi government
killed more than six million Jews as well as millions of people with
disabilities, LGBTQ people, Roma, Poles, Slovaks, Communists, and
others. To do this, Nazi leaders had to convince whole communities
of people to turn on one another and help them, or at least look the
other way as they eliminated those they labeled *Untermenschen*,
or subhuman (anyone who was not a straight, white, able-bodied
German Christian). That's where fake news came in.

In 1933, Hitler appointed Joseph Goebbels to set up and lead the Reich's Ministry of Public Enlightenment and Propaganda. (Another term for fake news is *propaganda*. Propaganda is the selective use of certain information in a biased way to encourage a particular reaction or view.) The ministry had the word *propaganda* right in its name, so you can probably guess what it did. The ministry spread fake, anti-Semitic information about Jews and other *Untermenschen* to incite violence and hatred against them. They did that by painting them as "the enemy of the people" to lay the groundwork for the violence that was to come. They said that Jewish people were greedy, corrupt, and trying to control the economy.[2]

As soon as Hitler was elected, he ordered all Germans to boycott Jewish businesses. When people refused to do so, his government started publishing fake crime statistics, including a weekly list of crimes Jewish people had supposedly committed, to convince the public that Jews were criminals. A German newspaper owned by a prominent Nazi Party official ran a section that featured stories contributed by readers about crimes supposedly committed by Jews. People could send in rumors or outright lies, and the paper would print them. The stories were not checked or verified in any way, which is not surprising, as the newspaper had started calling for the elimination of the Jewish people as soon as Hitler came to power in 1933. This newspaper was not looking for accuracy.

The Nazis also printed flyers and hung posters saying people with disabilities were a drain on Germany's economy and "unworthy of life." They would pair exaggerated illustrations of disabled people with headlines about how much money it cost Germany to keep them alive. The Nazis used this propaganda to later justify and carry out a program called T4, which called for the total elimination of anyone with a disability.[3] As many as three hundred thousand disabled Germans and Austrians were killed under T4.[4]

Another huge part of the Nazis' fake news strategy was to gain control of the media so they could publish all the propaganda they wanted.[5] Before Hitler was elected, the Nazis controlled less than 3 percent of Germany's approximately 4,700 newspapers. Once in power, the Nazi Party quickly forced the biggest newspapers in Berlin to close down, and then they set up their own newspapers and radio programs in their place. The Nazis also passed strict laws to take control over what independent newspapers and radio stations reported.[6] The Nazis' secret police (known as the SS) broke into the offices of newspapers that were considered unfriendly to the party and destroyed their printing presses. Journalists critical of the government fled Germany. Once they were gone, the Nazi Party ensured that any newspaper companies that remained open replaced their journalists with people loyal to the party. By the end of the war, in 1945, there were only 1,100 newspapers published in Germany, and the Nazi party directly owned 325 of them. For the entire war, Nazi-controlled press published and broadcast almost nothing but fake news.

One thing the Nazis could not completely control, however, was what the media outside Germany said about them. They did work hard to try to trick foreign press outlets into reporting fake news stories, however. In an elaborate attempt to hide from the world their mass murder of the Jewish people, in 1944 the Nazis invited the Red Cross to come to Germany to inspect one of their concentration camps, Theresienstadt, in what is now the Czech Republic. But first they had their prisoners build fake homes, gardens, and stores in it to make it look like a pleasant little town, hiding what it really was.

They even picked out some of the healthier prisoners to speak with the Red Cross delegation and forced them to tell them how happy they were to live there. The Nazis told the Red Cross it was a "spa town" where older Jewish people could retire, but the reality was that approximately thirty-three thousand people were killed there, and thousands more were shipped off to other camps to be killed. The elaborate scheme worked, and the delegation reported that they had not seen anything out of the ordinary on their visit.[7]

Whenever a foreign newspaper or reporter said something critical of the regime, the Nazis called them the *Lügenpresse*, or "lying press."[8] To be clear, the Nazis were not fighting against fake news—after all, fake news was an integral part of their strategy. Instead, the term was meant to discredit *actual* news so that Germans would not believe what was reported. For the Nazis, *Lügenpresse* came to mean any journalist—and then any person—who disagreed with or criticized the Nazi government or Hitler.

The Nazis understood the power of fake news like almost no other group in history, and their actions provide an important lesson for us now. They knew that for their lies to work—to get people to turn on their neighbors—they had to control the press and convince the public that the only information they could believe was what the Nazi Party told them. People or groups using fake news to influence public opinion will often claim that what they say is the truth, and that every other source of information is lying.

The Nazis also played on people's existing biases and the racism of the time. Fake news is not usually capable of changing our minds completely—it cannot usually get us to believe the complete opposite of what we believed before. Instead, it plays to our existing beliefs and just makes us more certain we are right. In the years leading up to and during World War II, many Germans already thought that straight, white, able-bodied German Christians were a superior race. Nazi propaganda simply nudged them into targeting everyone who did not fall into that category.

THE ALLIES FIGHT BACK

"THIS IS GUSTAV SIEGFRIED EINS. THE CHIEF IS speaking," a man said in German over the tightly controlled radio waves in Germany.[9]

It was May 1941 at the height of World War II. The Chief was a Prussian military veteran and a loyal member of the Nazi Party, he told listeners. Loyal as he was, he had been compelled to speak out against the corruption of Nazi officials because the public deserved to know the truth. The Chief's broadcasts came up every hour and lasted just six minutes each. In each one, he praised the vision of Adolf Hitler and then went on angry, curse-filled tirades about how Nazi officials had corrupted it. Hitler's Nazi party officials were incompetent, cowardly, and immoral, the Chief said. Through the fault of these terrible officials, he said, the war effort was falling apart and Germany was losing battles. He ended each message by reciting a secret code, which changed with every broadcast.

The Nazis were furious. One of their own dared to publicly criticize them? They launched a full-scale effort to identify and track down the traitor, scouring the country for him. The Chief knew too much about the party and about the war, so he had to be a disaffected military officer, they thought. They assigned their code breakers to crack the code from each broadcast. The Nazis also tried to interrupt the signal to stop the Chief's broadcasts from getting through, but they could not seem to do it. They were fairly certain he was using a mobile transmitter and changing his location for every broadcast so the SS would not find him.

The code breakers eventually figured out the codes. Each one was the name of a place—like a grocery store or a bus stop—but there were never any more details than that. The Germans believed the locations were secret meeting points for members of the anti-Nazi resistance and sent police out to look for the Chief all over Germany. But they did not have much information to go on. In all, the Chief did over seven hundred broadcasts over the course of two years, but the Nazis never tracked him down.[10]

Many years later, British intelligence declassified once-sensitive documents and the Chief's identity was revealed: Peter Seckelmann, a German exile who had been broadcasting from England. After leaving his home in Berlin during the war, Seckelmann continued to work as a journalist in England and also began to assist British intelligence. The information used for the broadcast came from intelligence the British had collected from German prisoners of war, members of the resistance in Germany, and German newspapers and radio broadcasts.

The broadcasts used a lot of true information about the war to add to the Chief's credibility and fool Nazi Party officials. Seckelmann convincingly painted himself as a faithful, though disenchanted, member of the Nazi Party who was speaking out for the good of Germany. By talking frequently about his love for Adolf Hitler, his loyalty to Hitler's vision, and his hatred of the *Untermensch*, he made the public believe what he was saying.

British intelligence and Seckelmann blended in false information, too, to make it sound as if the Germans were doing worse than they really were. The goal of the broadcasts was to hurt the German military's morale and to weaken public support for the Nazi Party. Seckelmann, aka the Chief, made it sound like the Nazi government was on the brink of imploding, the military commanders had no idea what they were doing, and there was no hope. That was because it was in the Allies' best interest to paint a picture of a government on its last legs. After all, if you were a German soldier and you thought you were losing the war, would you necessarily fight to the bitter end?

Radio was a useful tool for promoting fake news for both sides of the war. It came across as a more authoritative source of information because you could hear a real person talk, rather than simply reading something in a newspaper. It made people more confident about what they were hearing. But they really had no idea who the person was behind the voice they heard. They would have never guessed it was someone like Seckelmann, fighting the war from hundreds of miles away, inside a secure room with British intelligence officers.

Radio broadcasts were not the only way the Allies (the "Big Four" included France, the Soviet Union, the United Kingdom, and the United States) used fake news to deceive Germany. In 1944, after the United States joined the war, the Allies were getting ready to invade Normandy in northern France to make their big move against the Axis powers (Germany, Italy, and Japan). It would take everything the Allies had—soldiers, navy ships, and airplanes—to get into France. More important, they knew it would turn the tide of the entire war if they pulled it off successfully.

But the Allies had a very serious problem. Germany had built a long line of defense all along the French coast: There were thousands of troops and millions of land mines waiting for them. That's when military leaders decided their best bet was to trick the enemy—they would make a fake army and get the Germans to believe they were going to attack in the Pas-de-Calais area, about 165 miles away from Normandy. And so, the First United States Army Group (FUSAG) was created.[11]

FUSAG was supposedly stationed in England. To make it look as convincing as possible, the US had movie and theater set builders construct what looked like a real army base for nearly one million fake soldiers. They built fake tanks, barracks, tents, hospitals, ammunition depots, jeeps, and other military equipment. The tanks and vehicles were all inflatable, and the buildings were just wood and painted canvas. But to the German planes doing surveillance thousands of feet above it all, it looked entirely real. To make it even more believable, the Allies put a famous general, George S. Patton, in charge of it and announced his command publicly. If FUSAG had been real, it would have made the Allied forces as much as 70 percent larger than they really were—a figure sure to terrify the Axis powers.[12]

But the Allies did not stop there. They also broadcast fake radio transmissions to make it sound to the Germans listening in as if different FUSAG units were really talking to one another. Diplomats also passed one another fake information about FUSAG, knowing the Germans would catch wind of it. British intelligence planted fake stories in newspapers about the command, even at one point having a local priest write a story about the inappropriate behavior of FUSAG troops stationed there. The Germans were utterly convinced that FUSAG was real and about to attack Pas-de-Calais, so they kept a large number of troops there to defend it.

Instead, on June 6 the Allies invaded Normandy with more than 156,000 soldiers: the biggest amphibious invasion in military history. They suffered over 4,000 casualties on what became known as D-Day. But without FUSAG, there would have been a lot more, and the operation might not have succeeded. Even weeks after the invasion in Normandy, the Germans waited in Pas-de-Calais, certain that FUSAG was still planning to come there. The Allies kept up the ruse and said that FUSAG was simply folded into other operations because Normandy had been so successful that they did not have to attack Pas-de-Calais anymore.[13] As a result, the Germans long thought the Allied military was actually much larger than it really was.

IN 1941, AT THE HEIGHT OF WORLD WAR II, THE US ARMY FOUND SOME VERY UNLIKELY PARTNERS TO HELP WITH ITS PROPAGANDA EFFORT AGAINST GERMANY AND JAPAN: WALT DISNEY AND WARNER BROTHERS. Together they created animated films, posters, and advertisements. Mickey and Minnie Mouse told people that patriotism meant supporting the war.[14] Bugs Bunny encouraged people to buy war bonds to help pay for military operations. Donald Duck and an animated Adolf Hitler told viewers Germany was losing the war, and an animated Chicken Little showed viewers how Hitler had used panic and fear to come to power in the first place.

Pinocchio and Geppetto in a scene from Disney's 1941 short film *All Together*[15]

We know from history, of course, that the Allies ultimately won the war. But that outcome was certainly not guaranteed at the time. The Allies often struggled to gain support for the war, both from the public at home and from other countries. Some people questioned if the Nazis were really committing the atrocities newspapers reported. That skepticism was in part thanks to a fake news story, long before the war, that backfired. In 1917, during World War I, Britain was working to get China to join the fight against the Central Powers (Germany, Austria-Hungary, Bulgaria, and the Ottoman Empire). So the British government took advantage of a shocking rumor that had appeared in smaller newspapers across Europe. The rumor was that the German government was taking the bodies of its own dead soldiers to a factory and, to help them in the war, boiling them to turn them into products like soap.

The British government had the story planted in several news-papers, including an English-language Chinese newspaper.[16] One of the articles even included a gruesome cartoon of the boiling process. Chinese officials were justifiably horrified by the story and declared war on Germany that same year. But in 1925, the British head of intelligence admitted that the government had made the story up to get support for the war.[17] The government finally faced the conse-quences of the story years later when it tried to gain international and public support to stop Germany's very real atrocities against Jews and other communities. People thought it was just more of Britain's propaganda.

As we have seen, fake news has helped countries start wars and win them, too. Why? The answer is simple: Fake news is an effective weapon. It has been used to build support for wars and tricked whole militaries. But when fake news is used by a government, there is a huge risk of backlash, because it creates a cycle of distrust. People who feel they have been tricked no longer believe they can trust the elements of society traditionally counted on to tell the truth, such as the government or the media. That makes people question if anything they are told is true at all. But living in that kind of uncertainty is too uncomfortable for most people, so we go looking for answers elsewhere. And that is when fake news can take a stronger hold. We become an easy target for fake news pushers who want to take advantage of our distrust of the government or media. They are like a movie villain beckoning to us from a dark alleyway, saying, "Come this way! I know the real truth!" Fake news might help governments win wars, but when it is used against people, governments lose something else—public trust.

CHAPTER 8

WHEN RACIST CONSPIRACIES BECOME FAKE NEWS

I N 1942, THE FEDERAL BUREAU OF INVESTIGA-
tion (FBI) received an odd request from the White House: to
investigate rumors that First Lady Eleanor Roosevelt was trying to organize an uprising in the South. For months, local newspapers all over the South had reported that black women who worked
as maids were forming a secret network of groups called "Eleanor
Clubs." The story went that the goal of these clubs was to get black
maids to quit their jobs working for white families by 1943, and
that they were all organized by the First Lady herself, who traveled
from town to town setting them up. Supposedly it cost ten cents to
be a member, and the motto was "A white woman in every kitchen
by Christmas!"[1]

Because of harsh laws at the time that discriminated against
black people, black women had long been forced into working

low-paying domestic service jobs. But the fact that more and more women were quitting these jobs, the newspapers claimed, was evidence that the clubs were clearly working. One conspiracy reported by a town newspaper as real news said that a maid quit her job suddenly when she heard her white employers criticizing the First Lady and the president. It was a rule every club member—signing her name in blood—had pledged to follow: that if her employer criticized either of the Roosevelts, she would quit her job immediately.[2] Another newspaper told a story about a black maid in South Carolina who set the table for lunch for three people. When her white employer asked who the third place setting was for, she said, "In the Eleanor Club we always sit with the people we work for."[3] In Alabama, a rumor spread that members of the Eleanor Club wore wide-brimmed hats with a feather in them. The larger the feather, the more senior the person was in the club.[4]

CONSPIRACY THEORIES ARE NOT EXACTLY THE SAME AS FAKE NEWS. A conspiracy theory is a belief that a covert but influential organization is responsible for an unexplained event or circumstance, but without credible evidence. These are theories such as the US government faking the moon landing of 1969 or President George W. Bush and the CIA masterminding the terrorist attack on America on September 11, 2001. Or the government hiding aliens from us on a secret military base called Area 51, or the Earth actually being flat but all the world's space agencies lying to us. Each time there is a shooting in the US, conspiracy theories spread, claiming the shooting was actually faked by various groups or individuals that want to take away the right of Americans to own guns.[5]

True conspiracy theorists are usually not trying to deceive people by spreading conspiracies—they actually believe the theories and that they are revealing a hidden truth. However, conspiracy theories can turn into fake news when people report them as actual news, knowing there is no evidence that they are true.

The Eleanor Club rumors were not just about women quitting their jobs. Many of the stories claimed the First Lady was actively organizing black people to stage an uprising. One rumor said that a black woman was heard saying that the Eleanor Club would have enough power to control the outcome of the next presidential election. Other dangerous rumors spread at the same time claimed that black men were stockpiling guns, ice picks, and other weapons to use against white people. One reported story claimed that black men were going to cause a blackout in electricity and then take over the country.

In response to the rumors, a newspaper editor in Mississippi wrote about the First Lady that "more than any other person, [she] was morally responsible for race riots."[6] Most larger newspapers in the South discounted the rumors, but they still published articles about them, which only helped the rumors spread. Smaller local newspapers reprinted the rumors as actual news without giving any proof the stories were true. Another Mississippi newspaper said there "was conclusive evidence" that the Eleanor Clubs existed, though the article did not provide any of that evidence.[7] Local newspapers would often report that Eleanor Roosevelt had hosted a meeting in a nearby town to rally members or cite supposed police reports from neighboring cities she had visited as evidence of the rumored plans for an uprising.[8]

A professor from the University of North Carolina at Chapel Hill heard of these rumors in 1942 and recruited several other professors across the South to help him collect and document them all. Together, the professors received thousands of reports from white people containing stories they had heard about black people working to disrupt their communities. The details of each story changed from state to state. Sometimes the woman who planned to eat with her employers set the table for five people instead of three, for example. But researchers saw that the stories all had the same message—that white people believed black people were working to overturn society in ways that would harm them or diminish their power. They were stories intended to cause fear by playing on racism.

When the White House asked the FBI to investigate the rumors, they of course knew the First Lady was not secretly plotting a revolt in the South. They were simply baffled about how the conspiracy theories had started and whether there might be violence because of them. The FBI interviewed everyone: newspaper editors, local politicians and police, and local citizens all over the South. All these people said the same thing: They had heard the stories from a friend, who had heard them from someone else, who had heard them from someone else, and so on. No one who had heard the stories knew where they had actually started. At the end of the investigation, the FBI announced it had not found any evidence that any of the stories were true.

So where did the conspiracies come from, then? At the time, the American South was undergoing significant political, social, and economic change. The United States had just declared war against Germany and Japan after Japan's attack on Pearl Harbor in December

FEDERAL BUREAU OF INVESTIGATION

Form
This ... ORIGINATED AT   MEMPHIS, TENNESSEE   FILE NO. 100-1535

REPORT MADE AT	DATE WHEN MADE	PERIOD FOR WHICH MADE	REPORT MADE BY	
MEMPHIS, TENNESSEE	11-13-42	11-3,5-42	██████████████	JOS

TITLE	CHARACTER OF CASE
ELEANOR ROOSEVELT CLUB OF NEGRO WOMEN, Jackson, Tennessee.	INTERNAL SECURITY - X

SYNOPSIS OF FACTS:

Investigation based upon report by confidential informant that negro women of Jackson, Tennessee were forming a club whose slogan was "not a cook in the kitchen by Christmas" results negatively. Original informant states that there was no basis for such a report.

- C -

DETAILS:

Investigation in this case is predicated upon information furnished to this office by Confidential Informant A who advised that information had been received by that informant to the effect that the negro women of Jackson, Tennessee had organized an Eleanor Roosevelt Club. Membership was reported in this club to be ten cents a week.

It was further stated by the informant that a negro cook who had worked for a ████████ on ████ Street in Jackson, Tennessee for some time had resigned recently, stating she was a member of this club and that the slogan of this group was "not a cook in the kitchen by Christmas". The initials of the ██████ referred to and the house number were not given.

AT JACKSON, TENNESSEE

A check of the Jackson, Tennessee City Directory for 1942 lists only one family by the name of ████ residing on ████ Street in Jackson.

██████████████████████ was contacted and

APPROVED AND FORWARDED: *Perry Wing* SPECIAL AGENT IN CHARGE	DO NOT WRITE IN THESE SPACES	SE
COPIES DESTROYED █████████	*100 -139664- IX*	RECORDED & INDEXED
COPIES OF THIS REPORT 5 DEC 3 1942		
6 Bureau 2 G-2 (1 Atlanta; 1 Memphis) 2 Memphis	COPY IN FILE 13 NOV 16 1942	

U S GOVERNMENT PRINTING OFFICE

1941. The country had to quickly get ready for war, and the government had opened factories all over the South to make equipment. When America joined the war, millions of black men joined the military. Black men and women also went to work in the factories.[10] Both jobs paid higher wages than many other jobs, such as domestic service, to which black people had been limited because of systemic racism. With more opportunities, black activists and workers pushed for better pay and equal rights, and they formed workers' unions to help them achieve those goals.

After the Fifteenth Amendment was added to the Constitution in 1870, making it illegal to deny (male) citizens the right to vote based on race or color, many states implemented poll taxes instead, making people pay a fee to register to vote. It was a way to keep low-income people, and especially black people and immigrants, out of politics and without a voice in government. And it worked quite effectively for a long time. Before 1942, only about 20 percent of people who were eligible to vote actually did so.[11]

Better-paying jobs meant many more people could afford to register to vote. White people who believed the rumors saw their society shifting in ways they did not like, ways that would give black people equal rights and put an end to the South's Jim Crow laws— laws enforced until 1965 that allowed racial segregation.

The rumors also started because of the unpopularity of the Roosevelts in the South. The president was disliked, but as an outspoken advocate for civil rights and the end to segregation, the First Lady was even more so.[12] On a trip the First Lady took to North Carolina in 1942, she held a series of community events, including a dinner with black men and women from different parts of the community. The white hosts who were supposed to provide her with a place to stay for the night were so upset she had broken the law on segregation that they forced her to return to Washington, DC, the same night.[13]

That was absolutely true, and for many people, it was something that made the conspiracy theories all the more believable. Of course the First Lady was running around the South organizing a revolt! People who believed the rumors saw them as just more evidence that the First Lady was trying to meddle in their affairs.

The conspiracies that spread were not just harmless little stories. They had serious consequences for civil rights. Black men who had enlisted in the army had hoped that their participation as an essential part of the military during World War II would push civil rights forward. Black activists and journalists called out the similarities between the Nazi Party that the US was fighting in Europe and the white supremacy in the South that was at the heart of the Jim Crow laws.[14] But the rumors ended up leading to an increase of violence by white people against black people, especially in the areas across the South where black troops were stationed.[15]

As we have seen in previous chapters, minority groups are often the targets of fake news, especially in times of political and social change.[16] People look for information to explain what is happening, and rumors start about evil forces conspiring against them. These conspiracies turn into fake news when people know they are not true and pass them on anyway, as many newspapers did in the South. Fake news takes advantage of people's existing racism or other discriminatory beliefs about minority communities. The people who believed the rumors saw that black people were moving into better-paying jobs and steadily gaining more rights. Their racism led them to believe that the reason those things were happening was not because of the shifting economic and political landscape and the hard work of black activists and community leaders, but rather because of an evil First Lady in the White House and a minority group trying to overthrow the country.

THE ALIEN INVASION
THAT WASN'T

O
N THE NIGHT BEFORE HALLOWEEN IN 1938, a radio announcer interrupted a live broadcast of dance music over the Columbia Broadcasting System network to inform listeners that an astronomer had detected explosions "like a jet of blue flame shot from a gun" on the planet Mars. A few minutes later, a reporter interviewed the astronomer, Professor Pierson, live on the air—he said he did not know why the explosions had happened. He assured listeners it was nothing to worry about, even as he received a telegram while on the air that said something like a large earthquake had just been detected around Princeton, New Jersey.

The program returned to the upbeat music, but soon the announcer was back, informing listeners that the earthquake that had been reported was actually a meteorite, which had crashed into a farmer's field in Grover's Mill, New Jersey. The reporter and Professor Pierson raced to the crash site. With sirens blaring in the background, the two quickly determined it wasn't a meteorite at all, but a metallic cylinder thirty yards in diameter—an extraterrestrial object of some kind.

Panicked shouts filled the air as the object began moving and a figure emerged. "Ladies and gentlemen, this is the most terrifying thing I've ever witnessed," the reporter said in a quivering voice. "Good heavens, something's wriggling out of the shadow like a gray snake. Now it's another one and another one and another one. They look like tentacles to me. . . . I can see the thing's body now. It's large, large as a bear. It glistens like wet leather. But that face, it—it—ladies and gentlemen, it's indescribable. I can hardly force myself to keep looking at it, it's so awful. The eyes are black and they gleam like a serpent. The mouth is kind of V-shaped with saliva dripping from its rimless lips that seem to quiver and pulsate."

As police neared the crash, the creature revealed a mirrorlike object that sent fire roaring out of the pit. Screams erupted over the radio as the flames spread, and then the transmission from Grover's Mill went dead.

During the next few minutes, a series of news bulletins told listeners that officials had declared martial law in New Jersey and Pennsylvania. Aliens were invading Earth. A military officer gave an eyewitness account of a massive slaughter of nearly seven thousand armed guardsmen who had been deployed to New Jersey to fight the aliens. The aliens killed them all with their "heat rays" and rode "tripod machines" that were taller than skyscrapers. But the invasion didn't stop there. Soon, "Martian cylinders" landed in Buffalo, Chicago, and St. Louis and killed whole cities with poisonous black gas, the radio reported.[17] They were coming to destroy everyone and everything.

Now, if you're wondering why your history textbooks never told you about the Great Martian Invasion of Earth in 1938, that's because, as you might have guessed, it never happened. Before we had twenty-four-hour TV programming and hundreds of cable TV channels to choose from, families would gather around the radio. It was their main source for news and entertainment. They would listen to dramatic readings over the radio, the way we listen to audiobooks. At the beginning of this particular program, the announcer explained that a radio-acting troupe, led by a young actor named Orson Welles, would be doing a dramatic reenactment of a famous work of fiction: *The War of the Worlds* by H. G. Wells. The station had planned it as part of their Halloween series.

The program really was impressively innovative. If you listened to the recording now, you might be surprised at how convincing it sounds, in part because they used very sophisticated sound effects for the time,

Even though most of the program was structured as a series of news bulletins, the broadcast itself isn't a case of fake news. The radio company was not intentionally trying to pass H. G. Wells's fiction off as fact, and they informed listeners that it was a fictional radio play at the start of the program. But the way the newspapers reported on it afterward is. The day after the program aired, newspapers all over the country decried the program for being a deliberate hoax. Some listeners had tuned into the program after it had already started and so had missed that crucial opening caveat, articles said. As a result, thousands of people genuinely believed that Martians had invaded Earth. Newspapers reported stories about hours-long traffic jams because people were trying to flee the East Coast. The *New York Times* told a story about families in New Jersey rushing out of their houses with wet towels over their faces to flee the poisonous gas attacks. An article from the Associated Press claimed a man came home to find his wife ready to commit suicide to escape the invasion.[18] Even history books written after the fact bought into claims of mass hysteria.

Most of these claims were never proven, however. A survey conducted later showed that the percentage of people who actually listened to the broadcast was very small. So why all the dramatic reports? Well, print journalism and radio were competitors back then. Regular radio broadcasts had only started in 1920, so it was still a new thing at that point. It was in the newspapers' interest to make the station look as reckless and deceitful as possible so consumers might decide to rely on print journalism for their news.[19]

While fake news about the event has made it difficult for historians to determine how many people were actually fooled by the program, there is evidence that some listeners did indeed take the dramatization seriously. Listening to a few moments of a radio broadcast and running in panic is kind of like seeing a news headline that makes us angry or scared, and then sharing the whole article without reading the rest of it to make sure we should actually be worried. When information triggers strong emotions in us, it is important to make sure we have the whole story before acting on those emotions. If listeners had waited to learn more, they might have caught the reminder at intermission that the show was not real.

Years later, in 1955, Orson Welles himself offered similar advice during an interview with the BBC by revealing the true intentions of those involved in the broadcast. "We weren't as innocent as we meant to be when we did the Martian broadcast," he said. "We were fed up with the way in which everything that came over this new magic box, the radio, was being swallowed...so in a way, our broadcast was an assault on the credibility of that machine. We wanted people to understand that they shouldn't take any opinion predigested, and they shouldn't swallow everything that came through the tap, whether it was radio or not."[20]

CHAPTER 9

SMOKING IS GOOD FOR YOU AND OTHER FAKE NEWS ABOUT YOUR HEALTH

I N DECEMBER 1953, THE LEADERS OF THE SIX biggest tobacco companies in the United States held a series of secret meetings at the Plaza Hotel in New York City.[1] They had a big problem on their hands. In a report in *Time* magazine, scientists had announced that the tar and other chemicals used in cigarettes had given lab mice cancer. "Beyond any doubt," the magazine had said, "there is something in cigarette smoke which can produce cancer."[2]

In the United States around this time, about two thirds of men and one third of women smoked, and lung cancer became the number one cancer to lead to death. The cigarette business was booming, but now new reports were coming out about the health risks that could put everything in jeopardy. At the secret meetings, the heads of Big Tobacco—as the companies were called—agreed that they needed to develop a strategy, together, to keep people smoking. They needed to counter the new health reports, trick the media, and deceive the public.

To do that, they hired one of the most influential public relations firms in the United States: Hill & Knowlton. The firm had had years of experience working to boost the public image of other companies whose products carried big health risks, like those in the liquor and the chemical industries. If scientific research was what threatened tobacco companies, Hill & Knowlton said, then the key to the solution also lay with scientific research. With their help, Big Tobacco started finding and promoting the voices of researchers who had expressed doubt about the link between smoking and lung cancer. But the companies knew that was not going to be enough to counter the growing anti-tobacco voices.[3]

That was when it hit them: Big Tobacco had to undermine the public's trust in science in general. To do that, they needed their *own* research organization, which the companies themselves could direct and control. This research group would ultimately claim that science was really a matter of opinion. They set about hiring a team of scientists and founded an organization called the Tobacco Industry Research Committee (TIRC). At the time, John W. Hill, the head of Hill & Knowlton, wrote that "the word 'Research' is needed in the name to give weight and added credence to the Committee's statements."[4] In other words, they needed to make the TIRC sound independent and scientific so they could present its research as legitimate and unbiased, even though it was the opposite.

The heads of Big Tobacco put out a full-page ad in over four hundred newspapers nationwide announcing the creation of the TIRC in response to the new health reports on the effects of smoking. "We always have and always will cooperate closely with those whose task it is to safeguard the public health," they pledged in the ad. They also insisted, however, that links between smoking and lung cancer had not been proven, and that "there is no agreement among the authorities regarding what the cause is. . . . For more than 300 years tobacco has given solace, relaxation, and enjoyment to mankind. At one time or another during those years critics have held it responsible for practically every disease of the human body. One by one these charges have been abandoned for lack of evidence."[5] That was why they'd created the TIRC, they said—to get to the truth of the matter.

And what do you know, the TIRC did indeed find that smoking was not dangerous at all! People were developing cancer for other reasons, the TIRC said, none of which had to do with smoking. The findings were far from unbiased, of course. They left out that the tobacco companies were paying the TIRC researchers and that the whole thing was a publicity stunt to keep people buying cigarettes.

Next, Big Tobacco needed to get the media on board. Yes, thousands of scientists agreed that smoking caused cancer, but there were a few scientists who did not. These scientists needed to be heard, the companies said; there were two sides to the debate, and journalists were not doing their job of providing information objectively if they did not report both, even if the evidence on one side was overwhelming. One executive at Hill & Knowlton said in 1968 that "the most important type of story is that which casts doubt in the cause and effect theory of disease and smoking. Eye-grabbing headlines should strongly call out the point—Controversy! Contradiction! Other Factors! Unknowns!"[6]

A Frank Statement

to Cigarette Smokers

RECENT REPORTS on experiments with mice have given wide publicity to a theory that cigarette smoking is in some way linked with lung cancer in human beings.

Although conducted by doctors of professional standing, these experiments are not regarded as conclusive in the field of cancer research. However, we do not believe that any serious medical research, even though its results are inconclusive should be disregarded or lightly dismissed.

At the same time, we feel it is in the public interest to call attention to the fact that eminent doctors and research scientists have publicly questioned the claimed significance of these experiments.

Distinguished authorities point out:

1. That medical research of recent years indicates many possible causes of lung cancer.

2. That there is no agreement among the authorities regarding what the cause is.

3. That there is no proof that cigarette smoking is one of the causes.

4. That statistics purporting to link cigarette smoking with the disease could apply with equal force to any one of many other aspects of modern life. Indeed the validity of the statistics themselves is questioned by numerous scientists.

We accept an interest in people's health as a basic responsibility, paramount to every other consideration in our business.

We believe the products we make are not injurious to health.

We always have and always will cooperate closely with those whose task it is to safeguard the public health.

For more than 300 years tobacco has given solace, relaxation, and enjoyment to mankind. At one time or another during those years critics have held it responsible for practically every disease of the human body. One by one these charges have been abandoned for lack of evidence.

Regardless of the record of the past, the fact that cigarette smoking today should even be suspected as a cause of a serious disease is a matter of deep concern to us.

Many people have asked us what we are doing to meet the public's concern aroused by the recent reports. Here is the answer:

1. We are pledging aid and assistance to the research effort into all phases of tobacco use and health. This joint financial aid will of course be in addition to what is already being contributed by individual companies.

2. For this purpose we are establishing a joint industry group consisting initially of the undersigned. This group will be known as TOBACCO INDUSTRY RESEARCH COMMITTEE.

3. In charge of the research activities of the Committee will be a scientist of unimpeachable integrity and national repute. In addition there will be an Advisory Board of scientists disinterested in the cigarette industry. A group of distinguished men from medicine, science, and education will be invited to serve on this Board. These scientists will advise the Committee on its research activities.

This statement is being issued because we believe the people are entitled to know where we stand on this matter and what we intend to do about it.

TOBACCO INDUSTRY RESEARCH COMMITTEE

5400 EMPIRE STATE BUILDING, NEW YORK 1, N. Y.

SPONSORS:

THE AMERICAN TOBACCO COMPANY, INC.
Paul M. Hahn, President

BENSON & HEDGES
Joseph F. Cullman, Jr., President

BRIGHT BELT WAREHOUSE ASSOCIATION
F. S. Royster, President

BROWN & WILLIAMSON TOBACCO CORPORATION
Timothy V. Hartnett, President

BURLEY AUCTION WAREHOUSE ASSOCIATION
Albert Clay, President

BURLEY TOBACCO GROWERS COOPERATIVE
ASSOCIATION
John W. Jones, President

LARUS & BROTHER COMPANY, INC.
W. T. Reed, Jr., President

P. LORILLARD COMPANY
Herbert A. Kent, Chairman

MARYLAND TOBACCO GROWERS ASSOCIATION
Samuel C. Linton, General Manager

PHILIP MORRIS & CO., LTD., INC.
O. Parker McComas, President

R. J. REYNOLDS TOBACCO COMPANY
E. A. Darr, President

STEPHANO BROTHERS, INC.
C. S. Stephano, D'Sc., Director of Research

TOBACCO ASSOCIATES, INC.
(An organization of flue-cured tobacco growers)
J. B. Hutson, President

UNITED STATES TOBACCO COMPANY
J. W. Peterson, President

After years of yellow journalism tanking the credibility of the media, the number one concern of reporters in the 1950s was to be as objective as possible so they could not be accused of bias. Big Tobacco took advantage of that, and of the fact that reporters covering the issue were not scientists or experts in the field themselves. They could not verify the information or do their own lab research, so the best solution for most reporters was to present both sides and let the public (who, by and large, were also not scientists) decide for themselves.[8] The companies did not need to fully convince anyone; they just needed to sow enough uncertainty into the debate that people would keep smoking, and the media helped them do it. Suddenly, people were presented with contradictory information about smoking that made it sound as if the scientific findings really were up for debate. If you liked smoking and it seemed that scientists really didn't know the effects, the choice was an easy one—keep smoking.

Big Tobacco also worked to get politicians on their side. They donated to political campaigns that were friendly to their cause and then gave those politicians talking points to use when defending them against government agencies that wanted to implement regulations, such as the Environmental Protection Agency and the Food and Drug Administration.

Tobacco's fake news campaign went on for over four decades, even though more and more research proving the dangers of smoking came out over time. By 1964, when the US surgeon general first warned that smoking caused cancer, there were more than seven thousand published articles that said smoking was dangerous. Things were once again looking dire for tobacco companies, so they simply altered their strategy. Big Tobacco designed "low-tar" or "light" cigarettes that used filters, claiming they were the healthy option and providing the research (from TIRC, of course) to back it up. But in fact, low-tar cigarettes allowed more carcinogens to go deeper into the lungs, because people smoking them would take deeper puffs. In 1996, the American Cancer Society published a study that showed the rate of lung cancer deaths actually increased after supposed low-tar cigarettes came onto the market.[9]

It was not until the 1990s that secret documents started to become public that showed tobacco companies had long known the effects of smoking both regular and "light" cigarettes, even as they pumped out fake news saying otherwise.[10] And the US government decided there was something it could do about it. In 1999, in one of the government's biggest cases against a totally legal industry, the US sued the six biggest companies involved in the scheme. The Department of Justice spent years compiling evidence, including incriminating company documents that had been leaked. The lawsuit said that Big Tobacco had made cigarettes more addictive while claiming they were not addictive at all. It showed that the companies had targeted young people in their advertising campaigns in order to get people hooked on cigarettes at a young age. The lawsuit also showed that the companies had purposefully lied about the health risks of smoking when they knew the truth, and even destroyed documents to cover up their activities.[11]

In the landmark case, the judge found that the companies had engaged in racketeering—in other words, they'd been involved in a dishonest or fraudulent business. According to the judge, the companies had "marketed and sold their lethal product with zeal, with deception, with a single-minded focus on their financial success, and without regard for the human tragedy or social costs that success exacted."[12] The companies were ordered to stop lying to the public.

Despite the lawsuit, Big Tobacco is still—years later—fighting the US government on how it markets its products. Why are so many people taken in by fake news campaigns when scientific results are so clear on things like smoking? First, as we saw with Big Tobacco, many people believed the TIRC's research because it sounded independent and unbiased. Real scientists were saying smoking was safe. Would it have changed people's minds to know that those scientists were paid by tobacco companies to come up with those conclusions? Hopefully. But those people liked smoking, and the TIRC said what they wanted to hear.

The media also helped amplify the fake news voices out of an effort to appear unbiased and objective. There is a danger in reporting "both sides" of an issue without telling readers where the information comes from. It makes it sound as though the thousands of pages of scientific research proving something is the same thing as the statements of a handful of scientists paid by companies to create uncertainty.

Perhaps most alarming is that the four decades in which Big Tobacco successfully spread fake news to keep themselves from going out of business created a kind of road map for other industries to follow. In 1998, Dr. Andrew Wakefield published a research paper in a medical journal claiming that there was a link between the measles, mumps, and rubella (MMR) vaccine and autism. According to his study, eight of twelve previously healthy children studied contracted symptoms within two weeks of having gotten the vaccine.[13] Wakefield called for people to stop getting their children the MMR vaccine until more research could be done. That was all it took. Wakefield and his study were suddenly all over the news, launching a global health scare.[14]

Even when evidence started to arise that disproved Wakefield's analysis, the *Daily Mail* and other British newspapers published positive stories about his findings. Hollywood celebrities of the era, including Jenny McCarthy, Charlie Sheen, and Alicia Silverstone, jumped on the anti-vaccination movement, too. Wakefield's research was discredited within a few years, but MMR vaccinations declined so sharply that there were full-blown measles outbreaks in Canada, the United Kingdom, and the US starting around 2006 as the population of unvaccinated children grew.[15]

Years later the *Times* of London reported that Wakefield had apparently manipulated the data in his study and changed the results to purposefully show a link between the vaccine and the disease. What could be worth risking public health for? Money, of course! It was revealed that Wakefield was being paid by parents who believed the MMR vaccine had harmful side effects and were considering suing the makers of it. Did he believe that if he could force a link between the vaccines and diseases, he would get paid a lot of money from future lawsuits to continue doing research on the issue? It certainly seems likely. Wakefield's medical license was revoked, and he has since been barred from practicing medicine. The medical journal that published the original study retracted it in 2010, but by then the damage had been done. To this day, fake news sources still push Wakefield's research online, and he continues to defend his conclusions.

Big Tobacco's and Wakefield's fake news scheme provide an important lesson on knowing where our information comes from before believing it, and on looking at the motivation of the person or group producing it. Information produced by a biased author or a group that pays someone to say a certain thing is, by its very nature, not objective.

THE INTRODUCTION OF TELEVISION

THE FIRST TV NEWS PROGRAMS IN AMERICA began airing in 1940. They were short, fifteen- to thirty-minute spots, because stations were not convinced at first that people wanted that much news.[16] But the public loved it. They no longer had to simply read about events in faraway lands or listen to faceless voices on the radio talk, they could witness them firsthand thanks to foreign correspondents and camera crews bringing them to the frontlines. The public demand for news increased over the decades, becoming so high that CNN was established in 1980, becoming the first twenty-four-hour-a-day news network on TV and setting off the creation of other cable news networks.

The interest in TV news was driven in large part by the fact that after hundreds of years of sensationalized news, people liked to be able to visually verify what they were being told.[17] They wanted objective and factual news, and being able to see for themselves what was reported increased their confidence in the news. But there was a downside too. For a long time, people believed that, since they could see it for themselves, whatever they saw on TV was true.

That trust posed an opportunity for horror writer Stephen Volk and TV producer Ruth Baumgarten in 1992. On Halloween night, they aired a ninety-minute show on the BBC called *Ghostwatch*. It was marketed as a live broadcast investigating a home in northwest London that was said to be "the most haunted house in Britain."[18] The show followed Pamela Early and her two daughters, who lived in the house with a ghost they'd named Pipes, as it supposedly liked to bang on the water pipes.

The hosts were two of the BBC's most trusted presenters, and the whole thing was shot on videotape rather than the sixteen-millimeter film typically used then for TV shows. This made *Ghostwatch* look homemade and more authentic. The camera followed the Early family around the house, during which Pipes caused all sorts of havoc and even possessed the girls. As the hosts investigated, the camera cut back to the BBC studio to interview a paranormal specialist and take calls from viewers who shared their own personal experiences with ghosts. The show ended with the revelation that the investigation and the eleven million viewers watching around Britain had acted as a kind of séance that had released Pipes's evil spirit through the airwaves and into the homes of the viewers. The ghost then supposedly took control of the cameras in the BBC stations and TV screens went dark.[19]

Before the show aired, it was featured on the cover of a British weekly magazine that listed TV and radio schedules. The article about the show clarified that *Ghostwatch* was fiction. But the problem was that not everyone who watched the show had read the article. The BBC received over twenty thousand complaints for airing the show, which was later linked to multiple cases of children being diagnosed with post-traumatic stress disorder.[20] The show was also said to have been the cause of a suicide. Afterward, a British court found that the BBC had tried to "cultivate a sense of menace" and had neglected its "duty to do more than simply hint at the deception it was practising on the audience."[21]

GHOSTWATCH WAS NOT THE LAST ATTEMPT BY FILMMAKERS TO SPOOF PARANORMAL ACTIVITY ON FILM. In 1999, a low-budget independent horror film, *The Blair Witch Project*, hit US movie theaters, going on to make over $250 million worldwide. It followed three young filmmakers who went camping in a forest in Maryland to uncover the mystery of a local legend known as the Blair Witch. In the movie, the group gets lost in the woods, where they are haunted, and the witch ultimately kills the group. The actors shot the whole movie themselves on handheld cameras to make it look like a real documentary. Perhaps even more impressive, the IMDb acting pages for the three main actors even said "missing, presumed dead" before the film was released.[22]

CHAPTER 10

THE FAKE NEWS INTELLIGENCE BATTLES

IT IS TIME FOR A MASSIVE DISCLAIMER. Almost all governments, including the United States, have used fake news as a weapon to influence events in other countries, though they usually call it "disinformation" or "influence of information operations." Most countries use their intelligence services to do so, and in America's case, that means the CIA.

After World War II, the world suddenly found itself caught in a fierce tug-of-war between the Soviet Union and the United States, each trying to gain global dominance during a period known as the Cold War. They did not fight this war in actual military-on-military battles, at least not directly with each other; neither side really wanted to, despite how much they threatened to attack each other. Instead they relied a lot on disinformation to do the work, in part because it was so cheap and relatively easy to do.

Both sides especially wanted to increase their influence in the world's developing countries. Using the growth of the media to its advantage, the United States spread disinformation to fight the spread of Communism, erode the reputation of the Soviet Union, and even destabilize and overthrow foreign governments it deemed unfriendly to American interests.

When the CIA was created in 1947, one of its main missions was to conduct covert action overseas—secret operations to influence political, economic, or military conditions in other countries. It is used when government officials think covert action is the only way to advance US goals—rather than, for example, using traditional diplomacy or a military operation. And the White House used the CIA *a lot* during the Cold War. I have many stories about that, but, unfortunately, most of the good ones are classified. Instead, let's talk about the Soviet Union.

The same year the US created the CIA, the Soviet Union created a new foreign intelligence agency to run some of its secret operations called the Committee of Information (KI).[1] The Soviets started funding newspapers in Africa and Latin America, two areas where they wanted to increase their political and economic influence.[2] That way, they would be able to influence what stories were printed. Soviet officers then conducted a thorough analysis of what was already published and reported in the US news. Officers learned quickly that disinformation spread better when it was about topics that were both politically and culturally relevant, and touched on real events that were already happening.

In 1964, the Soviets forged documents to make it look like Western politicians had supported the Nazi regime in Germany, but they were quickly discovered to be fake. The Soviets also planted wild conspiracy stories in the newspapers they funded and recruited journalists to work for them to publish and promote the claim that the CIA had assassinated President John F. Kennedy and civil rights leader Martin Luther King Jr.[3] Another campaign the Soviets waged claimed that American couples adopted babies from other countries as part of a secret operation to harvest their organs. This disinformation campaign was so convincing that some countries stopped allowing Americans to adopt children.[4]

The Soviets learned something important from the success of these early disinformation operations—people could be fooled by stories about fake secret government plots. In fact, to this day there are still conspiracy-theory websites that promote all these stories.

In 1981, the Soviets watched carefully when the US Centers for Disease Control and Prevention (CDC) released a report on a sudden illness affecting five previously healthy gay men in Los Angeles.[5] The report said these men had multiple infections and pneumonia, and their immune systems were shutting down. The CDC did not know what the cause was, how the illness spread, or how to cure it, and by the time they wrote the report and published it, two of the five men had died. After the report was published, doctors around the United States flooded the CDC with reports of similar cases. A little over a year later, there was a name for the disease—Acquired Immuno deficiency Syndrome (AIDS)—and it had broken out, not just across the country but across the world, in a full-blown epidemic.[6] For the Soviets, this was the perfect opportunity to turn the world against the United States.

In the 1980s, the American public was very concerned about biological and chemical weapons.[7] (Chemical weapons are chemicals used to kill or maim people, such as mustard gas, which was used for the first time in World War I. Chemicals can also be used to destroy crops to starve a population during wartime. Biological weapons are infectious diseases intentionally spread through viruses, bacteria, and other toxins, such as anthrax.) Through several congressional investigations, the public had learned that the government was spending a lot of money on research into biological and chemical warfare. The public was weary from back-to-back wars in Europe, Korea, and Vietnam, and they did not trust the government to keep them out of another war.

The Soviets saw that Americans were paying more attention to what their government was doing because of this mistrust, and realized it was an opportunity. That is when they launched a secret disinformation campaign called Operation INFEKTION, claiming that US government scientists had created the lethal virus called AIDS. It was almost too easy for the Soviets. Two disinformation officers from the KGB—the Soviet's main security agency—later claimed that the idea "virtually conceptualized itself."[8]

As usual, the first step was to plant stories in media outlets outside the Soviet Union to hide the fact that it came from them. The Soviets had learned by then that disinformation worked best when they mixed true facts in with the fake information. The first article the Soviets produced appeared in 1983, in the *Patriot*, a small newspaper they had been funding in India, with the headline AIDS MAY INVADE INDIA: MYSTERY DISEASE CAUSED BY US EXPERIMENTS. It was supposedly written by a "well-known American scientist and anthropologist." The article included a number of facts about the virus. It cited real information that had been reported in America about US research into chemical and biological weapons. That is when they sowed in the fake information. "AIDS," the supposed

American scientist said, "is believed to be the result of the Pentagon's experiments to develop new and dangerous biological weapons" in a secret lab at Fort Detrick, an army medical base in Maryland.[9]

The Soviets published another article, this time in a Russian newspaper known to carry Soviet propaganda, titled PANIC IN THE WEST OR WHAT IS HIDING BEHIND THE SENSATION SURROUNDING AIDS. The article used real statistics about AIDS breaking out on the East Coast of the United States. It also listed secret biological-warfare programs to suggest the government was deploying the virus intentionally as a kind of genocide against the communities AIDS affected more than any other—gay people and African Americans.[10] It also cited the previous article in the *Patriot* to make both articles seem more credible. But the Soviets did not stop there.

One of the keys to getting fake news to spread is repeating the same message over and over in as many forms as possible, so the Soviets organized radio broadcasts, published more articles and papers, and printed leaflets and posters, especially in countries that were the most strategically important to Moscow, like Zaire (now the Democratic Republic of Congo), Argentina, and Pakistan. Some of those stories and posters claimed that American troops deployed overseas were secretly injecting local populations with the virus themselves.[11] And those efforts paid off. As fake news reports continued to appear, real news outlets started picking up the story, especially in developing countries where the AIDS virus was also spreading. The media was still growing in many of those countries, so it was often easier to get sketchy stories published there.

After media coverage, the second step of the Soviet operation was to use "agents of influence" to spread disinformation. These were KGB contacts who held important positions, including scientists, journalists, and public figures. In 1985, the Soviets reached out to the East German state security service—known as the Stasi—and asked for help with Operation INFEKTION. The Stasi was one of the most feared and hated parts of the Eastern German Communist government. It ran East Germany like a prison and had a huge network of secret informants, mostly just regular people forced into spying on their neighbors. And, as the KGB expected, the Stasi had the perfect person for the job—a retired East German biophysicist, Dr. Jakob Segal.

Segal was born in St. Petersburg, Russia, and living in Eastern Germany, with no connections, at least that he knew about, to the KGB. He was a respected scientist who could speak authoritatively and convincingly on health issues. This was a man people would take seriously. The Stasi made contact with Segal and gave him evidence— which was of course fake—that the US was responsible for the AIDS epidemic. By then, AIDS had broken out on every continent except Antarctica, with over 15,500 cases reported in the US and almost as many deaths.[12] Segal was convinced of the "evidence" and wrote a forty-seven-page report claiming that the US government had created and spread AIDS by experimenting on gay people in prison, so that they would later infect the gay population in New York City and San Francisco. By 1987, the report had been covered by the media in eighty different countries.

Besides Segal's report, one of the biggest successes in Operation INFEKTION came after the Stasi sent an anonymous package of (dis)information about the origin of AIDS to a bestselling author from Austria.[13] The author took the bait, and in 1987 he published a novel using the disinformation as the premise. In interviews with the media, he said his inspiration for the book came from the fact that the US had created the AIDS virus.

The US knew that the Soviets were behind the campaign and publicly called them out. Scientists from all over the world also spoke out against the stories. By 1987, AIDS had started to spread in the Soviet Union, too. When Soviet researchers reached out to the US for help treating the virus, the US realized it had some leverage. American officials told them they would not help until the Soviets stopped their disinformation campaign. And so the Soviets were forced to abandon Operation INFEKTION.

But the damage had already been done. Between when the first article was published in India in 1983 to when the Soviets ended the operation in 1987, media outlets in fifty countries had published news on the conspiracy.[14] Soviet efforts to push the conspiracy that the US military was spreading AIDS made countries afraid to let them in.[15] Moreover, the whole time the Soviets were running Operation INFEKTION, they were also secretly developing their *own* chemical and biological weapons. The world was so focused on watching the US, however, that no one was paying attention to what the Soviets were up to on that front.

The operation had an even longer-lasting impact at home in the US. In a survey in 1992, 15 percent of American participants said they believed the US government deliberately created the AIDS virus in a lab. Even years later, in a 2005 study published by the *Journal of Acquired Immune Deficiency Syndromes*, 15 percent of African Americans surveyed said they believed AIDS was a form of genocide against black people, and nearly 50 percent believed it was a man-made virus.[16]

Operation INFEKTION shows us how important it is to do a little investigating into where our information is coming from. Many of the stories that claimed the US invented AIDS hinged on that one original article published in 1983 by the Indian newspaper funded by the Soviets. Just as your teacher wants you to cite all your sources in your research paper, we should expect that real media outlets will do the same in their reports. Credible media will cite more than one source of information to demonstrate that what they are reporting is true. Especially if they are making as big a claim as, you know, a country attacking populations with weaponized viruses created in secret labs.

WELCOME TO THE INTERNET

IN 1937, H. G. WELLS (YES, THE SAME AUTHOR who wrote about alien invasions) predicted the creation of the internet. "The whole human memory can be, and probably in short time will be, made accessible to every individual," he wrote. And in a lecture that year, he said, "The time is close at hand when any student, in any part of the world, will be able to sit with his projector in his own study at his or her own convenience to examine any book, any document, in an exact replica."[17] The idea at the time was considered revolutionary by most people. But it was not too far off.

In the late 1960s, researchers at several universities, funded by the US Department of Defense, had the idea that people could more easily share information with one another if they created a network of computers all linked together. They called it the Advanced Research Projects Agency Network—or, ARPANET. The first internet browser, the World Wide Web, was created in 1989, but it was mostly for scientists.[18] When the internet became more widely available to regular users late in the mid-1990s, it was a little like the immediate aftermath of the invention of the printing press. Except that if the printing press had created a flood of information, the internet created a tsunami.

The internet went from 130 websites by June 1993[19] to almost 2 billion by 2019.[20] Suddenly, information and news was available in unprecedented amounts, and all at the click of a button (or maybe a little longer—dial-up internet was slow in the beginning!). In 1994, sensing the turning tide, Reuters became the first news agency to provide free access to news online.[21] Soon after, the other major media outlets followed suit. New, alternative media (that is, media outside the traditional news outlets) popped up, started by people or organizations that otherwise would not have had the funds to start a print newspaper, radio station, or TV show. Alternative media could provide much narrower coverage, sometimes on one specific topic or geared toward a particular interest of specific readers. There were now more choices than ever before of where people could get their news and information, and most of it was free. In 2000, just 46 percent of adults in the United States used the internet. But by 2008, more than 74 percent did.[22]

WHAT IS THE DEFINITION OF MAINSTREAM MEDIA?
The term *mainstream media* refers to the national news media outlets (including newspapers, radio, and television networks) that have the most influence on public views. Mainstream media outlets typically have millions of readers or viewers, such as NBC, the *Washington Post*, and the BBC. They also market themselves as being objective and politically neutral, although outlets like Fox News, whose creators in 1996 claimed it would be a conservative voice to counterbalance what they viewed as a left-leaning CNN, challenge that definition.[23] However, there is not a definitive list of which outlets are considered part of the mainstream media.

The surge of information online did have a negative effect on traditional media. People stopped buying print subscriptions to newspapers because there was so much free content available online. As a result, companies stopped buying advertising space in papers, since there were not as many readers to reach. Advertisers also had the ability now to reach potential customers directly online, rather than having to go through the media. In 1950, almost everyone subscribed to a newspaper, and some households had more than one. But by 2010, most newspapers had lost over 70 percent of their subscriptions.[24] Newspapers were gutted, and journalists were laid off in droves.[25]

Today, most news outlets have stopped printing hard-copy papers altogether and have turned to digital news only, which readers pay a subscription fee to access. But even that is a struggle, now that there is so much free information online. In 1994, newspapers printed about 60 million copies a year, but by 2018, newspaper circulation for both print and digital news *combined* was between 31 and 34 million a year.[26] Smaller regional and local news outlets around the world have taken some of the biggest hits, laying off staff or shutting down altogether. In the UK alone, more than two hundred regional and local newspapers closed down between 2005 and 2018.[27]

The internet also had a major impact on fake news. Ordinary people soon realized that there were no limits online, as long as they could afford an internet connection. The internet did not belong to anyone, really. With minimal web-design skills, a person could buy a domain and put up their own website or blog in no time at all, something that has only gotten easier as web-design companies have made templates that anyone of any skill level can use. Fake news pushers no longer had to go through the mainstream media outlets to get false information out. They could connect instantly with potentially thousands of people by just having an email address or website. And that is exactly what they did.

SECTION 3

Drowning in Fake News

CHAPTER 11

GOING DIGITAL

"I LIVE IN DAMASCUS, SYRIA. IT'S A REPRESSIVE
police state. Most LGBT people are still deep in the closet or stay-
ing as invisible as possible. But I have set up a blog announcing my
sexuality, with my name and my photo. Am I crazy?" wrote twenty-
five-year-old gay Syrian American Amina Arraf in 2011 in one of
her first posts on a blog titled *A Gay Girl in Damascus*.[1] The blog was
definitely a heroic act. The Syrian government had a long history of
limiting free speech and imprisoning anyone who spoke out against
its leaders. It was even more dangerous for Amina because being gay
was illegal in Syria.

At the end of 2010, large protests had erupted across the Middle
East and North Africa against corrupt authoritarian governments.
Media outlets called it the Arab Spring.[2] The protests started in
Tunisia and then spread to Libya and Egypt, and it looked like Syria
would be next. When nationwide protests broke out across Syria in
March 2011, Amina not only joined the thousands of people in the
streets demanding change, but she also documented the marches in
detail for her blog. She felt the Syrian people had been persecuted by

their government for too long, and enough was enough. "No conspiracy, no diabolical plot, but the slow accumulation of grievances and indignities and a people who'd outgrown its rulers," Amina explained on her blog. "We were still sleeping, but barely. And a spark was all that was needed to awaken us." [3]

The world was closely following the Arab Spring, and readers of Amina's blog were captivated by her detailed stories of what was happening. In some countries where protests had taken place, the governments had resigned. But in Syria, the government sent in the military and police, killing protestors or putting them in prison. Amina shared with her readers that before every protest she would write her name and phone number on her arm in case she was killed for participating. In one of her most shared posts, Amina told readers how the Syrian security services had finally found out who she was and showed up at her house in April to arrest her. Her father had bravely talked them out of it, but Amina had been forced to go into hiding.

In June, a post appeared that many of Amina's followers had long been dreading. It was written by her cousin, Rania, who said that three armed men had spotted Amina on her way to meet another activist and arrested her. Her capture made news around the world. In just the first three months of the Arab Spring in Syria alone, it was estimated that the Syrian government had imprisoned more than ten thousand people. [4] Now it looked like Amina was one of them.

Since she was also an American citizen, the US Department of State stepped in. But when they began investigating, they discovered that there was no record of Amina Arraf. When media outlets began to question Amina's existence, the truth came out. The gay Syrian American woman was actually Tom MacMaster—a forty-year-old straight, married, male American graduate student studying at the University of Edinburgh in Scotland who had made up the whole thing.[5]

There had been a few signs along the way that Amina might not really be who she claimed to be. Several journalists had interviewed her before she was supposedly taken, but when they compared notes, they realized that none of them had ever actually met her or even talked to her on the phone. All their communication had been over email. The *Guardian* newspaper had arranged to interview her in Damascus at one point, but she had not shown up to the meeting. "Amina" later sent the reporter an email blaming her failure to show on the fact that security had been following her and she could not move around the city safely. It had seemed to make sense at the time, but it became a red flag when reporters realized that no one had ever seen her in person. An investigative reporter also later discovered that the photos MacMaster had posted of Amina on the blog were actually of a Croatian woman living in London.[6]

After he was discovered, MacMaster claimed he had lied for a good reason. He said he had thought he was helping to draw international attention to the heroic activism of people in the Middle East and to the very real atrocities committed by the Syrian government. In a post he published on the blog, he wrote that even though he had made up Amina and all of her stories, the blog still represented the things real people were going through during the Arab Spring.[7]

But the true reason seems to be greed. MacMaster had previously written books about himself that he hadn't managed to sell. When he read about the protests breaking out, he saw an opportunity to create a more interesting and compelling story—one that might turn into an actual book deal someday, even if he did have to write it under a pen name.[8] He set about creating a character, writing down Amina's backstory to give her the feeling of a real, well-rounded person. MacMaster created social-media accounts under her name, using pictures of the same Croatian woman and also a Palestinian woman he later used on the blog. He even posted chapters of his book (under Amina's name), hoping to draw interest from publishers. But by doing so, he was speaking for an entire community to which he did not belong, and many of his posts were either factually inaccurate or played into stereotypes about Arab people.

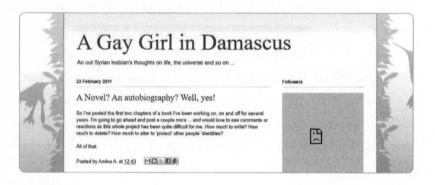

Screenshot of the blog *A Gay Girl in Damascus* on February 22, 2011, via the
Internet Archive Wayback Machine

MacMaster had realized that the anonymity of the internet pre-sented an opportunity to make money from fake content with very little personal risk. But he certainly was not the only one. When companies like Yahoo, Microsoft, and Google created pay-per-click advertisements (digital advertisements that direct visitors to other websites and then pay the owner of the original website a small fee for each ad clicked), internet users discovered they could profit financially if they could just get traffic to their ad-loaded websites.[9] Just as fake news sold newspapers, it could make money online.

The more sensational the content, the more traffic would come to a website, and the more clicks website owners would get on their advertisements.

In 2014, a deadly disease called Ebola broke out all over countries in West Africa, and people were concerned about it potentially spreading. A fake news website called the National Report took advantage of international hysteria by posting a fictional story about a family of five that had tested positive for Ebola in a small town outside Dallas, Texas.[10] It was easy for people to believe because a real person had died of the disease just a few days earlier in Dallas. The National Report website later added this disclaimer in tiny print on its homepage: "All news articles contained within National Report are fiction, and presumably fake news." But it did not matter. In just a few hours of the post going up, thousands of people had read the article and shared it, convinced that Texas was about to become overrun with Ebola.[11]

The National Report was just one website out of a whole network of fake news sites run by a man named Jestin Coler from Southern California under a company he created called Disinfomedia. Coler, who went by the pseudonym Allen Montgomery, was intrigued by the number of fake news articles he saw people sharing online and wondered what sensational claims he might be able to get the public to believe. Out of curiosity, Coler bought the domain NationalReport.net in 2013 and a dozen other what he called "sister sites."[12] It sounded like an official news website that could fool people. He filled the site with the most sensational fake news stories he could think of. Stories meant to scare people, like the one about Ebola. Racist ones, like an article about a bakery owned by Muslims who refused to bake an American flag cake for a veteran. And others that were just plain bizarre, like an article titled PRESIDENT OBAMA ADVOCATES EATING DOGS IN JULY 4TH ADDRESS. Coler almost could not believe it when his website started getting hits, but he did not waste a second before capitalizing on it. He filled each article with multiple digital ads, for which he received a few cents each time a user clicked on them. By 2017, Coler was making thirty thousand dollars a month and his websites received more than a hundred million views between them. His sites became so popular, he even employed staff to write the fake articles for them.[13]

Screenshot of NationalReport.net on July 7, 2015,
via the Internet Archive Wayback Machine

Coler's websites pretended to be independent news media outlets, but other successful fake news websites have copied the format of actual news outlets to get people to believe them. Take CNNews3.com, which appeared in 2016. Its home page looked exactly like CNN's (CNN.com), with the company's red logo and everything. One of the impostor CNN's most shared articles that year was published as a breaking-news story. It claimed that a ten-year-old boy had contracted HIV after eating a banana from Walmart that had somehow been contaminated with the virus.[14] Eight kids under the age of seventeen had gotten the virus. All supposedly ate bananas purchased at the same Walmart in Tulsa, Oklahoma. The story was undated and never said when any of the events occurred. Yet it was shared thousands of times on social media. And this was not the first time the story of mysterious poisoned fruit made the rounds online. Another story, years before, had said that someone was infecting bananas with HIV and cited the World Health Organization, which, of course, had said no such thing.[15]

Screenshot of CNNews3.com on April 2, 2016,
via the Internet Archive Wayback Machine

This particular story about the poisoned bananas was traced back to a Facebook post in 2015 where a woman claimed that her friend's sister, who lived in Nebraska, had found that blood had been injected into her bananas.[17] She showed pictures of a peeled banana with a deep red streak in it. The local hospital had tested the blood and discovered it was HIV-positive, she said. Her post went viral and got so much attention that Del Monte, the seller of the fruit, had to make a public statement that the discoloration came from a common—and harmless-to-humans—bacteria.

Fake news websites are not always about gaining attention or money. They are also often about promoting certain political ideas or parties. Since the early days of the internet, partisan fake news websites have been popular, particularly during elections. Early versions of these sites published fake statistics about government issues or policies to confuse voters, or gave inaccurate information about how to vote in order to stop people from actually voting. They also published false information about candidates running for office and often bought domain names similar to an actual candidate's website name just to mislead potential voters looking on the internet for information about the candidate.

In 1999, two websites caused then-presidential candidate George W. Bush serious headaches by each pretending to be his official campaign website. The first one, GWBush.com, was created by a twenty-nine-year-old computer programmer from Boston. The site did state that it was a parody website, but it featured a digitally altered photo of Bush doing drugs, which obviously wasn't exactly the message the candidate wanted to send to any voters tricked by the URL.[18] The second website, Bushcampaignhq.com, noted it was not the real campaign website and it included false and misleading information about

Bush, but it still drew a lot of attention.[19] It received nearly 6.5 million views in just the first month it was up, while Bush's actual website only got thirty thousand in that same period.[20] "There ought to be limits to freedom," Bush famously said about the fake websites.[21]

Hate groups also created fake political websites to spread their messages. MartinLutherKing.org was designed to look like the official website of the great civil rights leader Dr. Martin Luther King Jr., but it was actually created by a neo-Nazi white-supremacist website called Stormfront. The creators put up false information about Dr. King's personal life, his family, and his civil rights work to try to discredit him.[22] The only thing that identified the hate group as the creator of the website in its first version was the email address connected with it. But even then, most people would have had to research the name to know what Stormfront was. The fake website at times still will show up as one of the top links on internet searches for Dr. King.

There is more information on the internet than ever before. For fake news pushers, it offers not only a way to reach more people all at once, but it's also a way to do it all anonymously, for the most part. We might be tempted to believe whatever we find on a website or see on social media. But that can be very dangerous if we do not know who runs the site and where the information is coming from. At the same time, there simply is not enough time in our day to hunt down all the Tom MacMasters and Jestin Colers of the world before we let ourselves believe what we are reading. As a result, it is important that we develop a list of reliable news sources and websites we can count on to provide accurate information and to help us identify what is fake news. That way, we know where we can go to find accurate information, and then, later, investigate new sources of information we come across as you have the time.

FACT-CHECKING WEBSITES

AT THE SAME TIME THAT FAKE NEWS WEBSITES started popping up, so too did independent fact-checking organizations that rounded up the rumors, hoaxes, and false information circulating online to identify what was accurate and what was untrue. Organizations can now be found all over the world that specialize in checking information and media coverage in their regions. Many newspaper outlets also track the fake news stories that circulate online. The *Washington Post*, for example, does a weekly review of political statements made that are true or false. They rate those statements using icons of Pinocchio—the famous wooden puppet whose nose grew every time he lied. The more Pinocchio icons awarded, the bigger the lie.

It is important to understand the limitations of fact-checking. First, not every news story or website has been fact-checked. Organizations that specialize in fact-checking cannot keep up with the amount of information online, so they must decide what to prioritize each day. As a result, most of them focus only on content that has gotten a lot of attention online or gone viral. Fact-checking organizations must then fight to get the truth out about those stories or posts, which is difficult when they have already been shared widely. But it is easier when readers and social-media users help spread the word about things they have identified as fake news.

Here are five helpful websites that specialize in fact-checking of primarily English-language content:

1. *SNOPES.COM.* This independent organization fact-checks topics that are trending on social media or receiving significant media coverage.

2. *THE POYNTER INSTITUTE.* The website of this nonprofit journalism school maintains a list of verified fact-checking organizations around the world: *www.IFCNcodeOfPrinciples.Poynter.org/signatories*.

3. *POLITIFACT.COM.* A nonpartisan US fact-checking organization run by the Poynter Institute, it primarily fact-checks political issues.

4. *FACTCHECK.ORG.* A nonpartisan, nonprofit organization connected with the University of Pennsylvania's Annenberg Public Policy Center, it monitors the factual accuracy of statements made by US politicians.

5. *HOAX-SLAYER.COM.* An independent website out of Australia that identifies internet- and email-based scams and hoaxes from all over the world.

And a bonus recommendation:

6. *THE INTERNET ARCHIVE WAYBACK MACHINE.* This tool (found at archive.org/web) saves and then stores the internet so you can go back and look at web pages that no longer exist or at old versions of current websites. It will not tell you if something is true or false, but with 391 billion web pages saved (and counting!), it can help you do a little fact-checking yourself.

CHAPTER 12

FAKE NEWS GOES VIRAL

"IN THE PAST FEW DAYS, CHILDREN AGED FOUR, eight and 14 have disappeared and some of these kids have been found dead with signs that their organs were removed." The warning appeared as a message on WhatsApp to people in central Mexico. "It appears that these criminals are involved in organ trafficking."[1]

It was a terrifying prospect, and people forwarded the message right away to everyone they knew. The whole region was on edge as the message spread through private and public groups on WhatsApp in August 2018. Parents and neighbors kept a closer eye on children than normal, and everyone watched out for anyone who looked suspicious.

Then, one day, in the small town of Acatlán, some townspeople spotted two men in the center of town buying construction supplies. One was twenty-one-year-old Ricardo Flores, who had grown up nearby but was now a law student in another part of Mexico. The other man was Ricardo's uncle, fifty-six-year-old farmer Alberto Flores Morales. But to the people who lived there, the two men were strangers. After the WhatsApp message, they were not going to take any chances, so they kept a close eye on the two. The town was small, but visitors still passed through on occasion, so maybe the men would have been deemed ordinary travelers, if they had not started wandering toward the nearby elementary school after buying their supplies. That was the only sign the people needed—these men had to be the child traffickers they had been warned about.

Some townspeople started attacking the men until the police stepped in. There was no evidence that Ricardo and Alberto were there to kidnap children. The two men tried to explain who they were and that they had come to get materials for a well they were building nearby. Still, the police decided to bring the men to their station for disturbing the peace.

Word spread, and some people decided that the police involvement meant the men really were guilty. They began gathering outside the police station to wait for Ricardo and Alberto to arrive. Someone in the crowd started livestreaming everything on Facebook and encouraged other people to come join them. Others sent messages to their friends telling them that the police had caught the child traffickers. Another member of the crowd ran to the local church and rang the bell to get more people to come to the station. And come they did, in droves.

By the time the police arrived, there was already a large group of people waiting for them. Normally, crowds this size only showed up for holiday celebrations, and the crowd was getting bigger by the minute. The police took the two men inside and tried to make the crowd disperse. But the crowd said the men needed to be punished for what they had done. Things moved quickly then. A member of the crowd brought a can of gasoline; another got matches. Determined to protect their children, the crowd went wild and pushed through the small gate that was the only thing keeping them outside.

The mob dragged the two men out, overrunning the police completely. Without any evidence of a crime beyond a social media rumor and speculation, the crowd beat the two innocent men on the front steps of the police station and then burned them alive.[2] They livestreamed the whole thing on Facebook, where one of Ricardo and Alberto's relatives was watching. She left comment after comment, begging the crowd to stop and telling them the men were innocent. But it was too late.

How could this happen? Well, fake news can be powerful when it takes advantage of our emotions. In this case, it played on people's fear and anger. Creators of fake news do that intentionally. When people have a strong emotional reaction to what they are being shown or told, they care more about how they feel than whether the story itself is true. Strong emotions also mean we are more likely to share whatever caused them with someone else. We want someone to commiserate with us, to share in our fear. The people in Mexico were justifiably concerned for the safety of the town's children, but their fear made them share a completely made-up rumor that ultimately led to the death of two innocent men.

Also, the original message about child traffickers was spread among friends and neighbors. Since most people got the message this way, from someone they trusted rather than an anonymous phone number or website, they genuinely believed it was true. No one bothered to ask where the original information had come from or how anyone knew the men were guilty.

As we have seen, people have fallen for fake news throughout history. That much has not changed. Social media did not make that crowd in Mexico murder innocent people without any proof. But advances in technology and the creation of social media have allowed fake news to spread like never before, making social media like a megaphone for fake news. And that is where the real danger lies.

SOCIAL MEDIA MOVES SO QUICKLY THAT THE RUMORS IN MEXICO SPUN OUT OF CONTROL FASTER THAN THOSE FACT-CHECKING WEBSITES WE TALKED ABOUT IN THE LAST CHAPTER COULD KEEP UP. Complicating things even more in this particular instance was that WhatsApp, a messaging and voice app owned by Facebook, has end-to-end encryption, which means that no one outside a particular messaging group can see what has been said unless the chat group is open to the public.[3] When fake news is spread on encrypted apps, fact-checking groups and news outlets cannot always know which fake news messages are getting attention. This makes it much harder to head off false information before or even after it goes viral.

Social media is still a relatively new invention. Facebook was created in 2004, YouTube in 2005, Twitter in 2006, WhatsApp in 2009, and Instagram in 2010. And yet by 2019, approximately 3.48 billion people around the world used some form of social media.[4] And the really startling thing (at least for those of us who were born before the internet was a normal thing) is that, in 2019, 55 percent of American adults said they got their news from social media at least sometimes or often.[5] That means most of us rely on our feeds to keep us informed rather than going directly to news sources on our own.[6] Social media has become a significant part of our daily lives, and fake news has taken advantage of that. The creation of the internet allowed fake news pushers to post their content without having to use traditional media. But social media was the ticket they needed to get their websites and articles in front of the whole world.

WHAT ARE BOTS? There are many different kinds of bots, but in general, bots are automated programs created to perform a particular job, such as tweeting an article link a hundred times a day or posting inspirational quotes and memes.[8] Bots are not human. They are not the same as the internet trolls leaving nasty comments online, though some of the comments you see on articles might come from chatbots.[9] A chatbot is designed to simulate human conversation—to comment on articles, tweet at actual users, or DM back and forth with you. Vanity bots are fake accounts created to like, share, and follow things on social media to make the original post or poster seem more popular.[10] On social-media platforms, bots only share content that already exists. They cannot create new content.

While bots are automated, real people direct them, telling them what to do. Bots post fake news on social media, but they depend on real users taking the bait to help them really spread their posts.

Individuals, groups, and governments realized they could turn social media into a weapon, using fake accounts and whole armies of automated bots to influence things like politics, the economy, and, as a result, even the course of history. And they have been extremely successful. In 2018, MIT released the results of a study about the biggest news stories in English that were shared on Twitter from 2006 to 2017.[7] In all, the researchers looked at around 126,000 stories shared by more than three million users. The study found that fake news and rumors overwhelmingly reached more people and spread a whole six times faster than true stories. Fake political news, more than any other category of false information on social media, reached more people faster and went deeper into their personal networks.

Not only can fake news pushers reach a lot of people on social media, but their posts can also have significant impact quickly. In 2013, a group known as the Syrian Electronic Army hacked into the Associated Press's official Twitter account, which had almost two million followers. They did it by sending something called a phishing email to AP employees. The email looked like any other email, but its purpose was to get the readers to click on a link in the body of the message. Once they did, malicious software automatically began to download onto their computers so that the hackers could get access to all their files and, ultimately, the AP Twitter account.

At 1:07 p.m., the hackers tweeted this fake headline: BREAKING: TWO EXPLOSIONS IN THE WHITE HOUSE AND BARACK OBAMA IS INJURED.[11] By 1:10 p.m., the New York Stock Exchange had plunged, wiping out $130 billion in stock values. The tweet came just eight days after terrorists detonated bombs at the finish line of the Boston Marathon, killing three people and injuring hundreds of others. Panicked stock investors worried there had been yet another terrorist attack, this time against the president. The report came from the real AP, after all.

The AP quickly got word out that its account had been hacked, and other news outlets verified that there had not been an attack at the White House. Several journalists also took to social media to point out some suspicious elements of the tweet: For instance, the AP always referred to Obama as "President Barack Obama," whereas the tweet did not.[12]

Screenshot of the tweet posted from the Associated Press Twitter account on April 16, 2013

The AP quickly took back control of the account and the stock market rebounded, but the hackers dealt an impressive amount of damage in just those three minutes.[13] Many factors cause changes in the stock market from minute to minute, but one of them is how investors feel about economic and political stability in countries like the United States. An attack against the president was enough to make investors lose confidence in the market, and it was not even real.

Fake news on social media has also tricked world leaders. In December 2016, the Pakistani defense minister read a story on a fake news website called AWDNews.com that said the Israeli defense minister had threatened to attack Pakistan with nuclear weapons. He did not know it was fake, but there were multiple errors in the article that could have tipped him off. For example, the article gave the wrong name of the Israeli defense minister, and there was a typo in the headline. But he did not notice, and in response, he tweeted, "Israeli def min threatens nuclear retaliation presuming pak role in Syria against Daesh. Israel forgets Pakistan is a Nuclear state too."[14]

Soon after, the Israeli Ministry of Defense tweeted back, denying the report: "The statement attributed to fmr Def Min Yaalon re Pakistan was never said. Reports referred to by the Pakistan Def Min are entirely false."[15]

Screenshot of the AWDnews.com article posted on December 20, 2016, via the Internet Archive Wayback Machine

Luckily, things did not escalate between the two countries, but can you imagine if a nuclear war had started over a fake news article and a tweet?

DISAPPEARING AIRPLANES AND
FAKE NEWS COVER-UPS

IN THE LATE AFTERNOON ON JULY 17, 2014, SOME-where over eastern Ukraine, Malaysia Airlines flight MH17, traveling from Amsterdam to Kuala Lumpur, disappeared from the radar systems that track planes.[16] Air-traffic controllers tried to make contact with the pilot over the radio, but there was no response. Minutes later, wreckage from the airplane, the bodies of passengers, and luggage began to rain down from the sky, crashing into fields and houses twenty-five miles from the Russian border. None of the 298 passengers and crew members survived. An investigation into the cause began right away, and by the next day, it was clear that the plane had been shot down by a missile launched from Ukraine.

Earlier in February of that same year, Ukrainians across the country had staged a revolution and ultimately overthrown the government. In April, a pro-Russia armed militia group had taken advantage of unrest in the country to seize control of several cities in eastern Ukraine and declare independence. That was when Russia started quietly sending its own military into Ukraine to help the separatists. But the Russians were not doing it out of the goodness of their hearts. Russia had long believed that that part of Ukraine, called Crimea, belonged to them, and they used this as an opportunity to try to take it back for themselves. Moscow worked to hide its operations in Ukraine and denied having troops illegally in Ukraine every time leaders around the world accused them of it. They denied it even when a couple of Russian soldiers posted selfies from inside Crimea (whoops!) and others outright admitted to journalists that they were from Russia.[17]

After the downing of flight MH17, Ukrainian and Russian leaders immediately pointed fingers at each other. Ukraine's interior minister said that Russia had smuggled a missile launcher over the border into Crimea—a claim quickly proven true. Russia, on the other hand, began a massive fake news campaign to convince the world to ignore the evidence against them. First, Russian officials publicly denied they'd had any troops there at all to begin with. Military equipment and soldiers might have suddenly appeared in Crimea, but it had nothing to do with Russia, they said.

Then they presented their own version of events. In fact, they presented multiple versions. Russia claimed it had seen a Ukrainian military aircraft on the radar near flight MH17, so it must have been Ukraine that shot it down. Any evidence Ukraine presented about the missile belonging to Russia was fake, they said. Russia even concocted a story that an air-traffic controller working in Kiev, Ukraine, that day had come forward to verify he too had seen a Ukrainian jet on his radar at the time of the crash.[18] The Russian government then had the media outlets it controls spread the same stories. They even went so far as to produce a fake video interviewing supposed Ukrainians in the area of the crash who said they had seen a Ukrainian plane shoot down flight MH17.[19] Never mind the impossibility of someone on the ground being able to identify a Ukrainian jet thousands of feet above them in the clouds—the Russians did not really care about logic, in this case.

Russian intelligence services also launched a massive social-media campaign to back up their claims. They did not need air-tight stories. They just needed to create enough confusion to make people question the truth and ultimately allow Russia to get away with it. For a while, Russian intelligence had been working on creating fake accounts on Facebook and Twitter to help them spread disinformation when they needed it. The day after the crash, thousands of Russian bots and trolls took to Twitter to back up Russia's denial and support the claim that Ukraine was responsible.[20] In just one day, the accounts sent fifty-seven thousand tweets using hashtags like #KievShotDownTheBoeing, #KievTellTheTruth, and #ProvocationByKiev.[21] The accounts backed up the claims made by Russian media outlets, but also spread wild new conspiracies of their own. Perhaps the most ridiculous of all was that the airplane was already full of dead bodies and had been crashed on purpose to cover up a crime.[22]

> **WHAT IS AN INTERNET TROLL?** An internet troll is a real person who purposefully posts inflammatory content online to provoke, distract, or create discord with other users. Troll behavior may include spreading fake news, harassing others, and using racist and discriminatory language. A troll farm is an organized group of users who work together to spread fake news and information, with the goal of changing public opinion on an issue.[23]

Moscow knew that the key to really spreading their lies on social media was to tailor their posts in a way that would convince actual Russian citizens that Ukraine was responsible. This way, real people would be like a second army for them, helping to defend the government online. When the Russian government provided photos as supposed evidence—of course, it turned out they had been doctored—the fake and real accounts on social media helped spread them.[24]

Meanwhile, a team of people from several different countries was conducting an official investigation into the crash. With all the false information coming from Russia, it took a while to get to the truth. But the team finally released its findings in 2018.[25] It stated that Russia had brought the missile into Crimea and given it to the pro-Russian separatists. Those separatists shot down flight MH17 because they mistook it for a Ukrainian military plane. Russian officials strongly denied the report and worked to shift the blame to the investigators. They claimed that the photos and videos the investigators were using had been doctored, and that *they* were the real fake news. Russia also described an audio recording of a Ukrainian soldier talking about shooting down flight MH17, but did not share the recording with anyone, including investigators. To this day, Russia still denies the part it played in shooting down the plane.

It is not realistic to suggest that the answer to fighting fake news on social media is to just not use social media at all because it has become such a large part our lives. In addition, if we decided to block all social media, the fact is, most of the rest of the world will continue to use it and so it will remain a place for fake news. As a result, we have to learn how to figure out what we can trust from our feeds. Social-media platforms are fast-moving. Posts can go viral in just a few minutes. As a result, we can be so focused on getting likes, shares, and new followers that we do not stop to think about the content we are sharing and where it comes from before we pass it along. This is the case even more so when we have strong feelings about what we are sharing, like we talked about in the case in Mexico. The problem is, if we share something and it turns out to be false, there is not much we can do to take it back. With how much people depend on social media to get their news, it is worth it for all of us to stop and take a little time to figure out if what we want to share is accurate before we do so.

CHAPTER 13

FAKE NEWS TAKES
OVER ELECTIONS

I N EARLY DECEMBER 2016, LESS THAN A MONTH
after America's presidential election, a man from North
Carolina stormed a pizza restaurant in Washington, DC, armed
with an AR-15 semiautomatic rifle, a handgun, and a knife. He fired
into the air and then began searching the restaurant.[1] He was convinced that former president Bill Clinton and former secretary of
state—and recent presidential candidate—Hillary Clinton were running a child sex-trafficking business out of the restaurant's basement. He had come to free the kids and to make the Clintons pay.
The man searched the kitchen and behind closed doors, and even
shot off the lock to an office.[2] Then he looked for the basement,
but the restaurant didn't have one. He found no Clintons. And no
imprisoned children.

The man was shocked. He had been so sure he was about to
rescue a bunch of kids. The story about the sex-trafficking ring was
all over social media, after all. And he wasn't alone in thinking so. In

fact, the owner of the pizza place had been receiving death threats for weeks before the man showed up from people who believed the same thing. But where did the story even come from?

It started in July 2016 when a person claiming to be a high-level FBI analyst hosted an Ask Me Anything (AMA) on the imageboard (a forum focused on users posting images, sometimes with text) website 4chan. He said he was there to expose FBI secrets about the Clintons' charitable organization, the Clinton Foundation. Most users post anonymously, and the supposed FBI analyst did too. "Dig deep," he warned. "Bill and Hillary love foreign donors so much. They get paid in children as well as money."[3] It did not take long for that warning to spread. Through the end of summer and early fall, rumors filled social media and forums like Reddit that the Clintons were using their charitable foundation as a front for terrible crimes.[4] This was partially due to individual 4chan users posting about the AMA on other sites. But there were also coordinated efforts by groups on social media to spread the rumor. For example, a secret online activist group called "Trumps WarRoom" used its large bot network to share and boost fake news stories like this and political messages that were in support of Donald Trump and against Hillary Clinton throughout the campaign.

Accounts all over social media claimed to have evidence of the made-up crime, too. Earlier, a white supremacist had created a fake Twitter account pretending to be a Jewish lawyer in New York. He tweeted in October that the New York City police department had found evidence that several members of the Democratic Party, including the Clintons, were involved in a pedophilia ring. He cited a Facebook post from a woman in Missouri claiming to have sources in the NYPD, though she did not explain in the post how she had those sources. It did not matter: The posts went viral, shared by several fake news sites, conspiracy theorists, and bot networks.[5]

David Goldberg @DavidGoldbergNY · 11 ชม.

Rumors stirring in the NYPD that Huma's emails point to a pedophila ring and @HillaryClinton is at the center. #GoHillary #PodestaEmails23

Carmen Katz
My NYPD source said its much more vile and serious than classified material on Weiner's device. The email DETAIL the trips made by Weiner, Bill and Hillary on their pedophile billionaire friend's plane, the Lolita Express. Yup, Hillary has a well documented predilection for underage girls, and Mr. Weiner just could not bear to see those details deleted. We're talking an international child enslavement and sex ring. Not even Hillary's most ardent supporters and defenders will be able to excuse THIS!

Like · Reply · 👍 6 · 3 hrs

↩   ↻ 1.6 พ.   ♥ 1.3 พ.   •••

Image of the original tweet posted on October 30, 2016, on the fake account @DavidGoldbergNY, via the Internet Archive Wayback Machine[6]

Meanwhile, that same month, the Russian military hacked into the email accounts of Hillary Clinton's campaign manager and the Democratic National Committee. They then gave the emails to WikiLeaks, an organization that posts previously secret information online. WikiLeaks published all the hacked files. The ironic thing is that the emails were pretty mundane, nothing about secret plots or conspiracies. But those pushing the fake news stories about the Clintons were thrilled. Using the AMA from the summer, as well as all the work they had done since then to spread the idea of a pedophilia ring, fake news writers said the emails contained coded messages confirming their stories. They said that any time the phrase *cheese pizza* was mentioned in the Clinton campaign manager's leaked emails, it was a code for child pornography.

Fake news sites and bot networks spread the heck out of this story about the Clintons. Within days, it was all over right-wing fake news websites and on social media, even trending under #pizzagate. And when a fake account named a pizza restaurant in Washington, DC, as the site of the crimes, that story took off too. According to *Rolling Stone*, the Pizzagate story was shared approximately 1.4 million times by more than two hundred fifty thousand Twitter accounts in just five weeks.[7] It was later discovered that most of the users who'd shared the story on Twitter were bots, and that most of the bots were run by fake news writers living in the Czech Republic, Cyprus, and Vietnam. But it was also spread by regular social-media users, some key right-leaning political figures and media commentators, far-right news and opinion sites, and far-right conspiracy and fake news websites like Infowars.

As the story gained steam, it got embellished even further (as if the whole thing were not already bizarre enough), as tends to happen with rumors. Accounts claimed the walk-in refrigerator in the restaurant was actually a "kill room."[8] There were also reports that the Clintons were personally murdering and raping children, not just at the pizza restaurant, but all over the world.[9] A far-right conspiracy theorist went to the pizza place and recorded the whole visit on their Periscope account, narrating how the Clintons kept the children below the restaurant. That was when that man from North Carolina, the father of two kids, decided he had to act to protect innocent children from the former president of the United States and former secretary of state.

In what was considered a major success by the people pushing the fake news story, the *New York Times* published an article debunking Pizzagate a few weeks after the election in November.[10] We would not necessarily think an article proving something wrong could be seen as a good thing to the people spreading the lie, but to some, the simple fact that the article was published unintentionally implied that Pizzagate was a legitimate theory being discussed. Also, many of the people who were likely to believe conspiracy theories like Pizzagate already thought the *New York Times* was run by Clinton supporters, so in their eyes, a denial of the story by the *Times* was basically the same as a confirmation.

Pizzagate has been thoroughly discredited since 2016, but there are people who still swear the Clintons run child sex-trafficking rings. After the election, a poll conducted by the *Economist* magazine and YouGov, a research data company, found that a huge 46 percent of people who voted for Donald Trump in the election believed that the hacked emails from Clinton's campaign manager really did prove the Clintons had a child-trafficking operation.[11]

In a speech to Congress after the election, in December, Hillary Clinton called out "the epidemic of malicious fake news and false propaganda that flooded social media over the past year." She said, "It's now clear that so-called fake news can have real-world consequences."[12] She was talking about Pizzagate, but also about the other fake news stories that had become a prominent part of the election. It was such a defining issue, in fact, that Collins Dictionary named "fake news" its word of the year in 2017. Let's look at some statistics that break down just how *much* fake news there really was during the election.

The Knight Foundation, a nonprofit organization that promotes quality journalism, found that in the month before the 2016 election, over 6.6 million tweets provided links to publishers of fake news and conspiracy news. Interestingly, 65 percent of the fake news links that spread on Twitter during the election came from the same ten fake news websites.[13] While the majority of fake news came from pro-conservative and pro-Trump accounts, there was a smaller but still significant amount of fake news coming from liberal-identified accounts. *BuzzFeed News* also found that the top twenty fake news articles in 2016 got more shares on Facebook than the top twenty real news stories.[14]

What does all of this mean? First, it means that false information spread farther and reached more people than real news did ahead of the election. And it was not that there were thousands of fake news sites pushing it out. Most of the fake news came from the same key fake news websites and social-media accounts. But they would not have had the reach they did without real people who shared the articles on social media and visited their sites.

THE TOP TEN FAKE NEWS STORIES FROM THE ELECTION. Each of these articles received between half a million and one million views.

1. *Pope Francis shocks world, endorses Donald Trump for president.* Fake news website WTOE 5 News, which claimed to be a local TV news outlet, falsely claimed that "news outlets around the world" were saying this.[15]

2. *Donald Trump sent his own plane to transport two hundred stranded marines.* First announced by Sean Hannity, a Fox News political commentator, the story was later published as an article by Americanmilitarynews.com, and then removed when fact-checkers determined it was not accurate.[16]

3. Pizzagate.

4. Ireland is now officially accepting Trump refugees
    from America. **Published by a left-wing website, Winning
    Democrats, that produced sensationalized content, the story
    received almost a million views and was even covered by real
    news outlets.**[17]

5. WikiLeaks confirms Hillary sold weapons to ISIS . . .
    then drops another bombshell. **Published by the Political
    Insider fake news site, this story was based off actual (but
    false) comments made by the founder of WikiLeaks during an
    interview.**[18]

6. FBI agent suspected in Hillary email leaks found dead in
    apartment murder-suicide. **This story was published by the
    Denver Guardian, which claimed to be "Denver's oldest news
    source" but was in fact a fake news website (the address
    listed for its headquarters was actually a parking lot).**

7. FBI director received millions from Clinton Foundation;
    his brother's law firm does the Clintons' taxes. **Run by a
    Romanian man who was twenty-four at the time, popular fake
    news website Ending the Fed had four of the ten most popular
    fake news articles shared on Facebook in the run-up to the
    election and the website had millions of views in 2016.**[19]

8. ISIS leader calls for American Muslim voters to support
    Hillary Clinton. **Though it was published by the self-
    professed fake news website WNDR, this story was still
    reposted by hundreds of other fake news websites and shared
    by fake social-media users with the hashtag #ISISwithHer.**[20]

9. Hillary Clinton in 2013: "I would like to see people like
    Donald Trump run for office; they're honest and can't
    be bought." **This was published on a number of fake news
    websites, but it received the highest number of its views on**

ConservativeState.com, one of the top-performing fake news websites created by a group of teenagers living in Macedonia.[21]

10. *RuPaul claims Trump touched him inappropriately in the nineties.* This story was published by a satirical fake news website called World News Daily Report. Between October and November 2016, the article was shared 285,000 times on Facebook alone.[22]

BUT WHO WAS RESPONSIBLE FOR THE FAKE NEWS?

LIKE MANY PEOPLE FRESH OUT OF COLLEGE IN the United States, twenty-three-year-old Cameron Harris was loaded with student-loan debt as soon as he graduated in 2016. With a longtime interest in Republican Party politics, especially where he lived in Maryland, he closely followed the American presidential election.[23] In August of that year, Cameron Harris watched one of Donald Trump's campaign rallies in Ohio where the then presidential candidate told an excited crowd, "November eighth, we'd better be careful, because that election is going to be rigged. People are going to walk in and they're going to vote ten times, maybe, who knows?" (This claim was later proven false by PolitiFact.)[24] At the time, most major polls had Trump about nine points behind Clinton. That was when Cameron Harris got his idea—he could both get the money he needed and help his candidate, Donald Trump, win.

Harris bought an expired domain name for about the same price as a large double-shot caramel macchiato at Starbucks. From his own kitchen table in his apartment, he created a website: ChristianTimesNewspaper.com. This particular domain, he believed, would help him attract the kind of reader he thought would be the most likely to share his articles so that he would get more hits for his websites—conservative Christians. Harris was not a journalist and had no experience in the newspaper industry, but he made the website look exactly like any regular news site, with headlines and pictures. He also loaded the website with advertisements so that he would be paid each time someone clicked on one. If it all worked the way he hoped it would, those ads would give him the extra cash he needed. Most real news sites are full of digital advertisements anyway, so the ads made Harris's site look real. On September 30, Harris posted his very first article.

Harris's article claimed that an electrician in Columbus, Ohio—the same place Trump had held the rally where he'd suggested the election was rigged—had found a warehouse full of fake ballots all marked as votes for Clinton.[25] Clinton's campaign planned to use them to stuff the ballot boxes on Election Day to ensure she won, he said. Harris had made it all up, inventing the electrician and even posting a photograph of a man with boxes of the supposed ballots.[26] To reinforce the lie, he made it so a banner would pop up when a person clicked on the article. The banner said, "We already know that Hillary stole the primary. We can't let her steal the presidency."

Harris knew his claim was far-fetched, but he thought that, since Trump supporters believed in their candidate so much and had been so animated at his rallies when Trump talked about a rigged election,

SUNDAY, OCTOBER 2, 2016

NEWS　　ABOUT US　　POLITICS ⌄　　VIDEO ⌄　　RELIGION　　CHRISTIAN TIMES

Home > News > BREAKING: "Tens of thousands" of fraudulent Clinton votes found in Ohio warehouse

NEWS　**POLITICS**

BREAKING: "Tens of thousands" of fraudulent Clinton votes found in Ohio warehouse

By *admin1* - *September 30, 2016*　👁 *39645*　💬 *0*

SHARE　　f Facebook　　🐦 Twitter　　G+　　P

Screenshot of Harris's first post on ChristianTimesNewspaper.com, via the
Internet Archive Wayback Machine

his article might just get some attention. And he was right. It did not take long before the article went viral.

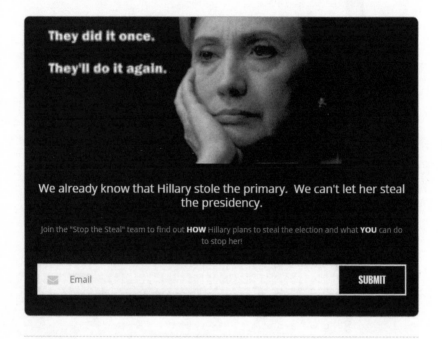

Screenshot of Harris's anti-Hillary pop-up ad via the Internet Archive Wayback Machine

Users across social media added their own versions of the story too. "Thousands of rigged ballots for Clinton have been found in five key swing states including Ohio thus far. Justice Dept. controlling them?" one Twitter user posted.[27] This user was not the only one to suggest that the Clinton campaign was secretly working with the federal government to get Hillary elected. In fact, Harris's story led to all kinds of theories about collusion between Clinton and the government.

In all, Harris's article was shared six million times. Harris made thousands of dollars off the ad revenue from just that one article in only a few days. But he didn't stop there. With the success of his launch, Harris went on to write even more stories, the vast majority of which were negative toward Clinton.[28]

Eventually, an investigative reporter at the *New York Times* uncovered the truth about ChristianTimesNewspaper.com and the man running it, and published a story exposing him. Google cut off Harris's ability to use ads so he could not make money from his site anymore and, eventually, he shut the page down. Harris walked away with his money free and clear. Even though the website is no longer active, a simple search on Twitter will show you that, years later, many people still believe that an unsuspecting electrician found fake ballot boxes in that fictional warehouse in Ohio.

Why did Harris's article catch on so quickly? Harris explained part of the answer himself when he told the *New York Times*, "Given the severe distrust of the media among Trump supporters, anything that parroted Trump's talking points people would click. Trump was saying 'rigged election, rigged election.' People were predisposed to believe Hillary Clinton could not win except by cheating."[29] In other words, people already believed Trump when he said the election would be rigged. Harris's article simply provided the "proof" they needed.

Young adults in the small town of Veles, Macedonia, in south-eastern Europe discovered that they too could make a lot of money off the American election. Before 2016, these teens made thousands by creating fake medical-advice websites and filling them with pay-per-click ads. But they saw a better financial opportunity with the American election. This group in Veles created more than a hundred fake news websites with articles about the election, including the one about the pope endorsing Trump.[30] Most of the websites published between eight and ten new articles a day to keep people coming back for updates, like a real news outlet.

It was easy for them to find content for their sites. Mostly they copied and pasted parts of existing articles or social-media posts. For example, one of the first articles published by an eighteen-year-old fake news writer from Veles for his Daily Interesting Things website was a story about Donald Trump slapping a man for disagreeing with him at one of his campaign rallies in North Carolina. The teen had found the story by randomly searching various American political groups on social media and simply copied it onto his website.[31] Other times, the Veles teens took stories from American far-right news websites and made simple changes, like adding more sensationalist headlines to make people more likely to click. To get more people to go to their websites, they would use fake social-media accounts to post links to their articles and run paid ads promoting their websites on Facebook.

It is not too hard to figure out why these teens did what they did. In Macedonia, the average monthly salary is about four hundred dollars. In contrast, one of them made sixteen thousand dollars between August and November 2016 by running just two fake sites. "The Americans loved our stories and we make money from them," another told the BBC. "Who cares if they are true or false?"[32] By 2017, the teens had already picked their next fake news target—the US presidential election in 2020.[33]

RUSSIA—YES, AGAIN

THERE WAS ANOTHER, MORE SERIOUS FAKE NEWS player that worked hard to take advantage of the political tension during the election—Russia. As we saw in previous chapters, the United States has often been a target of the Russian government, which long ago calculated that it could wage a war against America with disinformation. And Moscow did just that, in an unprecedented secret campaign to influence the results of the presidential election. During the Cold War, the Soviets had to find ways to get fake stories into newspapers and then hope they spread. Now they had social media as a weapon.

The seventeen agencies that make up America's Intelligence Community—of which the CIA is a part—published an unclassified assessment in early 2017 saying that Russian president Vladimir Putin himself directed an operation to influence the election.[34] The assessment said his goal was to undermine the public's faith in the US democratic process—things like voting—and to help get Trump elected. To achieve that goal, Putin relied on his own intelligence services, hackers, traditional media run and sponsored by the Russian government, social media, and fake news.

Part of Russia's strategy involved using a troll farm based in St. Petersburg, Russia, called the Internet Research Agency (IRA), starting as early as 2014. The troll farm spread fake news and disinformation about the election and the candidates. As we discussed earlier, there was already a lot of fake news online, much of it created by Americans themselves, and the IRA took advantage of that by boosting those websites on social media. But they also had their own campaigns. They created thousands of fake social-media accounts that looked like they belonged to real Americans, and they used YouTube videos, memes, websites, and digital ads on social-media sites.[35]

Ahead of the election, the IRA was tasked specifically with supporting Donald Trump and Bernie Sanders, to criticize Hillary Clinton, and to sow division among Democrats. Russia would then use its own government-controlled media, like the English-language TV news channel *Russia Today*, to report on the fake news as if it was legitimate to give their stories a thin layer of credibility. According to a *Time* interview with one of the IRA's former employees, the people who worked there were given instructions every day on what to write about and what political spin to give their fake news.[36]

When Bernie Sanders lost the Democratic Party primary election and Hillary Clinton became the Democrats' candidate for president, IRA accounts on social media and fake news websites started working on Sanders supporters. Their goal was to turn them against the Democratic Party and discourage them from voting for Clinton. That way, Trump would receive more votes.[37]

The IRA also targeted real people from marginalized communities. For example, they created fake accounts on social media that pretended to be tied to black or Muslim advocacy groups, including Black Lives Matter. Those accounts then worked to discourage specific groups of people from voting on Election Day, or to get them to vote for third-party candidates to pull votes away from Clinton.[39] IRA accounts also pushed the idea that the election was rigged. One of their most popular Twitter accounts was @TEN_GOP. Days before the election, when early voting was already underway, the account tweeted that election officials in a Florida county were counting ineligible mail-in ballots as votes for Clinton, even though they should not have been counted.

Tweets posted on May 14, 2016, by fake news account @MissouriNewsUS were designed to discourage Bernie Sanders supporters from voting for Hillary Clinton. It was later discovered that the account was run by Russia.[38]

Many of the fake accounts also posed as American political activists. These accounts contacted and recruited real people to carry out protests, campaign rallies, and other meetings all across the country. And they were pretty convincing. In a message to a Facebook group called "Florida for Trump," an IRA account posing as an American named Matt Skiber wrote:

> *Hi there! I'm a member of Being Patriotic online community. Listen, we've got an idea. Florida is still a purple state and we need to paint it red. If we lose Florida, we lose America. We can't let it happen, right? What about organizing a YUGE pro-Trump flash mob in every Florida town? We are currently reaching out to local activists and we've got the folks who are okay to be in charge of organizing their events almost everywhere in FL. However, we still need your support. What do you think about that? Are you in?[40]*

The events were not just in support of Trump, either. They also organized some that were against Trump in an attempt to increase tension between the two parties, even after the election. For example, on November 12, the IRA secretly hosted competing protests in New York, one called "Show Your Support for President-Elect Donald Trump" and the other "Trump Is NOT My President."[41] And people actually showed up, protesting with their respective groups and yelling at one another from opposite sides of the street not knowing that Russia had orchestrated the whole thing.

The IRA was a full-scale operation. Employees had to meet specific quotas for creating and posting online comments, blogs, and social-media posts. By the summer of 2016, the IRA was spending more than $1.25 million each month on their operations and had hundreds of employees.[43] By October 2017, Twitter had found nearly four thousand accounts that were run by the IRA.[44]

Facebook estimated that approximately 126 million people saw content the IRA posted on Facebook between January 2015 and August 2017, and 20 million people saw it on Instagram.[45] In January 2018, Twitter assessed that approximately 1.4 million people had retweeted, quoted, followed, liked, or replied to at least one account run by the IRA.[46]

Russia's efforts to influence the election results were so huge that the US Department of Justice appointed a special counsel to investigate the issue.[47] As a result of that investigation, thirteen Russian citizens and three Russian companies, including the IRA, were charged with conspiring to interfere with US politics and the presidential election.[48]

Researchers are still studying what impact fake news had on the election results. A study conducted by Professor Andrew Guess of Princeton University, Professor Brendan Nyhan of Dartmouth

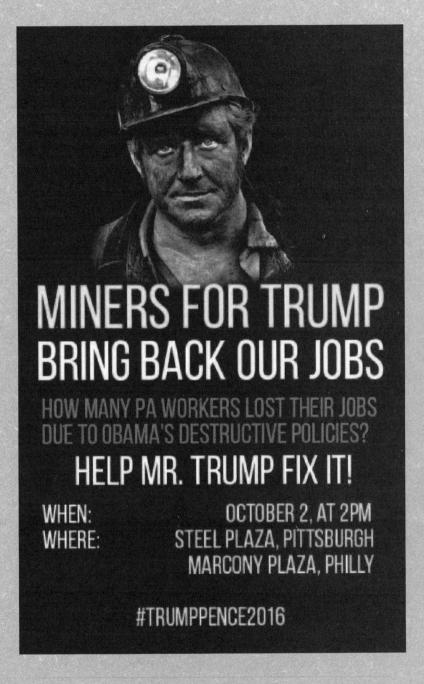

The IRA created this poster, highlighted in the special counsel's report, for its Pennsylvania rallies.[42]

College, and Professor Jason Reifler of the University of Exeter found that one in four Americans visited a fake news website between October 7 and November 14, 2016.[49] They also discovered that six in ten visits to fake news websites were by the same 10 percent of people. These people were older, on average, and were mostly Trump supporters visiting fake news websites that posted articles in favor of Trump and against Clinton. They also followed politics very closely from primarily conservative media outlets, on top of the fake news they consumed.

Perhaps surprisingly, given just how much fake news there was during the election, the study did not find evidence that fake news changed people's minds about which candidate to vote for on Election Day, even among "swing voters" (those who do not always vote for the same party). What it did do was reinforce people's existing beliefs, making them even more entrenched in their opinions and less willing to consider new evidence that did not support their views.[50]

Fake news did not stop after the election, though that's when a lot of people woke up to the extent of the problem. While the American election shined a spotlight on fake news globally and got companies and governments talking about possible solutions, the problem has only continued. In fact, as of October 2018, more than 80 percent of the accounts that had spread fake news during the election were still active on Twitter, according to the same study by the Knight Foundation. Those accounts published more than a million tweets per day.[51]

But perhaps the biggest effect of the heightened fake news during the election was that it eroded public trust in the real news media and made people question whether truth really existed. Along the campaign trail, Donald Trump used a different definition of "fake news." Instead of describing false information, he used the term to refer to true stories that were critical of him. "The FAKE NEWS media (failing @nytimes, @NBCNews, @ABC, @CBS, @CNN) is not my enemy, it is the enemy of the American People!" Trump tweeted in February 2017.[52]

Donald J. Trump ✓
@realDonaldTrump

The FAKE NEWS media (failing @nytimes, @NBCNews, @ABC, @CBS, @CNN) is not my enemy, it is the enemy of the American People!

4:48 PM · Feb 17, 2017 · Twitter for Android

47.3K Retweets   **146.9K** Likes

Screenshot of President Trump's tweet on February 17, 2017

In response to media reports about a poll that showed his public approval rating was below 50 percent, Trump tweeted in February 2017, "Any negative polls are fake news, just like the CNN, ABC, NBC polls in the election."[53] In July 2018 he told attendees at the annual Veterans of Foreign Wars conference not to believe what they were seeing happening in the country. "Don't believe the crap you see from these people, the fake news . . . What you're seeing and what you're reading is not what's happening," he said.[54] Earlier in 2018, it came out that, as a presidential candidate, Trump had told a *60 Minutes* reporter the reason he called the media "fake news." He'd said, "You know why I do it? I do it to discredit you all and demean you all so when you write negative stories about me, no one will believe you."[55]

In a 2018 survey conducted by Gallup, most American adults said they had lost trust in the media in recent years. Forty-five percent of those people said it was because the media was inaccurate, biased, or fake news, or because they believed in "alternative facts."[56] Part of this distrust came from the sheer amount of false information people saw on social media during the election. Many calculated that it was safer not to trust anything they heard or read than to believe something and find out later it was wrong.

But the distrust was also a result of the serious tension between political parties at the time. People were so committed to their chosen presidential candidate that they believed anything positive about their candidate was true, while anything negative was fake news. In this way, many people came to see legitimate media outlets—simply reporting the facts—as untrustworthy or as fake news. They also started to believe that their own personal opinions about things were more important and valid than reality. The Oxford Dictionary named "post-truth" as the word of the year in 2016, defining it as "relating to or denoting circumstances in which objective facts are less influential in shaping public opinion than appeals to emotion and personal belief."[57]

WHAT ARE "ALTERNATIVE FACTS" AND WHEN DID PEOPLE START USING THE PHRASE? In January 2017, the White House press secretary, Sean Spicer, claimed that the media was spreading fake news about the size of Trump's inauguration ceremony. It was "the largest audience to ever witness an inauguration, period," he had said without citing any sources. However, photos of the inauguration showed that the inauguration was actually quite poorly attended. Later, Kellyanne Conway, one of Trump's advisers, defended Spicer's lie by saying he had simply given "alternative facts."[58] Later, Spicer corrected his statement, but the idea of "alternative facts"—that facts were really just matters of opinion—took off.

FAKE NEWS WEAPONIZED AROUND THE WORLD

AS THE UNITED STATES DEALT WITH THE swell of fake news before and after the election, the rest of the world was watching closely. Some politicians, groups, and governments realized they could mass-produce fake content to influence their own elections and to win or maintain political power.

In the Philippines, spreading fake news was a key part of Rodrigo Duterte's successful campaign to become president in 2016, and it's a tactic he has since used to advance his agenda. An impressive 97 percent of Filipinos who use the internet have a Facebook account, and Duterte put that to use by unleashing thousands of fake social-media accounts to push fake news throughout the election.[59] Like one fake story that might sound familiar, a fake article said that the pope had called Duterte "a blessing." Another popular but fake story that spread on social media claimed that Prince Harry and Duchess Meghan Markle supported Duterte.[60]

Once Duterte was elected, he continued to use fake news stories and photos, but this time to justify a violent "war on drugs." He deployed death squads, which have murdered and imprisoned thousands of alleged drug dealers, addicts, and innocent people. In one instance, members of Duterte's administration posted a photo of a young girl and claimed she had been raped and killed by criminals in the Philippines. Officials used the photo to call out the media for supposedly "derailing" Duterte's drug war by criticizing it and to try to convince the public that his violent crackdown was needed. But the photo turned out to actually be of a girl who had been attacked in Brazil.[61]

His administration also actively encouraged and supported activists who waged vicious online attacks against Duterte's critics and pushed out fake news articles and videos supporting Duterte.

While he was waging his violent drug war, Duterte also worked to shut down media outlets that the government did not already control, including Rappler, an independent online news start-up. Rappler had partnered with Facebook to identify and remove pro-Duterte fake news pages, and had also reported extensively on Duterte's violent campaign against critics and his use of fake news.[62] To demean and discredit any media that criticized him, Duterte had started using a new term—*presstitute*, a combination of the words *press* and *prostitute*. He had also routinely jailed and killed activists who spoke out and warned journalists that they were "not exempted from assassination."[63]

In November 2017, President Trump held a meeting with Duterte on the margins of an international summit in Manila. At a press conference with Trump when members of the media asked about Duterte's human rights abuses, Duterte denounced the press as "spies."

When nervous laughter broke out, he said emphatically, "You are."[64]

WHAT DOES "FREE PRESS" ACTUALLY MEAN?

A free press means that people have the right to publish and share information and opinions without the fear of government interference, censorship, or retribution, such as physical violence or imprisonment. In many countries, the freedom of the press is guaranteed by specific laws. In America, for instance, freedom of the press is a right in the Constitution, and the media is often referred to as the "fourth branch of government," working as a necessary check on the government and other people and groups in power.[65]

As we saw when European monarchies tacked on all sorts of laws to limit what people could print with the printing press, governments now use "fake news" as an excuse to go after the media and to limit press freedom.

Governments have enacted laws to stop online critics. Just in 2018, Russia passed a law allowing the government to shut down websites that publish information critical of public figures, Malaysia outlawed fake news and swiftly used the law to convict a Danish citizen who criticized the government on YouTube, and Belarus amended its media law to let the government prosecute anyone believed to have spread false information over the internet.[66]

Also in 2018, Egyptian president Abdel Fattah el-Sisi passed a law giving the government sweeping power to remove, ban, and prosecute any social media account or blog owner with at least five thousand followers it judges has posted fake news without even obtaining a court order. The law also states that these accounts and blogs are legally considered media outlets and therefore must get a permit from the Egyptian government before they are allowed to create a website.[67] The government passed a separate law giving them the authority to block any website that it deemed a threat to national security without having to provide an explanation, and even set up a unit within the government to track rumors and the people spreading them online.

Egyptian officials claimed that fake news was sowing division in the country and threatening the rule of the Egyptian president, but the laws did not even define what was considered fake news. The government has since used the laws to crack down on journalists and other voices critical of the government. Anyone found violating these laws can be given heavy fines or be imprisoned, and in 2018, Egypt jailed more journalists on fake news charges than any other country.[68]

It is no coincidence that with increasing crackdowns on the media and free speech, the rate of violence against journalists worldwide has also gone up.[69] Since 2016, there has been a spike in the number of journalists jailed, and in 2018, more journalists were murdered than ever before, according to the Committee to Protect Journalists (CPJ).[70]

PART II

HOW WE FIGHT BACK!

Most people, in fact, will not take trouble in finding out the truth, but are much more inclined to accept the first story they hear.

—THUCYDIDES

CHAPTER 14

FACTS VS. OPINIONS

AT ITS CORE, A FACT IS A STATEMENT THAT can be proven, through either observation or experimentation. For example, the sun rises in the east and sets in the west. What makes that a fact? Well, if you wanted to, you could go outside with a little compass each morning and evening and watch it happen over and over again. Want to definitively prove the Earth is not flat? Become an astronaut and see it for yourself from space.

An opinion, on the other hand, is something you believe, think, or feel. You cannot prove an opinion, and someone can have the exact opposite opinion from yours. For example, summer is the best of the four seasons. This is an opinion. I can't prove summer is the best season: There is no universally accepted measurement of seasons or what makes them particularly good or bad. My statement is based on personal preferences: I love the sun, being warm, having leaves on the trees, and wearing flip-flops. Many people reading this book would choose another season as their favorite, and that would be fine—because it is their opinion.

THE WORD *FACT* FIRST APPEARED IN THE ENGLISH LANGUAGE AROUND THE SIXTEENTH CENTURY, ABOUT A HUNDRED YEARS AFTER THE INVENTION OF THE PRINTING PRESS.[1]

THE FACTS ABOUT FACTS:

1. Statements that you can (and should) verify.
2. Not based on a belief or feeling.
3. Do not try to argue in favor or convince the reader of a particular position.
4. Can be proven through experimentation or observation.
5. True regardless of what someone personally thinks about them.
6. Usually use precise language or measurements, such as dates, locations, or numbers.
7. Tend to stay away from absolutes like *everybody, always, never,* and *no one* unless those things can be measured or proven.

THE FACTS ABOUT OPINIONS:

1. Feelings, views, thoughts, judgments, and beliefs you cannot verify.
2. Sometimes based on a person's interpretation or analysis of facts and presented as a conclusion.
3. Sometimes presented as an argument in favor of one thing or another.
4. Cannot be proven, and someone can have the opposite view.
5. Frequently use buzzwords and phrases like *I think, you should, may, I feel,* and *I believe.*

6. Use descriptive, judgmental language, including *best* and *worst*.
7. Often use absolutes like *everybody*, *always*, *never*, and *no one*.

This might look simple, but in June 2018 the Pew Research Center asked over five thousand adults in America to take a simple survey. Participants were shown ten statements and asked to identify which were factual and which were opinions—regardless of whether they agreed with the statements. Only 26 percent of respondents could properly classify all the facts, whereas 35 percent could accurately identify all the opinions (the survey counted any time participants skipped a question as a failure to choose the correct answer). That means the majority of Americans cannot reliably tell the difference between opinions and facts.[2]

QUESTIONS FROM THE PEW RESEARCH CENTER SURVEY

Factual statements:

1. Spending on Social Security, Medicare, and Medicaid makes up the largest portion of the US federal budget.

2. ISIS lost a significant portion of its territory in Iraq and Syria in 2017.

3. Health care costs per person in the US are the highest in the developed world.

4. Immigrants who are in the US illegally have some rights under the Constitution.

5. President Barack Obama was born in the United States.

Opinion statements:

1. Immigrants who are in the US illegally are a very big problem for the country today.

2. Government is almost always wasteful and inefficient.

3. Democracy is the greatest form of government.

4. Abortion should be legal in most cases.

5. Increasing the federal minimum wage to $15 an hour is essential for the health of the US economy.

But why was it so difficult? First, politics. The study found that, regardless of what political party participants belonged to, they were more likely to say a statement was a fact when it appealed to their political beliefs. Similarly, they were more likely to classify it as opinion when it was something they disagreed with. For example, one of the statements was "President Barack Obama was born in the United States." A fact, and one you could check by looking at his birth certificate. In response, 89 percent of Democrats said it was a fact, but only 63 percent of Republicans did. A lot of different factors probably contributed to Republicans being skeptical, but at the most basic level, Republicans were more susceptible to believing Obama was not qualified to be president because he was a Democrat.

On the other hand, when looking at the opinion statement "Increasing the federal minimum wage to $15 an hour is essential for the health of the US economy," 37 percent of Democrats incorrectly said it was a fact, while only 17 percent of Republicans misidentified it. This statement is an opinion because a lot of different factors can contribute to a good economy, such as low unemployment or access to affordable health care. It is the view or conclusion of the person making the statement that increasing the minimum wage is "essential." Most Democrats believe in raising the minimum wage, so when Democratic participants heard the sentence, it sounded to them like a fact.

The study uncovered a couple of other important vulnerabilities we all have when it comes to telling fact from opinion. The first is that we can sometimes be fooled into thinking an opinion is a fact when it is presented to us in a declarative statement. For example, "Paris is the most beautiful capital in Europe" has the same self-assuredness to it as "Paris is the capital of France." But even if a person thinks or believes something (an opinion) and states it in a way that sounds true, that does not actually make it a fact.

The other vulnerability is that we often equate a conclusion with a fact. Opinions are usually conclusions we've drawn after conducting an analysis of actual facts. For example, someone might tell you that their favorite movie is the best film ever made. They might even provide facts to support that claim, such as how many Oscar nominations the director has received or how much money the film made opening weekend. Those are facts you can verify, yet they don't prove their conclusion. The person's claim comes from their particular interpretation or analysis of the facts, which they turned into a conclusion: that their favorite movie is the best film ever made.

Their conclusion is an opinion. Why? Well, if I don't agree with the opinion, I can provide my own series of facts to show why *my* favorite movie is actually the best film ever made. I can tell them about the actors in the movie and how many Oscars they won, or about how the film launched a whole new movie genre. All those things might be facts, but the conclusion would still be my opinion.

On TV news programs and in news articles, reporters often interview people considered to be experts to give their analysis of current events. Published opinions and TV commentators can both provide useful information, but it is important to note that they are giving their personal views and analysis—or opinions. These opinions are often a mix of facts, analysis, and personal views. Because of that, they are an excellent way to get insight into a world you otherwise would not see, but the conclusions drawn are not facts.

When you are reading the news, you will notice that legitimate media outlets take steps to help readers clearly identify fact from opinion. Most news articles are meant to simply report the facts journalists have gathered and observed about a particular topic. However, media outlets also publish opinion articles (commonly known as op-eds) and letters to the editor. Many news websites now keep these analyses and opinions under a separate tab, usually marking them as OPINION (or OP-ED), EDITORIAL, COLUMN, or LETTER TO THE EDITOR to show readers what is not standard news.[3] This is an easy way to quickly identify what you are about to read.

Let's look at how similar topics can be expressed with either fact or opinion.

OPINION	FACT
There are not enough female astronauts.	Valentina Tereshkova was the first female astronaut to go into space.
Abraham Lincoln was the most eloquent speaker of all American presidents.	Abraham Lincoln's Gettysburg Address was ten sentences long.
Everybody likes kangaroos because they hop.	The largest kangaroo species, a red kangaroo, can typically jump about twenty-five feet at its fastest speed.
Everyone knows that having access to affordable education is the solution to unemployment in America.	In 2018, the unemployment rate in America for people with some college or an associate degree was 3.5 percent, whereas the rate was 5.9 percent for people with less than a high school diploma.[4]

The statements on the left-hand side are all opinions—there is no way to prove them. I could give you several different pieces of evidence to support each statement, but you could turn around and give me several different arguments as to why the conclusion is untrue. The statements in the right column are all facts because you can verify them by looking in a history book, an encyclopedia, or a dictionary. In some cases, such as the fact about the kangaroos, you could even set up your own experiment to test it out (if you had access to kangaroos, that is).

When trying to figure out whether something is a fact or an opinion, ask yourself: *Is this something I, or someone else, can prove? Can I look it up in a history book or an online encyclopedia?* If so, you are probably looking at a fact. When you are talking with people, get in the habit of asking them how they know what they have said is a fact. If it is a fact, they can point you to the source of information. If they cannot point you to evidence, or if their statement comes from their analysis of different facts, what they have told you is their opinion. It does not mean what they have said is not important or valid, or that it is wrong, of course. It simply means they are giving you their viewpoint.

Learning how to tell the difference between fact and opinion is a really important first step in learning how to spot fake news. Remember the study from earlier in the chapter illustrating how hard it is for people to do it? There was some hope in the results too. The study found that people who were politically aware, digitally savvy (meaning they regularly used digital devices and the internet), and generally trusting of the media were more likely to be able to correctly tell the difference between fact and opinion statements. That means that all the things you're learning how to do from this book will make you less susceptible to mixing up fact and opinion, and, ultimately, to falling for fake news. Onward!

Exercise:
FACT OR OPINION?

_____

Read the excerpt below from the *San Francisco Chronicle*.[5] It contains both opinions and facts, but the original article was published as an editorial because it is making an argument. Underline the facts you spot, and circle all the opinion statements you find. Check your answers with mine on the next page.

EDITORIAL:

MANY OF THE PRODUCTS MILLENNIALS ARE KILLING DESERVE TO DIE

(https://www.sfchronicle.com/opinion/article/Many-of-the-products-Millennials-are-killing-13442886.php)

Dec. 4, 2018 • Caille Millner

. . . While I was reading this week's capitalist woe—canned tuna consumption is down 42 percent per capita over the past 30 years, and guess who's to blame?—I realized something.

Millennials have good taste.

This is a generation that's making far less money than their parents did. It can't afford big-ticket items like houses, marriages or children.

So the Millennials are spending their few coins on vacations and avocado toast. And honestly? Those are better choices than canned tuna, golf and fabric softener.

Many of the products that Millennials are killing deserve to die. The kids are more than all right—they're wiser than their elders, who should have left them a better country while they had the chance.

MANY OF THE PRODUCTS MILLENNIALS ARE KILLING DESERVE TO DIE

Dec. 4, 2018 • Caille Millner

. . . While I was reading this week's capitalist woe—**canned tuna consumption is down 42 percent per capita over the past 30 years,** and guess who's to blame?—I realized something.

FACT. This is a statistic you can verify with a little research.

Millennials have good taste.

OPINION. This is based on the author's personal dislike of products millennials are no longer buying, like canned tuna.

This is a generation that's making far less money than their parents did. It can't afford big-ticket items like houses, marriages, or children.

FACT. You could do research on income levels across time to verify this.

So the **Millennials are spending their few coins on vacations and avocado toast.** And honestly? **Those are better** choices than canned tuna, golf, and fabric softener.

FACT. You could do research on spending habits to verify this.

OPINION. Again, this is based on the author's personal interests.

Many of the products that Millennials are killing deserve to die. The kids are more than all right—they're wiser than their elders, who should have left them a better country while they had the chance.

OPINION. The writer's dislike of these products is not a verifiable way of measuring which products "deserve to die" and which do not.

OPINION. This statement is filled with descriptive and judgment-based language.

CHAPTER 15

I'M BIASED, YOU'RE BIASED, WE'RE ALL BIASED

I **AM GOING TO BLOW YOUR MIND RIGHT NOW.** Ready for it?

Fact-checking alone is not the solution to our fake news problems.

What? Confronting a lie with the truth should work, right? It *should*, but it often *doesn't*. When our friend down the street posts an article on social media that is not true, we cannot simply reply with a link to Snopes debunking the article and then tell ourselves our work is done. Unfortunately, even if our friend looks at the article, it probably will not change their mind at all.

There is a simple reason for that—people are biased. We all have biases, preconceived and sometimes unreasoned tendencies or inclinations. They are inescapable. The most freethinking, woke, open-minded person in the world will still look at information through a certain lens that affects how they interpret and trust (or don't trust) it. That lens comes from things like background, race, religion, gender, political identity, education, life experiences, and culture.

Biases affect what information we pay attention to. They can lead us to ignore important information or automatically accept other things because they confirm what we already believe. Biases can also cause us to fall for fake news. One would think that in the online age, people might have fewer biases. After all, we are exposed to so much information every single day. With the ability to livestream, to communicate with anyone, anywhere, and with Google to answer any question we could think of, we basically have the world at our fingertips. But that is not how our minds work, unfortunately.

With our lives so fast-paced, and increasingly spent online, we are inclined to go with our gut—trusting our preexisting opinions on things—rather than do the research to find the truth. So we side with what makes sense to us based on our current knowledge and beliefs. But that makes us more susceptible to fake news. If information challenges our beliefs, our gut will tell us it's not true. This is what fake news uses to trick us: Since it cannot supply actual facts to convince us, it plays to our emotions and biases.

Our biases also cause us to seek out information that reaffirms our own opinions and to tune out information that conflicts with them. In 1967, long before the internet or social media, an important study was conducted.[1] Researchers asked a bunch of college students to listen to recorded speeches covered with static. The students had to really pay attention to pick out what the person was saying. If they wanted to hear better, they could push a button to clear away the static for a few seconds.

There were four speeches altogether. Two were about Christianity, one positive and one negative. The other two speeches were about smoking. One said it caused cancer and the other claimed it did not. You know from an earlier chapter that there was a lot of fake news around this second topic. So it shouldn't come as any surprise that the students who smoked pushed the button more often than the nonsmokers to listen intently to speeches claiming there was no link between smoking and lung cancer.

The reverse was also true. The students who smoked had no interest whatsoever in hearing pesky facts about the negative effects of smoking, thank you very much! The nonsmokers, of course, were interested in hearing the recording because it confirmed their decision not to smoke was a good one. Similarly, students who did not go to church pressed the button more than devoted churchgoers when listening to speeches that were anti-Christianity. In short, the students automatically filtered out the things they did not agree with, while surrounding themselves with what they wanted to hear. We filter out information all the time for the simple reason that we don't agree with it.

Today, social media takes this automatic tendency to a whole other level. We friend people who agree with us, and mute, unfriend, or unfollow people we don't. And many algorithms for social media and search engines compound the problem. Internet companies want us to click on links because that is how they make money, so they show us what they think we are most likely to click on. And since they know about bias all too well, they know that showing us stuff they think we'll agree with is the best way of getting our clicks. All of this creates little information bubbles, where we only see information that matches our view, not things that will challenge it, and those information bubbles only make us more certain we were right to begin with.

Those students in 1967 could have kept pushing the button to clear away the static during those speeches—after all, it was pretty annoying to listen to. But they didn't, just like most of us do not follow news outlets we disagree with or friend people on social media who have different views from us. This is because of something called cognitive dissonance. Let's break it down.

COGNITIVE DISSONANCE

COGNITIVE DISSONANCE IS THE MENTAL DISCOM-fort we go through when our personal views and ideas about something do not match the actual facts or evidence in front of us. By and large, people do not like to be challenged or to be told they are wrong. When facts challenge our views, our brains automatically start searching for a way to reconcile the two in a way that will make us most comfortable. In fact, whether we are aware of it happening or not, we go to great lengths to convince ourselves we are right, even when we are not. Sometimes that means we do some Simone Biles–worthy gymnastics in our minds to rationalize our views, or to try to reinterpret the facts to better fit our beliefs. Other times, it means we outright ignore the facts or selectively forget any that may prove us wrong.[2] When we see something that does not conform to our existing views, our brains tell us, *Nope! That isn't right.*

SCIENTISTS HAVE USED MRI MACHINES TO SEE HOW PEOPLE'S BRAINS REACT WHEN THEY ARE GIVEN INFORMATION THAT CONTRADICTS THEIR VIEWS.[3] In one study, scientists tested how people responded when given negative information about their preferred political candidate. The MRIs showed that people naturally tried to rationalize or explain away the information.[4] On the other hand, negative information about the candidate they did not like made people even more convinced that they were a bad candidate.

In 1954, Dorothy Martin of Oak Park, Illinois, told local newspapers she'd received a message from extraterrestrial beings she called the Guardians warning her about a flood that was going to wipe out most of the Earth on December 21. But it was not all bad news. The Guardians would come with their flying saucers from their planet called Clarion and rescue her and other believers.[5] Martin was a member of a fringe religious group called the Seekers, and this was not the first time the Guardians had spoken to her. On the night of the twenty-first, a group gathered at her home on her sunporch to wait for their alien rescuers. Except the aliens did not appear that night. Or the three times afterward when Martin said they would.

Each time neither the Guardians nor the world-ending flood came, Martin and her group took it to mean they were doing something wrong. They believed that aliens existed and that they were coming for them, but they also had to face the reality that night after night the aliens did not actually show up. That's when their cognitive dissonance kicked in. First, the group decided that it wasn't that the aliens did not exist; it was because they would not take anyone who had metal on them. (Apparently, aliens don't like metal, FYI.) That night, the group removed all their metal—rings, necklaces, even bras. But the aliens still didn't come. So the cognitive dissonance kept going.

In interviews with the media afterward, Martin and her followers gave a number of different reasons why the aliens had not yet come to save them as they'd promised, and none of them had anything to do with the spacemen not actually being real. On Christmas Eve, when the group gathered for the fourth time and the Guardians did not show up, Martin announced that she had received a new message from them. The aliens had told her that Martin's group "had spread so much light that God had saved the world from destruction." The Seekers did not need their alien rescuers after all, because the Earth had been saved.[6]

SOCIAL PSYCHOLOGISTS LEON FESTINGER, HENRY W. Riecken, and Stanley Schachter first wrote about the theory of cognitive dissonance after studying Martin and the Seekers. Their 1956 book about the study, *When Prophecy Fails*, sums up cognitive dissonance this way:

A man with a conviction is a hard man to change. Tell him you disagree and he turns away. Show him facts or figures and he questions your sources. Appeal to logic and he fails to see your point. . . . Finally, suppose that he is presented with evidence, unequivocal and undeniable evidence, that his belief is wrong; what will happen? The individual will frequently emerge, not only unshaken, but even more convinced of the truth of his beliefs than ever before.[7]

This may sound utterly ridiculous to most of us, but the Seekers were totally convinced that the Guardians were real and that they were coming for them. No amount of time spent standing on the cold sunporch, never being picked up, never seeing the Earth-ending flood, could convince them otherwise. Cognitive dissonance was hard at work.

NEGATIVITY BIAS

WE ALL KNOW PESSIMISTS—THOSE PEOPLE WHO always see the cup half empty. In the middle of a beautiful, sunny day they will complain about the rain forecast for tomorrow. They are the Eeyores of the world. But it turns out, we all have a bit of Eeyore in us. We are more likely to click on a negative story about the world ending than one that says the world is doing great. We just *have* to know what terrible thing might be coming for us. It has been that way for humans since the beginning of time. When our ancestors were just people living in caves, they had to be more aware of negative things, such as wild animals that wanted to eat them. Our brains are literally wired to pay more attention to negative news or information than positive. You can actually watch parts of the brain light up on an MRI scan when the person is told negative news.[8] Our brains are trying to protect us from possible danger by zeroing in on the negatives. Not only are we more likely to pay attention to negative information than positive, but we are also more likely to *remember* negative things than positive ones. They just stick with us.

You might not remember what you had for lunch yesterday, but I bet you remember that time ten years ago when someone made fun of you. You probably even remember every word they said and what the bully was wearing. The memory might suddenly pop into your head when you are trying to sleep, making your chest tighten or your hands curl into fists. That is because our brains are constantly collecting information that will help protect us or warn us of danger, especially when we're young, because we don't know what our future will look like. Our brains think they are helping us prepare for all possibilities by storing the negative information for us so we know how to spot the signs of trouble in the future and how to respond appropriately.[9]

Negativity bias makes us more likely to believe fake news that promises us doom and gloom. It also makes us more likely to accept conspiracies, because we start to think, *Hey, maybe a terrible secret force of some kind really* is *trying to get us!*[10]

CONFIRMATION BIAS

CONFIRMATION BIAS MEANS WE ARE MORE LIKELY to seek out and agree with judgments or analyses that fit our own worldview rather than anything that challenges it. This makes us particularly susceptible to fake news. After we experience that discomfort of cognitive dissonance, confirmation bias can kick in to help us explain it away.[11]

This same phenomenon happens all the time to devoted sports fans. We align ourselves with teams that become so important to us that we take their wins and losses very seriously. It's a good day when the Red Sox win. It feels like the world is crashing down when they don't. (I'm just going to assume you're all fans, like me, because the Red Sox are awesome.) But our obsession also means that when we watch a game, we are certain it is the other team that always fouls, not *our* beloved team, which can do no wrong.

I'm not exaggerating. In a now-famous experiment, scientists showed fans of opposing football teams the same video footage of a game between the two. And what do you know—each side thought *their* team was always in the right and the opposing team was always in the wrong.[12]

Okay, so does all of this actually happen, or is this just a theory? Time for an example (and a bit of a confession) from my own life. In 2008 I read about the runner Oscar Pistorius, aka the "Blade Runner," for the first time. Pistorius was a decorated Paralympic athlete from South Africa who had both feet amputated as a child. He had been fighting a long legal battle against the International Association of Athletics Federations for the right to compete in the Olympics. The IAAF had barred him from even attempting to qualify because they believed that Pistorius's two prosthetic limbs could give him an unfair advantage against other athletes. Pistorius won the battle and made history in the 2012 Summer Olympics in London by becoming the first-ever amputee to compete in track and field in the Olympic Games. He ran the 400-meter race and was the anchor for the men's 4x400 relay.

As a disabled woman myself, I'll admit I watched his races with tears in my eyes. His long legal fight for the right to compete at the Olympics was symbolic of the fight so many of us have waged in our own lives for equal rights as people with disabilities. After the

London Olympics, Pistorius said he would compete again at the next one, in Brazil in 2016. I had all but packed my bags to go watch him run, when in February 2013 news broke that Pistorius had shot and killed his longtime girlfriend, Reeva Steenkamp.[13]

Pistorius claimed he thought an intruder had broken into his house in the middle of the night and that the intruder had locked themselves in the bathroom. He said he shot through the door at the person in self-defense. I followed the trial closely, certain he could not be guilty. None of it made any sense to me. Why would someone who had just made history and was getting ready to compete in the next Olympics intentionally kill someone? Pistorius was a hero, I thought. Heroes didn't go around intentionally killing people. It just had to have been self-defense.

I wanted to believe he was innocent, so I went searching for any articles that would back up that belief. The prosecution argued that one of the reasons they were sure it was an intentional murder was because Pistorius had on his prosthetic limbs at the time. If Pistorius had really woken up to the sounds of a burglar and thought he was in imminent danger, he wouldn't have taken the time to slip on his prosthetics, they argued. But my confirmation bias got to work. If an intruder came into my house, I reasoned, the first thing I'd do would be get into my wheelchair so I could move around. It had to be the same for Pistorius.

But a jury found him guilty of knowingly murdering his girl-friend after the couple got into a terrible argument. After a series of appeals, he was eventually sentenced to fifteen years in jail. As you probably noticed, my cognitive dissonance was hard at work from the beginning—I admired Pistorius, so of course he had to be innocent. The confirmation bias came into play when I actively went looking for anything that would prove me right. With time, I was able to see my desperate attempts to explain his guilt away for what they really were—bias. That meant coming to terms with the uncomfortable fact that someone could both do something heroic and, at the end of the day, be a murderer.

HOW TO CHECK YOUR BIASES

THE FIRST STEP TO FIGHTING BACK AGAINST biases is to recognize and accept that we all have them. Taking the time to uncover your own personal biases will help you more clearly assess the news and consider new ideas. We have to acknowledge that we will probably never feel good about facts that show us we are wrong. In fact, this will probably be a lifelong struggle. But confronting our biases head-on will make us less likely to fall for fake news.

You can start by making a list of all the things that make up the lens through which you, personally, look at information. For example, my list might look something like this:

- Female
- Middle-class
- Millennial
- Politically active, left-leaning
- Disabled
- Rural childhood, urban adult life
- American, East Coaster
- Former CIA
- White
- Terrible at science and math

There are probably another two dozen things I could add to this list, things about religion, my education, or my age. Next, underneath each item, write down how each factor affects the way you think about the information you receive each day. For example, I might write:

- *Disabled.* More likely to pay attention to news about disability rights, health care, and access to education, transportation, and communities. I am likely to be skeptical of stories about disability issues not written by disabled people.
- *Former CIA.* More likely to pay attention to news about national security or foreign policy. More likely to accept information produced by national-security agencies than to question it.
- *Terrible at science and math.* Less likely to pay attention to news about these topics because I am not as interested in them. More easily convinced by information or analysis rooted in either subject because I don't understand it.

Once you have completed your own list, the important thing is to remember those elements as you look at new information. We will always have biases. But being aware of your biases will help you make sure you don't fall for fake news because of them.

IDENTIFY YOUR
BIASES

———————

Following my example, make a list of things that make up the lens through which you view and interpret information. Then, next to each item, write out how it could influence the way you see information. Here are a few categories to get you started:

- Where you live

  _____

- Gender identity

  _____

- Race

  _____

- Age

  _____

- Religion

  _____

-

  _____

-

  _____

-

  _____

-

  _____

-

  _____

-

  _____

-

  _____

CHAPTER 16

UNDERSTANDING BIAS IN NEWS MEDIA

WE DON'T HAVE JUST OUR OWN BIASES to look out for. Bias can appear in news coverage, too. It is important to note that with media bias, unlike fake news, there is not an intent to deceive news consumers. However, sometimes journalists and news commentators *unintentionally* allow their personal biases to affect how they cover the news. If reporters do not strive to prevent their own biases from seeping into their work, it can affect what news stories are covered and how those stories are told.[1] Their biases might lead them to write very few news stories about certain communities or topics, or to write a lot of stories on a topic that would not get as much attention if the reporting were more objective. For example, bias might lead a media outlet run by white people to skip over potentially important stories about issues affecting communities of color. Journalists in the US also tend to live in major metropolitan areas, like New York City, Boston, and Los Angeles, so they may ignore more rural areas.[2]

OBJECTIVE NEWS COVERAGE IS SOMETIMES CALLED *FAIR* OR *BALANCED* REPORTING. That means that a media outlet tries to present all sides of a story without bias, aiming to be as accurate and truthful as possible without leading the reader to a reporter's predetermined conclusion.[3] In the English-language world, some of the more objective media outlets include Reuters, the Associated Press, the BBC, NPR, Bloomberg, *USA Today*, the *Washington Post*, and Agence France-Presse.[4]

In addition, reporting just the cold hard facts can make news coverage pretty boring. To make it more interesting, reporters often add in people's stories, quotes from interviews, and vivid descriptions of events. Personal biases can slip into the coverage as a result. Look at the difference between my strictly factual telling of a major news event compared to the more poetic coverage of the same event by the *New York Times*.

> **Me:** *A fire burned down part of the Notre-Dame cathedral in Paris, France, on April 15, 2019. The roof and spire collapsed. No one was injured. French officials said the fire probably started because of a short circuit.*

> **The *New York Times*:** *Notre-Dame cathedral, the symbol of the beauty and history of Paris, was scarred by an extensive fire on Monday evening that caused its delicate spire to collapse, bruised the Parisian skies with soot and further disheartened a city already back on its heels after weeks of violent protests.*

The spectacle of flames leaping from the cathedral's
wooden roof—its spire glowing red then turning into a
virtual cinder—stunned thousands of onlookers who
gathered along the banks of the Seine and packed into the
plaza of the nearby Hôtel de Ville, gasping and covering
their mouths in horror and wiping away tears.[5]

There is no question which version of the same event is more exciting and interesting to read. My version is accurate and un-biased, and that's about all it has going for it. The *New York Times* excerpt, on the other hand, paints a vivid picture and makes us feel something in response—sadness, mostly. It is when the news tries to make the basic facts of a story more interesting that bias can unintentionally slip in. Feeling something is not a sign that what is reported is wrong. It just means we need to pay close attention to what is being said.

That leads us to the second kind of media bias we will encounter —*intentional*. Intentional media bias is when a media outlet tells a news story a certain way to influence the audience's opinion about something. Bias from a media outlet can look or sound a lot as though a media outlet is arguing for or against a particular position.

Bias in the media is often discussed in terms of political affilia-tion. A media outlet may be described as left- or liberal-leaning, neu-tral, or right- or conservative-leaning. Sometimes the media outlet will make it easy for you and claim its bias up front, telling you on its website that politically it leans one way or another. For example, the FAQ page for the *National Review* magazine states that it is "of conservative opinion" and that its readers are primarily American conservatives.[6] Similarly, the left-leaning *Nation* says on its site that it is part of a "progressive journalistic community that is challenging the right."[7] If a media outlet claims to be a conservative or liberal voice, that does not necessarily mean that what it says is inaccurate. But it does mean that it is reporting the news with a specific agenda and through a particular political lens.

Consider this example of intentional bias. President Barack Obama announced in June 2011 that the United States would gradually begin withdrawing military troops from Afghanistan and would hand security responsibilities over to the Afghan government by 2014. The *New York Times*, which leans slightly left of center politically, published an article about the announcement with the headline OBAMA WILL SPEED PULLOUT FROM WAR IN AFGHANISTAN.[8] The article talked about America's timeline for withdrawal and how the Afghan military was getting ready. Covering the same announcement, *Fox News* took a very different approach. Their article was titled OBAMA DOESN'T THANK PETRAEUS.[9] General David Petraeus commanded US military forces in Afghanistan at the time, and the article that followed focused on criticizing Obama for not mentioning him in his speech. It included very little information from Obama's actual announcement on Afghanistan.

Reading it, you could see that the *Fox News* article was written with a purpose—to make Obama seem ungrateful. Was it accurate that Obama did not thank Petraeus in his speech? Yes. But the fact that the article focused on that one element of the speech instead of anything potentially positive, or even on the facts of the military withdrawal, was very deliberate and part of a larger pattern at the media outlet. The Center for Media and Public Affairs found that in the first fifty days of the Obama administration, only 13 percent of Fox News coverage on the president was positive, compared to a 73 percent positive coverage rate by the *New York Times*.[10]

A quick internet search would show you that *Fox News* markets itself as a conservative voice in news, meaning it tells the news through a conservative lens. But if a news outlet does not openly claim to have a particular political leaning or bias, what can you do to find out for yourself if it does?

1. *Break out of your own news silo.* We have so much information at our fingertips, but we often create information bubbles or news silos for ourselves. That means we find a few sources of information, usually the ones we agree with, and then we stick only to those. When we do that, we do not see other points of view. Being able to compare the information you are seeing with other trusted news sources will help you better spot bias. Look at which journalists, experts, and media outlets you follow and ask yourself if you follow them because they keep you well informed or only because you agree with what they report.

   Imagine trying to put together a super complicated puzzle. You might eventually be able to solve it on your own. But if you brought other people in to help you, you could probably do it faster and more easily. Reading a wide range of news sources is like that. It helps you put together a clearer and more accurate picture of what is being reported.

2. *Be wary of "news reports" that read more like opinion pieces.* As we discussed in chapter 14, reputable news outlets will separate opinion articles from news reports to help readers know what is factual reporting versus what was written based on personal views and analysis. Sometimes, however, media outlets that intentionally lean one way or another politically will blur the line between news reporting and opinion. If you are reading an

article marked as a news report, but it has a lot of the charac-
teristics of opinions that we talked about before—such as using
a lot of judgment-heavy language—your potential media bias
radar should go off.

3. *Check the evidence given.* Looking at what sources a media outlet
    regularly cites can tell you a lot about what biases may be at work
    in its reporting. If a news outlet only ever uses information from
    organizations or individuals that lean one way politically, that
    may be a sign of bias.

    Looking at sources, you might also uncover something called
    cherry-picking: making a claim and then only citing evidence
    that supports it. For example, if I'm saying summer is the best
    season, I might try to convince you that I'm right by talking about
    the warm weather, vacations, and outdoor activities. I would
    definitely not mention mosquitoes or how there are days when
    the sun and humidity make it too hot to go outside. Ask yourself
    if the evidence you find really does support what the outlet is
    saying, or if there are things it is leaving out.

4. *Look for the other side of the story.* Pretend you're part of a jury in
    which you will have to decide at the end of a trial whether or not
    a person is guilty of a crime. If only the prosecutor is allowed to
    provide evidence against the person, you are only getting part
    of the story, and it definitely is not a fair trial.

    To make sure they're telling the full story, balanced news
    outlets seek a comment from the subject of their news coverage.
    For example, if the CEO of a company publicly said something
    inflammatory, a reporter might offer that CEO an opportunity
    after the fact to make a comment explaining what they meant

or why they said what they did. If it looks like a news outlet is only covering one part of a story, ask yourself why and if there are larger biases at play.

5. *Give government-run media outlets the side-eye.* In many countries, the government either runs, sponsors, or plays a large role in directing certain media outlets. That means they tell the outlets what to report (such as positive news stories about their political leaders) and what to stay away from (such as news that would cast a bad light on the government). You should not rely on those outlets for unbiased news coverage. Some foreign outlets, including the Iranian government-owned Fars News Agency[11] or Chinese government-owned Xinhua, often help their governments spread false information.[12]

6. *Watch out for "loaded" terms.* Good reporters know that their choice of words is incredibly important, and they work hard to be as precise and neutral as possible. Loaded words are the opposite of precise and neutral. They inspire either a negative or a positive response.[13] Saying that someone "admitted" something is using a loaded term, since it can suggest that the person was originally trying to hide something. The word makes us automatically suspicious of the person in question. Loaded words can also be found in how we refer to people. For example, some news outlets describing people who live and work in a country where they do not have a visa or citizenship have started using the term *undocumented immigrant,* since the older term *illegal alien* can make a news story sound more negative.[14]

_____

Below are excerpts from two articles written about climate change from two different media outlets. As you read through them, underline all the potential signs of media bias—intentional and unintentional—that you can spot. Compare your answers with mine after.

https://dailycaller.com/2019/03/15/children-strike-school-climate-change/

JUST 12 YEARS LEFT? LET'S BREAK DOWN THE ALARMIST TALKING POINT FUELING KIDS' CLIMATE CHANGE STRIKES

March 15, 2019

Thousands of students will skip school Friday over global warming as part of an international movement backed by adult activists and based on a misreading of the latest United Nations climate report. . . .

The student strikes were inspired by 16-year-old Greta Thunberg, who began ditching school in August to sit in protest outside Swedish parliament. . . .

Student activists' alarm isn't surprising—it's been nurtured by the media, climate activists and politicians in the wake of a U.N. report released in October.

The U.N. special report stated emissions needed to fall 45 percent below 2010 levels by 2030, and then for emissions to reach zero by 2050 to avoid warming above 1.5 degrees Celsius by 2100. . . .

(And that's if you put faith in the U.N.'s climate models, which have been shown to overestimate warming by as much as 50 percent.)

Is 1.5 to 2 degrees of warming catastrophic? The U.N.'s projections suggest no, but the media framed it as a 12-year deadline to prevent climate change catastrophe . . .

YOUTH ACTIVISTS ACROSS GLOBE PROTEST FOR CLIMATE ACTION

MARCH 15, 2019

Protests erupted across the globe on Friday led by youth activists demanding governments take action to thwart the inevitable effects of climate change.

From Israel to South Africa to the U.S., thousands of student protesters rallied at school campuses and their civic centers asking for federal and international action to address global warming—the effects of which could greatly impact younger generations. . . .

In Cape Town, students in uniforms held signs, one which read, "Denial is not a policy."

In Lebanon, a sign at a rally announced, "You really know how to make me cry when you make those oceans rise."

In Hong Kong, it was reported that Friday's climate strike amounted to the city's largest environmental rally in history, with an estimated 1,000 students taking to the streets holding signs including one reading, "Our children will be endangered species."

In many instances, students skipped school to attend protests. . . .

Friday's protests also come the same week that the United Nations released two new scientific reports warning that the effects of global warming and sea level rise may be even more unavoidable than previously measured.

JUST 12 YEARS LEFT? LET'S BREAK DOWN THE ALARMIST TALKING POINT FUELING KIDS' CLIMATE CHANGE STRIKES

March 15, 2019

Thousands of students will skip school Friday over global warming as part of an international movement backed by adult activists and based on a misreading of the latest United Nations climate report. . . .

The student strikes were inspired by 16-year-old Greta Thunberg, **who began ditching school in August to sit in protest outside Swedish parliament. . . .**

Student activists' alarm isn't surprising—**it's been nurtured by the media, climate activists and politicians in the wake of a U.N. report released in October.**

If you do a quick internet search on this outlet, you'll find that it is frequently characterized as an American conservative news and opinion website founded by conservative media personalities. That tells you right away that what it reports caters to a particular audience and that its reporting has a particular political bias.

The headline is based on the author's own personal views. We know that because the word "alarmist" is not attributed to an expert or cited with evidence.

This is one of several instances where the author uses judgment-heavy language—"kids," "children," "skip school"—to paint the strike participants as immature, striking only to get out of going to school (rather than being serious activists), and manipulated by adults, environmental organizations, the UN, and the media.

It is factually true that participants were kids and that many left school to join the strikes, but the author uses language like "ditching school" in a way that's meant to tell us this is all a bad thing.

The author does not provide evidence of this, such as statements from the media or climate activists, or show a direct connection from those statements to those being made by student activists.

The U.N. special report stated emissions needed to fall 45 percent below 2010 levels by 2030, and then for emissions to reach zero by 2050 to avoid warming above 1.5 degrees Celsius by 2100. . . .

(And that's if you put faith in the U.N.'s climate models, which have been shown to overestimate warming by as much as 50 percent.)

Is 1.5 to 2 degrees of warming catastrophic? The U.N.'s projections suggest no, but **the media framed it as a 12-year deadline to prevent climate change catastrophe . . .**

Here the author calls into question the legitimacy of the UN's environmental work, but again does not give evidence, suggesting this is based on the author's own personal views.

The author suggests there is evidence the UN report was inaccurate, using the phrase "which have been shown" to discredit this and previous UN reports. But he does not provide the evidence or link to a source. We should be asking ourselves "shown by whom?"

Here the author could have included evidence—direct quotes from the report or from the media outlets—but doesn't. This suggests he is cherry-picking and interpreting information that supports his own claim, rather than laying out the facts and leaving readers to draw their own conclusions.

We come away from this article feeling a certain way about the event in question—a bunch of immature students have been manipulated into cutting school, all based on the sinister intentions of outside groups and the intentional misreading of a report. The article is full of judgment-based language that makes this "news report" read much more like an editorial or opinion article. All of these are signs of possible media bias.

YOUTH ACTIVISTS ACROSS GLOBE PROTEST FOR CLIMATE ACTION

MARCH 15, 2019

Protests erupted across the globe on Friday led by youth activists demanding governments take action to thwart the inevitable effects of climate change.

From Israel to South Africa to the U.S., thousands of student protesters rallied at school campuses and their civic centers asking for federal and international action to address global warming—**the effects of which could greatly impact younger generations. . . .**

An internet search will show you that this publication is sometimes characterized as leaning slightly left of center, which means its coverage may have a left-leaning bias. It does not mean that what it reports is not factual, but it does mean the outlet may be more likely to cover topics of interest to the political left.

Language like *inevitable effects of climate change* is a sign that you are probably not reading an article from an overtly conservative media outlet, because conservative outlets tend to question the existence of climate change.

This is not an outright sign of bias, but the author could have attributed this fact to experts who have written extensively on the effects of climate change on younger generations so that it did not look like a personal view from the author.

In Cape Town, students in uniforms held signs, one which read, "Denial is not a policy."

In Lebanon, a sign at a rally announced, "You really know how to make me cry when you make those oceans rise."

In Hong Kong, it was reported that Friday's climate strike amounted to the city's largest environmental rally in history, with an estimated 1,000 students taking to the streets holding signs including one reading, "Our children will be endangered species."

In many instances, students skipped school to attend protests. . . .

Friday's protests also come the same week that the United Nations released two new scientific reports warning that the effects of global warming and sea level rise may be even more unavoidable than previously measured.

> Since much of the language up to this point has painted a vivid picture of a worldwide movement in which the students are brave heroes—*rallied, taking to the streets*—the mention of *skipping school* doesn't carry the same judgment. By the time readers reach that phrase, they already believe the protests are for a good cause, because the paragraphs before got us emotionally invested.

We come away from this article with a very different feeling about the protests than we had from the previous article. In this one, we think of student protestors as mature and brave for fighting against the very serious threat of climate change.

CHAPTER 17

HOW TO SPOT FAKE NEWS ARTICLES

I HEAR THIS KIND OF CONVERSATION A LOT.

> **Person 1: Oh my gosh, did you hear that [fill in the blank with some current event/celebrity-couple breakup/natural disaster]? I saw it [in the news/when someone posted about it].**

> **Person 2: No way! What happened?**

> **Person 1: I'm not really sure. I only read the headline.**

Person 1 learned something they found interesting, and they wanted to pass along that information. But the problem is, Person 1 really did not learn anything at all. They read a headline that said something that may or may not have really happened, and may or may not have been supported by the information in the article that followed.

The truth is, most of us have done it. In fact, a 2018 study by the Media Insight Project showed that only four out of ten Americans said they read more than just the headline of a news article.[1] An earlier study showed that 59 percent of all the news articles shared on social media did not receive an actual click, meaning people shared the article on the headline alone and never read the article itself.[2]

Those biases we talked about in chapter 15 kick in even when we are doing something as quick as reading a headline. If it interests us and seems to fit with what we already believe, we tend to trust it. We also assume the article will say exactly what the headline said, so there is no reason to read more.[3] After all, headlines are supposed to quickly summarize the article in a way that makes readers want to read it.

But, if we actually read the article, we might quickly discover it doesn't really say what the headline suggested it would. News stories are almost always more complex than headlines suggest, and for an understandable reason—headlines have to be short. They can only call out one aspect of an article that usually is about a lot more than that.

Fake news sites and some media outlets often use misleading or sensational headlines to drive people to their websites, or to get people to share an article without ever looking at it. They'll sometimes start with THE SHOCKING TRUTH! or WHAT THEY DON'T WANT YOU TO KNOW ABOUT . . . to gain your interest. This kind of headline is sometimes called *clickbait*—the exciting or sensational headline is the bait they are using to get you to click on the link. Clickbait headlines are designed to get a strong emotional reaction from us, because that's when we are more likely to click on them or share them.

PSYCHOLOGISTS SAY THE IMPRESSION MADE ON OUR MINDS BY HEADLINES CAN ALSO CHANGE HOW WE READ THE ARTICLE THAT FOLLOWS.[4] And since the headline made the first impression, we are more likely to recall it than what was actually said in the article. For example, a headline might say that a war is going to break out, while the article itself explains that ten really big things have to happen first and some of them are really unlikely. But the headline will make such an impression on us that we might unintentionally miss or ignore the part in the article that says the war is not very likely.[5]

So how do you spot fake news headlines? Some are outrageous enough that you might spot them right away: for example, NINE-YEAR-OLD ACCIDENTALLY DISCOVERS CURE FOR CANCER THROUGH SCIENCE-FAIR PROJECT and SCIENTISTS PREDICT WORLD-ENDING FLOOD IN TWO YEARS. But in cases where you are not sure, there are a few questions you should consider that can help you spot a fake news story from just the headline. Ask yourself:

- Does what the headline says make sense, given what I know about this topic? For example, is what the headline describes even possible?
- Is the headline too outrageous or too good to be true?
- Could this story possibly be a joke or satire?

What about headlines that sit somewhere between outrageous and just bonkers enough that they might be true? Consider these fake headlines from the last few years:

1. PALESTINIANS RECOGNIZE TEXAS AS PART OF MEXICO.[6] This headline came from satirical website the Beaverton in 2017 after President Trump announced that the United States was going to move its embassy from Tel Aviv to Jerusalem and recognize Jerusalem as the capital city of the state of Israel. Many people never looked past the headline to figure out the Beaverton was satire.[7]

2. REPORT: KID ROCK BEING DISCUSSED AS GOP SENATE CANDIDATE. The idea of American musician Kid Rock in politics could have been enough for people to think the story was fake news, but reality stars and movie stars had been elected before. Why not Kid Rock? It was suddenly all over the news that he was considering running for the Michigan Senate seat. Most major news outlets dismissed it as a hoax, in part because Kid Rock's supposed campaign website simply linked to his merch store. He also released two new songs at the same time and announced a music tour instead of a campaign tour. But Kid Rock's mixed past (he'd gotten in trouble for several physical brawls, and he'd starred in a sex tape) excited some media outlets, and even news site Politico, which is typically respected by serious politics watchers, insisted it was real.[8] It soon came to light that the whole thing was in fact a publicity stunt to sell his new album and boost ticket sales for his concert tour.[9]

3. OBAMA SIGNS EXECUTIVE ORDER BANNING THE PLEDGE OF ALLEGIANCE IN SCHOOLS NATIONWIDE.[10] The article from 2016 came from abcnews.com.co, a fake news site designed to look like ABC News. The article that followed said not only that Obama had banned the pledge, but also that he had made it illegal for any federally funded agency to display, recite, or encourage others to

recite it. Readers who were fooled by the headline could have quickly figured out the article was fake news by reading all the way through it—it cites sources that are obviously made up, like Fappy the Anti-Masturbation Dolphin, the supposed mascot of an unnamed Christian organization. It also lists a phone number for a hotline where people can call to express their views of the Executive Order, but the number is for the Westboro Baptist Church, an organization known for protesting against minority groups, other religions, and military funerals. Over two million people liked, shared, or commented on the article on Facebook, but the article itself was only viewed 110,000 times. That means more than 1.9 million people reacted based on the headline alone.[11] For those who disapproved of President Obama, this would have seemed right in the realm of possibility, and it appears the headline was enough to convince them it was real.

4. TRUMP ORDERED EXECUTION OF OBAMA-PARDONED TURKEYS. In America around Thanksgiving, it is a tradition for the president to hold a ceremony to pardon a turkey—to keep it from being killed for Thanksgiving dinner. This headline came from a site that specializes in satire (which it hints at on its website, though it's hard to find).[12] But some people took it seriously when it was posted in 2017, in large part because Trump had been working on rolling back legislation and policies Barack Obama had passed when he was president.[13] *Why wouldn't he also un-pardon the turkeys Obama had saved?* some people thought. When we already feel one way about something, we will believe almost anything that fits within that view.

But even reading these examples and going through the questions we talked about will not make you totally immune to eye-catching fake news headlines. There is simply not enough evidence in most headlines to prove they're true or fake. But don't worry. There are many more clues to look for in an article or on a website. That is why we need to read more than just the headline.

So, now that we've committed to actually reading the article, what do we need to look for? Let's talk about some of the red flags that can tell you when something is fake news. Sometimes fake news will be obvious from the very first sentence. Other times, the first paragraph might sound reasonable, but then it will abruptly shift into outrageous halfway through. But sometimes fake news writers will copy and paste from legitimate sources to make an article sound more plausible to the reader, and then mix in lies and inaccuracies with the actual facts. But even in those harder-to-spot cases, you can find those red flags in a number of ways. You just have to do a little intelligence-analyst work.

First, here is what you *shouldn't* do. Even once you have read the article, *don't* go with your gut. As we discussed in chapter 15, our gut is not always the most reliable source when it comes to figuring out what information is true because all our personal biases are at play. Saying *Yeah, that sounds right to me* and then moving on once you've read something could make you miss all those signs that what you read was not actually true.

On the other hand, *don't* let yourself dismiss something as fake news simply because you do not agree with what it says. We already know that we are naturally programmed to do this. So when our inclination is to dismiss an article or a piece of information right away, instead taking the time to really consider it may show us we've been wrong all along.

Now for what you *should* do. Following these steps will help you figure out not only if something is fake news, but also which real news outlets are good sources of information.

1. *Check the URL.* First, take a look at the domain name. A domain name can sometimes tell you things about the website, such as the creator, the purpose, and often the country where the website was created. It can even alert you to possible fake news. These are the general kinds of domains out there:

   .com: This is for commercial websites that promote particular products. The website may not be trying to sell you something for money, but it is still promoting something, even if that something is information.

   .edu: This is for educational institutions, from kindergarten to higher education, but be aware that it can also be used for students' personal websites.

   .gov: This is a domain for American government agencies only. The real White House page ends with .gov because it is a part of the US government. When Whitehouse.com, on the other hand, was first created, it was actually a porn website[14]—and boy, were people surprised to find that out!

   .org: Traditionally, nonprofit organizations use this domain, but anyone can buy a .org domain without providing any proof the organization actually exists. Many nonprofits are unbiased and publish factual reports and good analyses of particular issues. But many others advocate for specific things or have partisan views, so the information published there may be skewed. RealTrueNews.org was a website that fooled thousands of people with fake stories about the US presidential election in 2016.[15]

   .biz, .net, .info, .xyz, etc.: These domains are for sites that do not really fit under the others. Most legitimate news sources will not use these domains, and if they do own one of these domains, they will usually have the page automatically redirect you back to their main .com address.

Often, fake news websites use domain names that are close to an actual news-website domain to try to trick people, like BuzzFeedUSA.com or NBCNews9.net.

2. *Check the date.* Quickly checking the date and time an article was published can save you a lot of grief later. Sometimes, fake news starts with someone recycling old news. Sure, the event everyone is suddenly raging about online might have happened, but it happened five years ago or more and no one who's sharing the article has bothered to check the publication date. Fake news writers also sometimes recycle old fake news stories after a couple of years, when people have forgotten the last time they made the rounds. Remember the HIV-filled bananas? The first version was written years before, and featured HIV-filled oranges. You can expect to see it pop up again in another year or two—this is your warning. But next time it might be HIV-filled papayas.

3. *Investigate the source.* Figure out where the news comes from. That means investigating the media outlet or the individual sharing the content. Ask yourself:

- Was the article or post written by someone who claims to be a journalist, or by something that calls itself a news organization? If so, you can do some research on the relevant outlet.
- Was it created by a non-news organization, a government agency, a company pushing a product, or an individual? A little investigating on the website can also tell you a lot.

Most often, you can see who the publisher of an article or report claims to be on the header of the website. Most legitimate news websites have an "About Us" section or something similar describing the company's history that will give you more information. Satire or news-joke websites will often say that they are not real news. The look of the website can also be a sign. If it only has four or five other articles, that in and of itself is a red flag. You have probably stumbled across fake news.

Additionally, a simple internet search can pull up a lot of useful information about a source's background. For example, when I looked up Infowars, Google showed me the following Wikipedia explanation: "Infowars is a far-right American conspiracy theory and fake news website," a good indication not to take anything from Infowars seriously, at least not without more research. It will also often tell you things like who or what company owns the publication, which will help you figure out what biases or motives the publication may have for publishing what they do. If you cannot find any information at all about the publication after you do a search, you should treat it and any news posted on it with a high degree of skepticism.

Finally, fake news articles sometimes make up experts or cite anonymous experts to prove their claims. It is worth checking on any experts cited to make sure that, first, they really exist, and, second, that they actually have the expertise with which they were credited.

4. *Watch out for spelling mistakes and poor grammar.* Now you are into the actual text of the article or post, and you come across a spelling mistake. One spelling mistake might be an oops, but then you find another and another. When you look closer, it turns

out the grammar is not great either. That is a big sign you have stumbled across fake news or, at the very least, a personal blog or website. Either way, it is not real news. Reputable media outlets have multiple layers of editors, copy editors, and fact-checkers, so it is very unlikely that an article riddled with mistakes like that would have been published.

5. *See if other news outlets are reporting on it.* If a news story is big enough, most media outlets will be covering it. If you encounter a story that has some earth-shattering news, a quick online search will show you if other outlets are reporting on it. Sometimes, however, fake news writers own more than one fake news site and will publish articles across all the websites to make them look more credible. In this case, check with a news outlet you already know is real to see if it is covering what the websites in question claim. Think again of the HIV-filled banana story. If there were really a nefarious person running around with syringes of HIV-positive blood trying to infect people, it would be a global story. Every single news outlet would be covering it. The fact that only one website wrote about it should have been a giant warning sign to readers that the whole thing was made up.

6. *Identify who is telling the story and why.* Every legitimate news story should have the author listed. You should be able to click on their name and see what else they have written or published previously. Often, news outlets will also include relevant information about the author's professional background. This will help you know their level of expertise and give you a sense of whether or not they are qualified to be writing on that particular topic.

But having an author listed on an article, in and of itself, is not a sign they are reporting real news. For example, the story about Obama banning the Pledge of Allegiance was supposedly written by a person named Jimmy Rustling.[16] You could even click on his name to go to his author page. On that page, it claimed Jimmy was a medical doctor. Okay, it might seem slightly odd that a doctor is writing on a political issue, but that is not necessarily cause for concern. But then the bio said Jimmy had won the biggest prizes in American journalism several times. Many people might take that as impressive evidence and conclude Jimmy was reporting the truth. However, that would be a mistake. With a simple internet search, you would find out that no one named Jimmy Rustling has ever won any of the awards his bio claimed. The whole thing was made up to make the story look more credible.

Doing a little research on an author's background might also tell you about possible motivations or biases that might have influenced what they reported. Remember the scientists paid by Big Tobacco to report that there was no link between smoking and lung cancer? If we had had Google back then, it most likely would not have taken so long to expose their research as fake news.

7. *Look at where the author got their information.* That means paying attention to the sources they cite and what level of access they have to the information they are giving. Real news is made up of facts and information gathered from people or groups involved, so articles should be full of sources, background information, and quotes. When specific names are given for sources, you should take the time to verify first that they actually exist, and then that they have the background attributed to them.

Sources should also be relevant to the topic discussed in

the article. An article discussing climate change, for example, should be based on information from scientists, studies, and people who work on climate change. Citing a dog groomer or a fiction writer is a sign the information may not be accurate (unless, say, that dog groomer or fiction writer also has a PhD in environmental science and spent thirty years working in the field before changing professions). Typically, real news will give a short explanation of a source's background, even something as simple as "Jane Smith, a professor of economics at the University of Fill-in-the-Blank."

Beware of articles making big claims that cite only one source, or that do not list any sources at all. A lack of sources means the article is probably not based on research or interviews. At least some of the sources used should also be firsthand accounts of people involved in the event, meaning they witnessed it or were personally involved in some way. Remember how newspapers reported on rumors about Jack the Ripper? Basing a whole story just on people who only heard the information from other people does not mean a report is wrong, but it may mean some of the details have probably gotten muddled.

In some cases, real reporters leave out a source's name because the source would face retribution of some kind if their name were reported. That's when you'll see phrases like "a source speaking on condition of anonymity." Even then, most reputable news organizations will explain the background of the source— for example, "an anonymous source in the White House"—to show that they have some level of knowledge about the issue. If a story makes an explosive claim based off one anonymous source, with no information about that source's background or access to the information, that is reason to treat the article with a healthy dose of skepticism.

Online articles will almost always include hyperlinks to other articles so you can find out where they got their information and also go to find out more if you want to. If they do not, that is a reason to be very suspicious. But even fake news often has hyperlinks, especially when it's making a big claim. Sometimes fake news articles insert hyperlinks that lead nowhere to make it look like the article is credible—if you find this, it is a dead giveaway you have encountered fake news. And even links that actually lead to reputable websites might not support or say what the article claims they do. The story about Obama banning the Pledge of Allegiance linked to an executive order he signed that had nothing to do with the pledge.

8. *Ask yourself if there is more to the story.* Sometimes fake news is based off real events and real news articles, but since the author copied and pasted only parts of the story, it is not accurate anymore. Even when reading an article from a reputable news source, you should ask yourself if it contains the whole story or if there is important context missing. When journalists report current events, particularly when they have word limits and deadlines to contend with, it can be easy to exclude relevant history and context.

Fake news often pulls actual quotes from real experts, but uses only parts of them to make them seem to say what the author wants them to say. Or they will make up quotes and attribute them to real people. You will recall that reporters made up quotes by famous scientists in the Great Moon Hoax and in the article about the telegraph putting Earth on a collision course with the sun. Take the time to check the quote and see if there might be more to the story, or if it was pulled out of context or made up to fit what an article is trying to say.

9. *Go to fact-checking websites.* Still in doubt whether something you read is fake news? Look it up on one of the many fact-checking websites that debunk the biggest conspiracies, hoaxes, and fake news stories making the rounds online.

The people who push out fake news are going to try their very best to fool you, and let's be honest—they're pretty good at what they do. So it may take you going through this whole list before you know if you've found fake news. But when you do, feel good about it and what you've done. You are one less person they will be able to trick!

The other bonus of going through this list to verify information is that when you're done, you will have your own list of those important trusted news sources you can turn to for information.

Exercise:
REAL OR FAKE?

Below are three excerpts from articles. Using the list of strategies we've discussed in this chapter, go through and mark up any signals you can spot that indicate the article is either fake or real. If you cannot decide if it is real or fake, make a list of things you would need to investigate further. Check your answers with mine at the end.

http://www.rilenews.com/stories/us-international/
federal-technology-grant-to-provide-e-cigs-for-inner-city-
students#sthash.iVQIfooS.dpuf

FEDERAL CLASSROOM TECHNOLOGY GRANT GUARANTEES E-CIGS FOR ALL INNER CITY STUDENTS

TECHNOLOGY FINALLY MAKES ITS WAY TO THE STUDENTS WHO NEED IT

By Sarah Connor | 2014.08.03

Some of the lowest performing schools in the country received a pleasant surprise this week when word of a new Federal technology grant was announced to the public. Much like the suburban programs that provide iPads to students, this program will finally put electronic cigarettes in the hands of trouble youths that are desperate for technology in the classroom. It is expected that the move will a game-changer in evening the playing field between suburban and urban schools.

Emma Harris, a principal in one of Detroit's worst school districts applauded the move. "We've been fighting for years to get more advanced technology available to the kids. I never thought I would see the day when I could bring in the teachers for a meeting and tell them that we finally accomplished what we set out to do. We all just cried tears of joy." . . .

ENTERTAINMENT

BEYONCÉ, JAY Z TO LAUNCH ONLINE CONTEST TO DETERMINE BABY NAMES

FEBRUARY 31, 2017 by R. HOBBUS J.D.

LOS ANGELES, Ca.—Less than twenty-four hours after Beyoncé's earth-shattering announcement that she and Jay Z are expecting twins, a source close to Queen Bey has revealed that the superstar couple plans to launch an online contest in which fans can submit and vote on potential baby names, the entertainment news website TMZ reported on Thursday.

"The Carters have always felt a strong connection to their fans and this is a way for them to truly give something back," the source told TMZ. The contest, which is scheduled to go live in the coming days via beyoncesbabynames.com, will begin with a three-week submission period followed by several days of voting. . . .

. . . A close friend of the Carter family, who spoke to *Real News Right Now* on condition of anonymity, has confirmed that the person responsible for submitting the winning names will receive a personal letter of gratitude from Beyoncé along with an invitation to be present for the twins' delivery. . . .

23 INJURED AFTER EXPLOSION REPORTED IN PLANTATION

2 PEOPLE SERIOUSLY INJURED, AUTHORITIES SAY

By AMANDA BATCHELOR-*Senior Digital Editor,*
ROY RAMOS-*Reporter,* PARKER BRANTON-*Reporter,*
TRENT KELLY-*Reporter*

Posted: 12:00 PM, July 06, 2019

PLANTATION, Fla.—A total of 23 people were injured Saturday during an explosion at a shopping center in Plantation, authorities confirmed.

Plantation Fire Department Deputy Chief Joel Gordon said two people suffered serious injuries in the blast that was reported just before 11:30 a.m. at the Market on University shopping center on South University Drive. . . .

Broward Health Medical Center officials confirmed an adult was taken to the hospital as a trauma alert. . . .

http://www.rilenews.com/stories/
us-international/federal-technology-
grant-to-provide-e-cigs-for-inner-city-
students#sthash.iVQIfooS.dpuf

The URL should raise a question in your mind. Is rile a misspelling of real or someone's name?

FAKE

FEDERAL CLASSROOM TECHNOLOGY GRANT GUARANTEES E-CIGS FOR ALL INNER CITY STUDENTS

Does this sound like something the Federal government would do?

TECHNOLOGY FINALLY MAKES ITS WAY TO THE STUDENTS WHO NEED IT

By Sarah Connor | 2014.08.03

Actual media outlets would provide a hyperlink to the announcement because it is evidence of their claim.

Some of the lowest performing schools in the country received a pleasant surprise this week when word of a new Federal technology grant was announced to the public. Much like the suburban programs that provide iPads to students, this program will finally put electronic cigarettes in the hands of **trouble** youths that are desperate for technology in the classroom. It is expected that the move **will a** game-changer in evening the playing field between suburban and urban schools.

A typo sometimes happens, but *trouble* where it should say *troubled* is the first of a few in this article.

Another typo—a missing word this time

Does it really sound possible that the government would think giving kids e-cigarettes is a good idea or that this is the kind of technology students needed? You could double-check by searching for other news outlets that might be reporting on the story.

Emma Harris, a principal in one of Detroit's **worst** school districts applauded the move. "We've been fighting for years to get more advanced technology available to the kids. I never thought I would see the day when I could bring in the teachers for a meeting and tell them that we finally accomplished what we set out to do. We all just cried tears of joy." . . .

A journalist reporting the facts would not typically refer to a school this way because *worst* is a loaded term. Instead they would give information about the school to indicate it is struggling—low test scores, lack of money, high dropout rates. However, they might quote someone else who calls it the *worst*.

http://realnewsrightnow.
com/2017/02/beyonce-jay-z-launch-
online-contest-fans-submit-vote-baby-
names/

ENTERTAINMENT

BEYONCÉ, JAY Z TO LAUNCH ONLINE CONTEST TO DETERMINE BABY NAMES

FEBRUARY 31, 2017 by R. HOBBUS J.D.

LOS ANGELES, Ca.—Less than twenty-four hours after Beyoncé's earth-shattering announcement that she and Jay Z are expecting twins, a source close to Queen Bey has revealed that the superstar couple plans to launch an online contest in which fans can submit and vote on potential baby names, the entertainment news website **TMZ** reported on Thursday.

"The Carters have always felt a strong **connection to their fans** and this is a way for them to truly give something back," the source told TMZ. The contest, which is scheduled to go live in the coming days via **beyoncesbabynames.com**, will begin with a three-week submission period followed by several days of voting. . . .

. . . A close friend of the Carter family, who spoke to *Real News Right Now* on condition of anonymity, has confirmed that the person responsible for submitting the winning names will receive a personal letter of gratitude from Beyoncé along with an **invitation to be present** for the twins' delivery. . . .

The URL should raise flags because legitimate media outlets are not going to have to try to convince you they are real in the URL.

First, February does not have thirty-one days in the month. Second, if you did a search on this writer's name, you would find that no one with this name has written a real news article before, just a series of articles as suspicious as this one for the same website. Additionally, J.D. stands for Juris Doctor, which means the person has a law degree. Of course lawyers can turn into entertainment journalists, but it's not very common and should lead you to do some more research.

If TMZ really reported this story, then this article would include a hyperlink to the report. Since it does not, you could go to TMZ's website to see if there is a report. There isn't.

Although it may be true that they feel connected to their fans, does it seem likely that they would let the public pick names for their twins?

You could click on this hyperlink to see if a real site exists.

Even if it were possible the celebrity pair would turn baby naming over to their fans, does it seem like Beyoncé and Jay Z would allow a stranger into the delivery room for the birth, given what you know about them and their privacy?

FAKE

23 INJURED AFTER EXPLOSION REPORTED IN PLANTATION

2 PEOPLE SERIOUSLY INJURED, AUTHORITIES SAY

By AMANDA BATCHELOR-
Senior Digital Editor,
ROY RAMOS-*Reporter,*
PARKER BRANTON-*Reporter,*
TRENT KELLY-*Reporter*

Posted: 12:00 PM, July 06, 2019

PLANTATION, Fla.—A total of 23 people were injured Saturday during an explosion at a shopping center in Plantation, authorities confirmed.

Plantation Fire Department **Deputy Chief** Joel Gordon said two people suffered serious injuries in the blast that was reported just before 11:30 a.m. at the **Market on University shopping center on South University Drive.** . . .

Broward Health Medical Center officials confirmed an adult was taken to the hospital as a trauma alert. . . .

You might not have heard of this outlet before, so you would want to do an internet search to find some information about it.

You can quickly verify that this happened by checking with other news outlets, especially ones based in Florida, where the event is said to have taken place.

You can do a search on each of these people and see that they have all written many other news articles.

There are not hyperlinks to check, but the article cites an expert as evidence, and you could verify that he really is the fire department deputy chief by looking online.

This gives you the exact location of the event, which is something you could easily verify by looking it up.

Again, the authors cite experts as sources.

CHAPTER 18

73% OF PEOPLE SAY THEY DON'T UNDERSTAND POLLING, AND OTHER FAKE STATS

A RECENT POLL FOUND THAT 62 PERCENT OF people do not actually love ice cream. How did it make you feel when you read that? Poll results like this typically elicit three kinds of responses from people.

1. "That can't possibly be true. Who are these lunatics who said they don't like ice cream?" (That would have been my response if I hadn't written the sentence myself.)

2. "Yep, that sounds about right."

3. "You know, come to think of it, ice cream makes me freezing

and it is usually too sugary, and if everyone else doesn't like ice cream, maybe I shouldn't either."

If we, ourselves, like ice cream, our response is likely to be number one—if we like it, we think everyone else should too. If we don't like ice cream, we will probably respond with the second statement. But there are also people who are likely to be influenced by learning the views of the supposed majority. For these people, poll results work kind of like peer pressure. These people want to be part of the popular group or the winning team. Is it any wonder, then, that fake news writers frequently use made-up poll results to make their articles appear more credible and have more of an impact on readers? This is true especially on issues like elections, crime, and race, when there are many different polls circulating at the same time that say different things.

So, what was the correct response to seeing the (totally made-up) ice cream poll result? The right answer is actually secret option number four: "This poll seems weird. I have questions."

Polls measure how the public or a certain subset of the public feels at a specific point in time about particular topics. How the polls are conducted can have a huge impact on their findings and, as a result, their reliability. In 1948, the Republican governor of New York State, Thomas Dewey, was running for president against the incumbent, Harry S. Truman. Most of the major polls predicted that Dewey would win by at least several points. After all, Truman was having problems keeping support from members of his own political party. He was also president at a time when the economy wasn't very good, which always makes it harder to run as the incumbent. Most newspapers said it was not looking good for Truman.

On Election Day, ballot counting went late into the night, and the *Chicago Daily Tribune* was in a hurry to get the paper printed and out in time for the next morning. The editors decided the polls were so convincing that they could go ahead and project the winner. DEWEY DEFEATS TRUMAN, their front-page headline read. Except, in one of the biggest election upsets in history, Truman won.[1]

How did the polls get it so wrong? Most polls were conducted over the phone. But in 1948, only wealthy people could afford a phone. So the polls really did not represent people from different backgrounds. The other problem was that the groups conducting the polling stopped doing their surveys two weeks before the election. In those two weeks, Truman's campaign buckled down even harder and energized people to come vote for him on Election Day. The polling stopped right when it mattered most.

A smiling Harry S. Truman holds a copy of the famous *Chicago Daily Tribune* declaring, erroneously, his defeat.[2]

So how do you make sense of it when news, real or fake, starts throwing polling results around? Here are the things to look for.

1. *Beware of how polls are framed.* Watch out for poll results that are labeled "historic" or "shocking," or that show something very unexpected. Most polls are simply a way of taking a snapshot of a certain group of people on a specific topic at a particular point in time. But attitudes can and do change. The poll results that matter most evaluate opinions over time to identify patterns and trends, rather than a sudden significant change in views. If the topic of the poll is important enough, like an election, there are probably several different organizations conducting polls. Do some research and see how the supposed "historic" poll compares to what other organizations have found.

2. *Investigate who conducted or sponsored the poll.* All sorts of organizations conduct and sponsor polling—nonpartisan organizations, partisan organizations, companies trying to find out what people think of their products, organizations tied to political candidates, and governments. Some organizations are looking for an accurate reading of public opinion. Others are looking to achieve specific results from the polls so they look like they have evidence to prove whatever point the organization would like to make. The fact is, with websites like SurveyMonkey, anyone can create an online poll these days. Do some digging on the background of who created and conducted the poll to see if they might have wanted to obtain the results they found.[3]

    In 2016, a British marketing firm conducted a poll showing that 52 percent of British people believed the first time astronauts walked on the moon in 1969 was a hoax. They claimed to have surveyed more than 1,003 people eighteen years old or older. Their announcement came just in time for the forty-seventh anniversary of the moon landing and made newspaper headlines around the world. Suspiciously, the company refused to release any of the data or information on the methodology to show how they conducted the poll, and with a little investigation, journalists discovered that the marketing company was doing it to get media coverage for one of their clients.[4]

Fake news writers will sometimes make up polling firms, so when you come across the name of one you have not heard of before, be skeptical and go research it.[5] If you search online for a polling firm cited in a poll and nothing comes up, congratulations— you may have just encountered a fake poll. Another trick is to take completely real poll results from a reputable polling organization and manipulate them to tell a fake news story. Real news articles will provide a hyperlink to the organization that conducted and published the poll so you can verify the results.

3. *If you can, look at the data for yourself.* You will not usually have access to all the data from a poll, like the questions that were asked and the demographics of the respondents. But if you do, the data can tell you if the way the results are framed is correct and whether the sample size was large enough and participants diverse enough to really be reflective of the population the poll is trying to measure. One problem polls often have is the questions they ask. For example, spot what is wrong with this question: "How furious are you to know 62 percent of people dislike ice cream?" Your options are very mad, pretty mad, or neutral. This is called a leading question: The question itself tells you you're already at least a little mad about those people. On top of that,

the responses do not give you a full range of options, including "I'm not mad at all and this is a weird question."

Here is a problematic question that's more serious: "Who do you plan to vote for in the next election?" The problem is that the question presumes that everyone who answers will vote. Hopefully the poll has asked previous questions that weed out people who are not planning to vote by the time they get to this question. But if it has not, there will be a whole group of participants who pick a candidate even though they are not planning to vote, therefore skewing the results.

4. *Check the sample size.* To get an accurate reading of public opinion, you have to have a large enough number of participants. That size is going to vary depending on the size of the population you want to know about and what your polling question is. For example, if you want to know how Americans across the country feel about something, you will need a large group of survey participants from all over. However, if your question is how residents of Chicago, Illinois, feel about the city council approving a new housing development, the sample size can be smaller and limited to just residents of Chicago (after all, you don't need to know how someone from Portland, Maine, feels about the issue). Even if you do not have access to the polling data, a story from a real news outlet will almost always tell you the sample size.

5. *Look at how the poll was conducted.* Polls are conducted in three main ways. First, a pollster will randomly call people on the phone and ask them questions. Some polling organizations only call people who have landline telephones, not cell phones. Since people with landlines are disproportionately older, pollsters have to adjust the weighting of the results. Response rates are

very low for phone polls in general because most people do not pick up the phone for phone numbers they do not recognize.[6]

Second, some organizations conduct polls online. Internet-based poll results are highly unreliable, because these polls typically depend on people to volunteer to participate and they can be easily manipulated to ensure a particular outcome. They also often depend on people finding them, so they do not represent all the people who could not find them. And they depend on potential participants having an internet connection. The most unreliable polls are internet polls posted on a website for anyone to complete. Only people with the strongest opinions typically respond, and it is very easy for people looking for a particular result to send their like-minded friends to it to vote how they want them to. For example, in 2016 the United Kingdom's Natural Environment Research Council launched an internet poll to name its new $288 million polar research ship. The poll went viral and internet users flocked to it to ensure their name of choice won—Boaty McBoatface.[7] And it did, although the council decided not to use the name.

Third, there are exit polls. These are polls taken on the day of an election to try to estimate who the ultimate winner will be. Pollsters physically stand outside voting locations and ask exiting voters a series of questions, the most important one being who they voted for. Exit polls can be misleading because pollsters cannot be at every polling station and the demographics of the people surveyed may not be an accurate representation of all the people voting.[8]

6. *Look at when and over what period of time the poll was conducted.* If an article is using polling results to talk about what people think about a topic, make sure that the polling was conducted recently enough to still be accurate. Participants might have said they felt one way five years ago, but the chance that they feel exactly the same way now is pretty small, whether the topic is about ice cream or politics. (I used to like strawberry ice cream but have very sensibly switched to chocolate peanut butter in recent years.) Another thing to consider is the length of the polling period. Were the questions only asked once over a couple of days or multiple times over the course of a month or a year? A poll concluding that people feel gas prices are too high has less weight if it was conducted the day after a major gas price hike than if the results covered a longer period of time. After all, gas prices fluctuate all the time.

7. *Look at the margin of error.* Pollsters only survey a sample of the population, so they know their results will only approximate reality. That is why every poll that's been done correctly will have a margin of error (if there is a graphic showing the results, you can usually find the margin of error listed below it, or sometimes right in the article). The margin of error shows how close we can reasonably expect the poll's results to be to the truth.[9] So, for example, if a poll says Political Candidate 1 is probably going to get 48 percent of the vote and the poll has a margin of error of +/-3 percent, that means they think the candidate could actually get anywhere from 45 to 51 percent of the vote.

8. *If you can, find out if the poll was random.* The only way a survey of 1,500 people polled can come close to representing the general public's views is if the people who participate have been selected randomly. That means those taking the poll cannot just survey their friends and neighbors and expect to get an accurate view of

what the rest of the country thinks about something. In general, participants must come from a diverse range of the population, including different ages, races, genders, and locations. The people conducting the poll can decide to only survey a certain kind of audience, like women ages eighteen to thirty-five, for example. But that means they cannot say the poll showed what fifty-year-old men think about the topic. Put another way, if a polling firm only interviews straight white men, even if they're randomly selected, the results will only be representative of straight white men, not the broader public.[10]

9. *Pay attention to the "undecided."* Most polls offer participants the opportunity to answer a question by saying that they are undecided or do not know how to answer. In any poll, a large number of "undecided" responses—or no answer—can make the result pretty useless. For example, if a poll finds that 30 percent of people like country music, and 30 percent like R&B, but 40 percent of people couldn't decide, the poll gets us no closer to figuring out which kind of music people prefer.

In elections especially, when candidates are very close, undecided voters can be the deciding factor. If 34 percent of voters say they are voting for Candidate 1, and 37 percent say they are voting for Candidate 2, but 29 percent of people say they have not decided yet, we really cannot draw any conclusions about who might win.

10. *Remember to look at the results from another angle.* Gallup, a very well-respected polling organization, released a poll in 2015 showing that 36 percent of millennials in America were not affiliated with a particular religion.[11] Afterward, several news outlets came out with articles exclaiming that the poll proved

religion was dying.[12] What those articles did not note (but you might have if you've done the math) is that about 64 percent of people who responded to the poll said they *did* still have a religion. Additionally, among the people who did not identify with a particular religion, two thirds of them said they still believed in a god. So why was none of that mentioned in the articles about millennials killing religion? There were probably a lot of different reasons, but one of them no doubt was that the slow death of organized religion made for a more exciting story and, therefore, more clicks. This is not necessarily an example of fake news, but it does show how easily data can be manipulated to tell a very different story than the results actually show. Sometimes real poll results from reputable firms can be manipulated to spin a certain story.

Exercise:
POLLING PRACTICE

Here are two polls. Using the information in the previous chapter, and the checklist below, can you tell which one is credible?

POLL I:

In 2017, this poll graphic accompanied an article with the headline KID ROCK AHEAD IN HYPOTHETICAL MATCHUP WITH DEBBIE STABENOW.

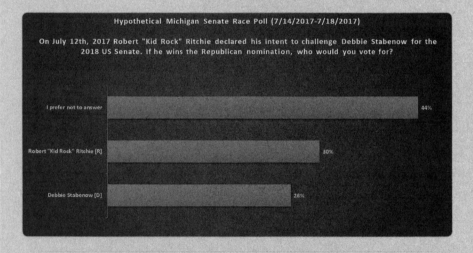

Hypothetical Michigan Senate Race Poll (7/14/2017-7/18/2017)

On July 12th, 2017 Robert "Kid Rock" Ritchie declared his intent to challenge Debbie Stabenow for the 2018 US Senate. If he wins the Republican nomination, who would you vote for?

I prefer not to answer	44%
Robert "Kid Rock" Ritchie [R]	30%
Debbie Stabenow [D]	26%

Screenshot of poll graphic from article posted by Delphi Analytica on
Medium.com on July 23, 2017

The following information was included in the article about the poll results:

> Debbie Stabenow is the incumbent Democratic Michigan senator
> who is scheduled to defend her seat in 2018. Ritchie intends to
> run as a Republican who would likely have to defeat a crowded
> primary field to challenge Stabenow. The margin of error for
> the poll is 3.2% at 90% confidence. To gauge Ritchie's chances
> in a hypothetical general election matchup, Delta Analytica
> conducted a poll from July 14–18 of 668 Michigan residents.[13]

CHECKLIST:

_____ Includes the dates the poll was conducted

_____ States the name of the polling firm

_____ Lists question(s) the participants were asked

_____ Shows the sample size

_____ Gives the margin of error

_____ Provides background on how the poll was conducted

_____ Results match the claim made about the poll

POLL 2:

This poll report came with a lengthy methodology note that included the following information:

> This particular survey featured interviews with 920 teens ages 13 to 17. Interviews were conducted online and by telephone from Sept. 17 to Nov. 25, 2018. . . . Sampling errors and statistical-significance tests take into account the effect of weighting. The following table shows the unweighted sample sizes and the error attributable to sampling that would be expected at the 95% level of confidence for different groups in the survey: [14]

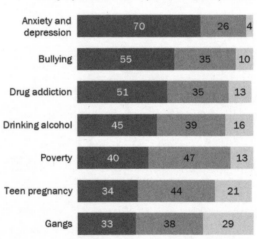

Anxiety and depression top list of problems teens see among their peers

% of teens saying each of the following is a ___ among people their age in the community where they live

■ Major problem ■ Minor problem ▪ Not a problem

	Major problem	Minor problem	Not a problem
Anxiety and depression	70	26	4
Bullying	55	35	10
Drug addiction	51	35	13
Drinking alcohol	45	39	16
Poverty	40	47	13
Teen pregnancy	34	44	21
Gangs	33	38	29

Note: Share of respondents who didn't offer an answer not shown.
Source: Survey of U.S. teens ages 13 to 17 conducted Sept. 17–Nov. 25, 2018.
"Most U.S. Teens See Anxiety and Depression as a Major Problem Among Their Peers"

PEW RESEARCH CENTER

Group	Unweighted sample size	Plus or minus ...
Teens ages 13-17	920	4.8 percentage points
Boys	461	7.0 percentage points
Girls	454	6.6 percentage points
Household income		
Less than $30K	210	10.1 percentage points
$30K to $74,999	326	8.5 percentage points
$75K and up	384	7.1 percentage points

CHECKLIST:

_____ Includes the dates the poll was conducted

_____ States the name of the polling firm

_____ Lists question(s) the participants were asked

_____ Shows the sample size

_____ Gives the margin of error

_____ Provides background on how the poll was conducted

_____ Results match the claim made about the poll

POLL 1: NOT CREDIBLE

✔ Includes the dates the poll was conducted

✔ States the name of the polling firm

✔ Lists question(s) the participants were asked

✔ Shows the sample size

✔ Gives the margin of error

_____ Provides background on how the poll was conducted

_____ Results match the claim made about the poll

There is a lot of information in Poll 1, but there are a couple of important red flags, such as the fact that it doesn't include information on how the poll was conducted. Additionally, 44 percent of respondents said they did not know who they would vote for—a larger percentage than the other two responses. So the claim in the headline that Kid Rock was ahead isn't accurate, given the large percentage of undecided voters. Once you noticed things were not quite right with this poll, you might want to do a little more investigating. If you did, you would discover that the website for Delphi Analytica went live just weeks before the poll was released and only ever conducted one more poll after this one.[15] Their Medium page only had two followers and Delphi Analytica did not seem to know its own name: In the article with the results, they refer to themselves as "Delta Analytica." These are not signs of a well-established polling firm that knows what it is doing.

POLL 2: CREDIBLE

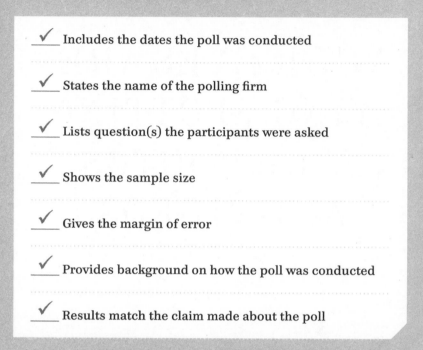

✓ Includes the dates the poll was conducted

✓ States the name of the polling firm

✓ Lists question(s) the participants were asked

✓ Shows the sample size

✓ Gives the margin of error

✓ Provides background on how the poll was conducted

✓ Results match the claim made about the poll

The second poll report has all the key information we need to determine if the results are credible. By including things like sample size and margin of error, it lets us decide if there is sufficient evidence to support the overall claim—that young adults are most concerned about anxiety and depression. If we wanted to do additional research on the polling firm, we would quickly find that the Pew Research Center is a nonpartisan think tank (an organization of experts that researches and advocates certain political or economic issues) that has a long history of conducting polling and other research. In fact, you may have noticed that I have referenced their polls in previous chapters!

CHAPTER 19

YOUR EYES ARE LYING: SPOTTING FAKE PHOTOS AND VIDEOS

PHOTOS AND VIDEOS ARE ONE OF THE BIG-gest reasons fake news ends up going viral. People think they are "evidence"—something must be true if we can actually visually verify it on our own. Except technology has made it so easy to make digitally altered photos and videos look real that we can no longer trust a quick glance to verify them.

After a school shooting in Parkland, Florida, that left seventeen people dead in 2018, many of the survivors became politically active, calling for gun-safety reform. That is when a doctored photo of one of the survivors, Emma González, went viral. It showed her ripping up the Constitution (the Second Amendment gives citizens the right to bear arms). A GIF version of the alleged act soon followed, showing her physically doing it, and it set off a firestorm online among pro-gun advocates. But none of it ever actually happened. In reality, the picture was from a photo shoot González did for *Teen Vogue*, and in it she was ripping up a paper gun target. As revealed by then *Teen Vogue* editor Phillip Picardi, the fake news photo manipulator simply slapped an image of the Constitution over it.

Phillip Picardi ✔
@pfpicardi

At left is @tyler_mitchell's photo of @Emma4Change for the cover of @TeenVogue. At right is what so-called "Gun Rights Activists" have photoshopped it into. #MarchForOurLives

1:26 PM · Mar 25, 2018 · Twitter for iPhone

Screenshot of then *Teen Vogue* editor Phillip Picardi's tweet on March 25, 2018, exposing the origin of the fake Emma González meme

Some governments use digitally altered photos to deceive and intimidate their enemies. In 2013, the North Korean News Agency, which is run by the government, released a photo showing its military practicing for a possible invasion of South Korea.[1] Most news agencies know not to believe anything that comes out of North Korea's official media, but the picture still spread online. In the picture, soldiers stormed a snowy beach; behind them were eight hovercraft in various stages of transporting the troops across the water and onto the sand. Except several of the craft were copies of the others—they had simply been altered in size and pasted into the picture to make it look like the force was bigger than it actually was.

The fastest way to tell if a photo has been altered is to do a reverse image search, where the search engine shows you all the times the photo you're looking at has been posted online. You can trace a photo all the way back to the original one and then compare the two to see if the photo you first saw was altered. You can do a reverse image search on Google, or through an image database such as TinEye. However, there are also a number of things you can look for on your own to tell if an image is fake.

1. *Watch out for photos without attribution.* Reputable news outlets have their own professional photographers, or use photojournalists from other outlets. News articles will credit the photographer in the caption of the photo. Photos that appear on social media and without attribution are not all fake, but you should ask the poster where the image came from.

2. *Check out the edges of an object.* Cropping around an object to add it to another image can be really hard to do. If you zoom in on the photo and check out the edges, you might find that they are

quite jagged. That is a sign the object was cropped and slapped onto another image, meaning the whole thing is fake.

3. *Look for wavy or mismatching lines.* One of the easiest ways to tell if an image is a fake is to check out the lines in the picture. Often, they will not match up or will be out of place. That can happen when you try to layer one image over another.

4. *Check to see if the lighting matches up.* If there are shadows from something in one part of the picture, but not in the other, that can be a sign the image has been altered. In 2016, a doctored photo of Michael Bennett, the defensive end for the Seattle Seahawks football team, went viral. It showed him burning an American flag in the locker room. The photo received so much attention because during this time, Americans were in heated debate about football players kneeling at games during the national anthem as a form of protest against racial inequality.[2] The light could have tipped people off to the fact that it was fake. If the football player really had been burning a flag so close to his body, his body would have been brightened by the light of the flame—but it wasn't. The real photo was of Bennett leading his team in their traditional postgame locker-room victory dance.

5. *Investigate whether parts of the photo are a different quality.* When pictures are added on top of pictures, sometimes they are not blended together well. Parts of the final image may have a different quality. It might be more pixelated or blurry in some places. The sizes of parts of the image may vary, and the color may also be brighter or lighter in some parts.

6. *Think about how it fits with what you already know.* Like you do when spotting fake news headlines, ask yourself, *Does this make sense given what I know about the topic?* In the case of

survivor-turned-activist Emma González, no it did not. Students from Parkland like González were advocating for gun safety reform to keep students safe, not for the destruction of the Constitution. Beware of images that feel like they are trying to go viral or create outrage. Images that create strong emotional reactions are not ones we usually take the time to carefully study, but they are the ones we definitely should.

And remember, even if a photo or video is real, it can still be taken out of context by fake news. For example, every time there is a hurricane in the southern United States, you will find photos of boats overturned, houses demolished, and sharks swimming along waterlogged city streets. But chances are that some of these pictures are from other places, from years before, or have nothing to do with the current natural disaster. During Hurricane Sandy in 2012, photos of flooding all over New York City circulated online before the storm even hit the city. Most of them were photoshopped, and some were even stills taken from the disaster movie *The Day After Tomorrow*. Although a lot of the photos went viral because people believed them, most of the fake reports did not fool the media. Except for one. A Twitter account using an anonymous handle took advantage of all the fake photos and photos taken out of context swirling on social media to report that the New York Stock Exchange (NYSE) was under three feet of water.[3] Other parts of the city nearby had flooding from the storm, so the news seemed plausible and quickly spread across social media. It was even reported on CNN and the Weather Channel, and it caused financial analysts to worry the stock market might plunge because of it.[4] The tweet was not referenced when the story about the NYSE made it on TV, but for the journalists who were combing through the photos circulating on social media, a reverse image search would have shown many of them for what they were: fake. This would have been the first clue that maybe anonymous Twitter users might not be a reliable source.

Sometimes a photo doesn't really provide any evidence for what a fake news article claims, but simply having it next to the text tricks us into thinking it does.[5] Take, for example, a claim that cheetahs are the only mammals that can run at fifty miles per hour or higher, paired with a generic photo of a cheetah running. Even though the photo does nothing to prove or disprove the claim, we are naturally more inclined to believe it simply because of the picture. (The claim about cheetahs is false, by the way.)

In fact, researchers have found that a photograph (not even one that has been altered) can make us 60 to 70 percent more likely to believe a claim. As Australian National University researcher Dr. Eryn Newsman explained, "Adding a photograph to a message, even when that photograph provides no evidence, actually systematically shapes people's beliefs."[6]

When you see a photo alongside an article, do not let yourself be fooled. Stop to consider whether or not the photo proves anything at all. If the article is real, the most important evidence will be in the actual text.

WHAT ABOUT FAKE VIDEOS?

ON SEPTEMBER 13, 2018, FACEBOOK USERS watched in total horror a video that showed a commercial airliner flipping over in the air.[7] In the video, the plane is tossed around by intense winds and does a complete 360-degree roll in the air before righting itself and landing. The video was posted on a page called Time News International with this caption: "A Capital Airlines Beijing-Macao flight, carrying 166 people, made an emergency landing in Shenzhen on 28 August 2018, after aborting a landing attempt in Macao due to mechanical failure, the airline said." The video got over 14 million views. The video looks real, and if you were a little skeptical and decided to do some digging, you would discover that an airplane really did make an emergency landing in Macao that day.

Yet, the video is totally fake. Or at least the context it was given was fake. The video had been made a year earlier by a film director and computer-graphics expert who animated the whole 360-degree roll and then posted the video to YouTube for people to see his animation skills. The maker never intended for it to be labeled as real; it was the fake news writers who did that. Enough people shared and viewed the video that even though Facebook was trying to crack down on fake news, the social media platform started displaying the video on people's news feeds as something users might be interested in viewing. Several days later, Snopes.com labeled the story as fake.

Okay, so you have never flown a plane, and maybe you are like me and not great at physics. What are you supposed to do when you see a video and do not know if what was shown really could have happened or if the was edited in some way? First, check the actual news. Many fake news videos are edited a little, sometimes called a cheap fake, to show something almost impossible to believe—that is how they go viral. If an eagle really did swoop down and carry off a kid in its talons, or if a girl caught on fire while twerking (both actual videos, both completely fake), at the very least your local news station would be covering it.

You should also look at who posted it and trace it back to find the original poster of the video. Was it a news outlet, or was it the YouTube channel of FancyDude247 who only just created that account and happened to go viral on his first post, but then never posted again? If the latter, alarm bells should be going off in your head. Finding the original video will also allow you to compare it with the first version you saw so you can note any changes that may have been made to it. You should also investigate the quality of the video, like if it flickers. You can also pause the video and run through the steps you would use when looking at an image to see if anything is off about it.

Technology is improving every day, and people are already working on software and apps that make it easier for even those without graphic-design or computer-animation skills to splice together fake videos or audio clips that are almost indistinguishable from real ones. These manufactured videos are called *deep fakes*, and they are meant to look or sound like the real thing. The software lets the user lay digital copies of pictures and sometimes audio over one another to create what looks like a moving, talking person. For example, a program called FaceApp created by a company in Russia allows users to create realistic videos that put people's faces on other people's bodies. You can also alter the look of a person to change things like signs of their age, gender, and facial expressions. It probably will not surprise you to learn that as soon as the technology was available, people started creating videos with celebrities' faces on the bodies of porn stars to create fake porn videos. Websites including Twitter and PornHub have banned the doctored videos over concerns that users would use them for revenge porn.[8]

It is not hard to guess that the next real concern of technology experts is that makers of deep fakes will next turn to making videos that could lead to violence or even start wars. As it gets easier to alter videos, not only can deep fakes make people look like they said something they never did, but they can provide "evidence" that someone said something they never actually said. This is another reason why those trusted sources of news you are going to build up over time are so important. They will help you verify what is real.

The people who make this kind of video content know how easy it is for us to get sucked into sites like YouTube, where the next recommended video is queued up and ready to go as soon as the last one you watched ends. Before moving on to your next video, stop and take the time to consider what you just watched and who created it.

Study the following pictures. Each of them has been digitally altered in at least one way. Can you tell how? Circle the changes you find.

Lake Batur

One thing has been changed in this photo, and that's me! My picture was cut out and added. Although I've been on a lot of mountains, I have never seen this one. One clue that something is amiss is the lighting. I look like I have the sun shining right on me, but there does not seem to be any sun in the picture. Also, I look like I'm dressed for summer, Which doesn't make much sense given the cold, dark, and misty mountain scene behind me.

Two things have been edited into this photo. You would not necessarily need to know that dolphins do not live in Bali's freshwater Lake Batur to see that it does not belong. If you look closely, you will notice that the dolphin looks too big compared to the size of the boat. The edges of the dolphin also look a little jagged—a key sign that someone edited the dolphin into the picture. Finally, the words *Lake Batur* were added to the top of the boat.

Two things have been edited in this photo. First, the numbers on the real clock are Roman numerals. You can tell because the font just does not look right. Also, this is Big Ben in London, England. So the American flag should definitely not be flying on that flagpole.

CHAPTER 20

MEMES AREN'T NEWS AND OTHER SOCIAL-MEDIA TIPS

THIRTY-FIVE-YEAR-OLD BUSINESSMAN Eric Tucker was walking in downtown Austin, Texas, the day after the 2016 presidential election when he came across a long line of buses parked on the street.[1] He remembered seeing on the news somewhere that anti-Trump protests were happening that day. *Could the buses and the protests be related?* he wondered. It seemed possible. Just to be safe, Tucker did a quick Google search to make sure there were not any conferences or other big events that day that might have used buses like the ones he had found. He didn't find anything, so that was enough evidence for him. Tucker tweeted the pictures along with the only conclusion that seemed reasonable: "Anti-Trump protestors in Austin today are not as organic as they seem. Here are the busses they came in. #fakeprotests #trump2016 #austin."[2]

erictucker @erictucker · Nov 9
Anti-Trump protestors in Austin today are not as organic as they seem. Here are the busses they came in. #fakeprotests #trump2016 #austin

↩   ⇄ 16K   🛡   ♥ 14K   •••

Screenshot of Eric Tucker's tweet on November 9, 2016

Even if he got it wrong, it did not really matter, Tucker thought. He only had around forty Twitter followers, after all. No one would probably even see his post. "I did think in the back of my mind there could be other explanations, but it just didn't seem plausible," he said later in an interview.

The next day, an anonymous Reddit user posted a screenshot of the tweet on the main pro-Trump Reddit channel, saying: "BREAKING: They found the buses! Dozens lined up just blocks away from the Austin protests." From there, conservative-leaning internet forums, social-media pages, blogs, and conspiracy websites shared the link, generating hundreds of thousands of views and likes. The story snowballed from there, with social-media users and fake news websites that posted conservative stories claiming the people that had come to Austin on the buses were being paid by George Soros to protest. Soros is a billionaire Jewish hedge-fund manager who has long been a popular target of extreme right-wing, anti-Semitic groups and conspiracy theorists, who believe he is secretly controlling the global economy and politics.[3]

The manager of the bus company in Tucker's pictures started getting calls from people all over the country who were angry that the company had supposedly been used to transport protestors, and from journalists who were trying to see if there was any truth to the story. Even President Trump shared the story and tweeted: "Just had a very open and successful presidential election. Now professional protesters, incited by the media, are protesting. Very unfair!"[4]

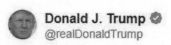

Donald J. Trump ✔
@realDonaldTrump

Just had a very open and successful presidential election. Now professional protesters, incited by the media, are protesting. Very unfair!

♡ 205K   10:19 PM - Nov 10, 2016

💬 119K people are talking about this

Screenshot of President Donald Trump's November 10, 2016, tweet in response to the bus story taken September 20, 2019.

Three days after tweeting the original post, Tucker admitted on Twitter that he had no concrete proof of his claim, and that he had never seen people getting on or off the buses. They just happened to be parked near where protests were taking place. He tried to correct his post by deleting the original and tweeting a new one that said his tweet was false. But how much attention did the new tweet correcting the record get? Just twenty-nine retweets and twenty-seven likes. It was far too late. Many far-right politicians in America still claim that people protesting against President Trump are paid to do so.

Later, Tucker told the *New York Times*, "I'm also a very busy businessman and I don't have time to fact-check everything that I put out there, especially when I don't think it's going out there for wide consumption."[5] But even the busiest people in the world have a responsibility to make sure that what they post is accurate. It does not matter how many followers you have, because anything on social media can quickly go viral and take on a life of its own we cannot control.

Have you ever played the game telephone? You line up side by side in a long row. The first person whispers a sentence into the ear of the person next to them—"I had pancakes for breakfast this morning," for example. You can only say the sentence once, even if the person did not quite hear or understand you. That person repeats what they think they heard into the ear of the person next to them, and so on down the row. The last person must say aloud what they heard. Almost always it is nothing like the original sentence, and often it's totally unintelligible, like "Mike ran ransack while drowning."

Social media can be like that too. It is a snapshot of what its users want the world to see, know, hear, and think, and all of it gets shared and reinterpreted over and over again. Someone gives their take on something. Then a person shares that post and gives their own take on it. Then someone shares that and gives *their* take on the previous take, and on and on until the original message has become quite muddled. That is certainly how things turned out in Eric Tucker's case.

Social media plays a significant role in generating and spreading fake news. Although bots, trolls, and foreign governments can be involved, the blame mostly lies with individual social-media users. In a Pew Research Center study conducted in December 2016, 23 percent of people admitted they had shared fabricated news stories on social media, sometimes even intentionally.[6] It does not sound that bad until you consider there are nearly 2.5 billion active Facebook users and 330 million Twitter users worldwide, and those aren't the only social-media platforms people use.[7] That means that at least 499,100,000 people have shared fake news—and those are just the ones who will admit it!

It matters how we behave on social media because, as we talked about in chapter 12, it's been proven that lies spread faster than truth there. And people's views are affected by what they see on their feeds. In a different Pew Research Center study in 2018, 14 percent of Americans said they had completely changed their minds about an issue as a result of something they saw on social media.[8]

While technology companies are working on ways to stop fake social-media accounts and to stop fake news from spreading, we cannot count on them to fix the problem on their own. Each person needs to take responsibility for their own social-media behavior.

So, how do you not only spot fake news on social media, but make sure you do not inadvertently have a hand in spreading it yourself?

Follow these rules:

1. *Figure out what kind of post and account you are looking at.* Social media is where we talk about everything—from what our dog ate for breakfast to our opinions on upcoming elections—all blended together. Everyone can have their say. But social-media posts do not come with labels, so it is up to us to sort out fact from opinion and find the truth in the clutter. It's pretty easy to spot the difference between things like updates from your friends, cute animal pictures, and popular memes, but other posts can be a bit trickier.

   - An official news post will come from the respective news outlet, even if it's then been shared by normal social-media users. You can trace a linked article back to the original outlet. If a social-media user is a journalist and works for a media outlet, they will usually say so in their bio.

   - A *hot take* is a person's immediate reaction or commentary, usually in response to something that has just happened. It is usually an opinion or a rant, though it may be based on the person's own experience or written by an expert on the issue. It can be difficult to verify the accuracy of a hot take unless the writer documents their evidence. If they do not, it may be best to wait to share their post until you can verify their claims.

   - A quote is something someone has actually said or something pulled from an article, book, video, or interview. Sometimes social-media users give a link to where the quote came from, but sometimes they don't. You can quickly check to see if the quote is accurate by doing a simple internet search.

   - An advertisement is meant to promote a business, organization, product, or person. It is often labeled on social media as "sponsored content." That means the account is paying the social-media platform to show you the content for a particular reason. The platform will list the name of the company or group that paid for the ad (though it may be in small print and hard to find), which you then can use to investigate the source.

* *Commentary* on social media is when experts post their informal analysis, sometimes with sources and sometimes not. These are like the op-ed articles we discussed earlier—typically based on facts and the person's expertise, but opinions all the same.

Knowing what you are looking at will help you determine how seriously to take it.

2. *Find the real experts.* Thanks to social media, experts are more accessible to us than ever before. If you have questions about astrophysics, you can follow real astrophysicists on social media. Want to know what it is like to work at the CIA? You can find me on Twitter. Experts on social media can help us make sense of important events and issues by using their professional experience and skills to put them into context.

Of course, anyone can create an account and claim to be an expert, so it is worth it to verify who you follow. If I wanted to pretend to be a nuclear scientist (which I am not), I could probably get a pretty impressive following simply by copying and pasting things from articles on the subject and changing my bio on social media. Check to see if an account is verified (marked by a blue check mark next to the person's name) to make sure you are following a popular expert and not an impostor, fan account, or a fake news site. Verification can tell you that the million Beyoncé fan accounts always circulating on social media are not the real Beyoncé, or that @BBC is the actual BBC news account.

It is important to note that just because your favorite celebrity has been verified, it does not mean that what they post is always true. Just because @ChrisEvans really is the account for Chris Evans (aka Captain America) and he has gone to space in the Avengers movies does not mean I would look to him for accurate information on astronomy (sorry, Chris!). For that, I would follow someone like Neil deGrasse Tyson, who is an astrophysicist and an expert in his field. I can double-check that I'm following Neil deGrasse Tyson's actual account (@neiltyson) by looking for the verification mark on his social media.

But don't rely solely on that blue check mark. Not all experts in every field have been verified, but a lack of verification does not mean the account is fake. In that case, you can look up the people claiming to be experts and see if their background checks out. And don't just rely on a personal website where they wrote their own biography. Just like on social media, anyone can say anything about themselves on their personal website, so try to find another source to back it up.

Finally, be wary of social-media users who post in a way that makes them look like they might be journalists, but they do not provide an actual source for their information or appear to work for a media outlet. For example, they might start a post with "Breaking News!" but do not actually provide a link to a news article. Those people got that information from somewhere, but without a citation you cannot verify what they have posted. Often, these social-media users are trying to make themselves look like a news source so that you will check their accounts regularly and share their posts. Ultimately, they want more followers. However, until you know where their information comes from—legitimate news reports or a rumor they heard from their neighbor down the street—treat them with skepticism.

3. *Don't be fooled by the number of likes, shares, and comments on a social-media post.* As we have already seen, just because a post has gone viral does not mean that what it says is accurate or true. Most social-media posts go viral because they are clever, invoke a certain emotion, are controversial, or have a strong image, not necessarily because they are accurate. But our brains sometimes make us think that a social-media post with more engagement must be right, or at the very least be important. This is a trap. Not all that engagement may be from real people. If you are looking for social-media fame, you can buy the likes to get you there. People have found ways to manipulate every social-media site. From YouTube to Facebook to Instagram, it's possible to buy thousands of fake likes and followers for social-media posts. And influencer wannabes are not the only ones using these services. Fake news posters also use them to make their posts go viral.

4. *Learn to spot fake accounts.* Fake social-media accounts are everywhere. In May 2019, Facebook announced it had found and removed 3.4 billion fake accounts in just one six-month period. The company estimated that 5 percent of its 2.4 billion active monthly users were fake.[9] As we discussed earlier, bots were designed to get real social-media users to engage with them in order to amplify what they are saying or the links they are sharing. Whether they are promoting a product, a person, a conspiracy theory, or fake news, people who push fake news want their message out there. Foreign governments use bots and trolls to spread fake news and stir up discord on the most politically sensitive topics. It can be tough to tell a fake social-media user

from a real one. But there are a couple of red flags to look for.

- Accounts that only share posts and never create original content might be bots. Most real humans using social media post original content about some element of their actual lives, like their interests, so an account that only shares other people's posts should raise concern. And be aware, some fake accounts will sometimes post a random-looking assortment of pictures—like a dog, a forest, and then a car—on their pages to try to make it look like they are actual people.

- If a (noncelebrity) account posts and immediately gets thousands of likes and shares, but not many comments, it may be because the likes or shares are from automated bots.

- If a social-media account has a large following but not a lot of engagement (original posts, likes, and shares), that can mean it purchased fake followers or is a fake account.

- Fake accounts often have the same or similar bios and profile pictures as other fake accounts. Oftentimes, profile pictures will be of inanimate objects or scenery, rather than people, because that makes it harder to spot a fake account. If the pictures are of people, they are often taken from stock images or are pictures of models or celebrities easily found online.[10]

- Fake news pushers will often create accounts the same day as a big news story. If an account was created the same day as a big story and only shares posts about that topic, you might have found a bot or a troll.

- People using bots and trolls want their content to spread to real users, so accounts will often include a lot of hashtags in their posts and their bios to try to make content go viral.

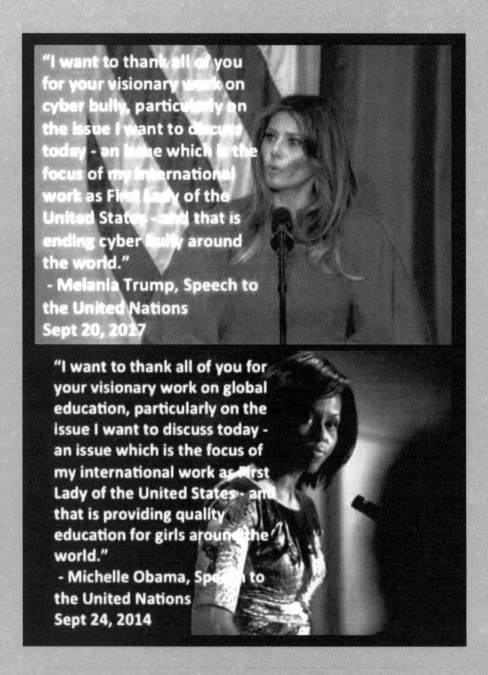

Screenshot of a widely spread political meme—later disproved—implying that Melania Trump plagiarized Michelle Obama's speech[15]

5. *Watch out for political memes.* All you have to do is click on the comments section of a social-media post to find that people debate issues more with memes than with actual words these days. But memes are often fake news traps. They can stir up our emotions simply by pairing short text with an image or a GIF. Memes can look authoritative, but they rarely provide actual links to source material, and they are not a reliable form of news. They contain no nuance or context—they are sound bites—and frequently include false statistics, quotes misattributed to celebrities or historical figures, and fake images. It is also very difficult to trace a meme back to the original creator, making it nearly impossible to figure out what motivation the poster might have had for creating it.

In September 2017, a meme spread like wildfire claiming that First Lady Melania Trump's speech to the United Nations earlier that month had been copied from former First Lady Michelle Obama's speech to the United Nations in 2014. The meme showed two quotes, one allegedly from each speech, but the quote attributed to Melania was not actually in her speech. Still, the meme went viral. Most people did not bother to look at the speeches and compare them. And, at the time, the White House had not posted the First Lady's speech, so even if you'd wanted to check whether the meme was true, there was no transcript or video to look at, so people simply believed it.[11]

One of the reasons people were so quick to jump onto the idea that Melania Trump had plagiarized her speech is the result of something called the illusory truth affect. Articles and memes had appeared earlier claiming that she had plagiarized other speeches from Michelle Obama. For example, a speech the First

Lady gave at the Republican National Convention in 2016 used several of the same sentences and phrases from Michelle Obama's speech in 2008 to the Democratic National Convention.[12] As a result, the news about the First Lady's speech at the United Nations sounded completely consistent with what we had heard before. Our brains had been trained by previous accounts to think Melania—or more accurately, her speechwriter—couldn't come up with original words of her own. So when we saw the claim this time, our brains automatically accepted it as true.

When you come across a political meme, use the same techniques we talked about for verifying articles claiming to be news—things like looking for the source of the information and investigating who originally posted it. Verifying statistics or quotes is even easier because you can just Google them.

THE WORD MEME IS RELATED TO THE GREEK WORD *MIMEME*, MEANING "IMITATED THING." It was first coined by evolutionary biologist Richard Dawkins in 1976, who defined a meme in an interview in 2018 as the "cultural equivalent of a gene. So anything that gets passed from brain to brain, like an accent, or a basic word, or a tune. It's anything that you can say spreads through the population in a cultural way, like an epidemic."[14]

6. *Don't share things you already know are not true.* There are all kinds of reasons we share things online even though we know they're false. Sometimes, fake news stories are so ridiculous that they're funny and we want our friends to join in on the laugh.

Other times we might get angry about a deliberate lie we see someone spreading, so we share it to call it out. In that case, we want our friends to join in on our outrage. If we agree with the sentiment being expressed in a story or post, even if we know the actual facts are wrong, we might even think we're doing a good thing by sharing it. One of the most infamous fake news writers in America claims to be politically liberal, but writes fake news that appeals to the far right.[15] He says his articles are meant to be satire and that he is actually fighting fake news by showing what the far right will fall for. But the fact of the matter is that people believe what he writes, and each of his posts gets thousands of likes and shares. His "fight" has really only helped to spread fake news.

You can never assume that since you know something is fake, everyone else must know too. Even if you start a post with "This isn't true, but . . . ," some people will never read your caveat. One of the memes that went viral during the 2016 US presidential election claimed Trump had once told *People* magazine, "If I were to run, I'd run as a Republican. They're the dumbest group of voters in the country. They believe anything on Fox News. I could lie and they'd still eat it up. I bet my numbers would be terrific."[16] Comedian Amy Schumer posted it on Instagram, saying, "Yes this quote is fake but it doesn't matter."[17] But it does matter. Many people did not read the part about it not being true. That meme is still circulating on social media to this day among people who believe it is actually true.

7. *Share good sources of news and information.* Once you have spent enough time verifying who you follow, you will start to find the people you can count on to provide helpful and accurate

information. Part of fighting fake news is also elevating and promoting those reputable sources, which means sharing the work of good journalists. Just as we try to root out inaccurate information, so too should we work to encourage and amplify the voice of those who provide accurate and unbiased information.

8. *Don't feed the trolls.* Unlike bots, trolls are real people. They try to stir up trouble by picking fights online and posting controversial material they know will make people angry. Trolls succeed when they get other social-media users to respond to them. Block, mute, report, or ignore them, but don't play into their hands by engaging because it helps to amplify the message they are trying to push.

9. *Flag fake news.* If you are sure you have found a fake account or a fake news story on social media, report it. Social-media companies are still working on ways to stem the tide of fake news. You can help them refine the algorithms that determine which content to promote by flagging articles and links that you know are fake.

Exercise:
TO TRUST OR NOT TO TRUST?

────────────────

Keeping in mind the tips we discussed earlier, can you identify whether each account is real or fake? You may not be sure about an account without doing some additional research to verify if the information the account gives about themselves is correct. In those cases, underline the information you could follow up on to check if the account is real.

PrinceHarry Charles ▢ 🔒
6 Tweets

PrinceHarry Charles ▢ 🔒
@PrinceHarry778

🗓 Joined November 2017

231 Following   **642** Followers

Shelly LaMonica
Realtor®

C: 912.312.3404   O: 912.445.2230
shelly@integritynewhomes.com

integritynewhomes.com

integrity
real estate llc

Shelly LaMonica - Real Estate Expert ···
· April 22 · 🌐

👍❤️ 13

👍 Like   💬 Comment   ↪ Share   😊 ▾

Write a comment...   😊 📷 🎬 🎁

7,465
Posts

1.9M
Followers

262
Following

NBC News
Broadcasting & Media Production Company
The official Instagram account of @NBCNews. A
visual digest of the top #news across 🇺🇸 and the 🌎
| 👇 LINK IN BIO
linkin.bio/nbcnews

Follow   Message   Contact   ⌄

Climate teens   Itta Bena, M...   Hunger CA   PR protests   D-Da

Holly West

Timeline | About | Friends 1 Mutual | Photos | More ▼

Intro

Senior Editor at Swoon Reads and Feiwel & Friends. Geek and fangirl. AKA That-Girl-Who-Reads-A-Lot.

⊟ Senior Editor at Feiwel & Friends / Macmillan Children's Publishing
⊟ Former Administrative Assistant at St. Martin's Press
🎓 Studied at NYU
🎓 Studied at University of the Cumberlands
🎓 Went to Wayne County High School
🏠 Lives in New York, New York
📍 From Monticello, Kentucky

Photos

✏ Create Post | 📷 Photo/Video

Write something to Holly...

📷 Photo/Video | 👥 Tag Friends | 😊 Feeling/Activ... | •••

Post

Holly West
2 mins · 👥

Found a new friend at #GenCon2019 and he's enjoying hanging out at the office with me today!

← **Keanu Charles reeves**
4 Tweets

••• Follow

Keanu Charles reeves
@KeanuCharlesr12

📍 Canada 🇨🇦 📅 Joined September 2018

190 Following   **83** Followers

Not followed by anyone you're following

Tweets | Tweets & replies | Media | Likes

Keanu Charles reeves @KeanuChar... · Sep 14, 2018 ⌄

💬 1   ⟲   ♡ 4   ⬆

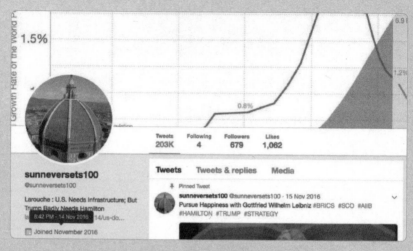

Tweets 203K   Following 4   Followers 679   Likes 1,062

Tweets   Tweets & replies   Media

Pinned Tweet
sunneversets100 @sunneversets100 · 15 Nov 2016
Pursue Happiness with Gottfried Wilhelm Leibniz #BRICS #SCO #AIIB
#HAMILTON #TRUMP #STRATEGY

← **Tasman Kekai (semi-hiatus)**
5,155 Tweets

Following

Tasman Kekai (semi-hiatus)
@m_kekai   Follows you

月亮代表我的心 // 20 – she/they – bi – writer // icon by @hexaes

📍 20 – she/they – bi – writer   🔗 tasmankekai.carrd.co   🎂 Born November 27
📅 Joined October 2015

1,204 Following   **1,019** Followers

Screenshot of Twitter account
@PrinceHarry778 taken on
September 28, 2019

FAKE. You might be fooled into thinking that a locked account with a low follower number might be real—maybe the prince likes his privacy. But the biggest sign that this is a fake account is that it is not verified. The blue-and-white circle icon is trying to fool you because it's similar to the blue check mark. Someone as famous as Prince Harry would definitely have a verified account.

Screenshot of Shelly LaMonica's Facebook
page, taken on September 30, 2019

REAL. You might wonder if this page is real because the banner picture does look like it has been digitally altered (the edges around her hair and the banner are the clue) and the business only has a few recommendations. But to check, we could call the phone number provided. We could also do a search for the business and see if she is listed as an employee. If we did, we'd discover this page is real.

Screenshot of the NBC News Instagram
page, taken on September 20, 2019

REAL. You can quickly see that this Instagram belongs to the real NBC News because of its verification. But there are other signs too. For example, click on the news stories and you'll be taken right to the NBC website. The account also has 1.8 million followers. A fake NBC would have to be pretty good to dupe that many people.

Screenshot of the Facebook profile for Holly West, taken on September 29, 2019

Screenshot of Twitter account @KeanuCharlesr12, taken on September 29, 2019

REAL. If you looked through Holly's profile, you would quickly see she's real. She lists things like where she lives, where she is from, and where she went to school. Holly also posts pictures of things she's interested in, along with actual original content, rather than just sharing other people's posts. You could double-check that she's real by looking into the employer she lists right on her profile or where she went to school. In short, Holly's account looks real because she posts the full range of human activities, including details you can verify.

FAKE. The real Keanu Reeves would have a verified account and more than eighty-three followers. I think we can safely say he'd also know to capitalize his last name. Also, fake account creators will often post random pictures of things on their pages to simulate human behavior—in this case, a weird picture of the belly of an airplane.

Screenshot of the Twitter page for @sunneversets100, taken on August 28, 2017

FAKE. Between the creation of this account in November 2016 and the time of this screenshot, less than a year later, the account tweeted 203,000 times. That's a little over seven hundred posts a day (or about one per minute during a twelve-hour period), way more than even the chattiest human posters. Also, the vast majority of these posts were retweets, rather than original content, and most were shares of articles by Russian government-owned news outlets.

Screenshot of Twitter user Tasman Kekai's profile, taken on July 21, 2019

REAL. This account has an average number of tweets given when it was created, and most of the tweets are original content rather than retweets. You could also click on Tasman's website link, where she gives more information about herself and links to her other social-media accounts.

CHAPTER 21

MANAGING THE CHAOS OF THE BREAKING-NEWS CYCLE

IT IS LATE ON A SUNDAY NIGHT AND YOU CAN'T sleep. You have a quiz at school tomorrow and you are worried you did not study enough. To distract yourself, you decide to check social media, and right away, your feed is filled with posts that start with:

BREAKING NEWS!

Not again, you think. Was it a terrorist? An earthquake? Or did another politician resign in disgrace? There was breaking news about something else just a few hours ago, wasn't there? Warily, you decide to read on.

It is another shooting, this time in Las Vegas at a concert. You can feel your chest tightening. You have friends who live there. What if something happened to them? Wrong place, wrong time—it happens. You quickly head over to Twitter to find out what the news is saying. A journalist from CNN tweeted that the shooting was on the Vegas strip. A gunman fired on a crowd from somewhere, but no one knows from where yet because the killer is still on the loose. At least a dozen people have been killed or injured, the news report says. #LasVegas is trending, so you click on it and start scrolling through the latest posts.

Most of the tweets are people praying for Vegas or saying they have friends at that concert. It makes you feel a little sick to read them all. But then another tweet says the cops are in the middle of a shootout with the killer. Wait, when did they find the gunman? You don't recognize the name of the person who tweeted it, but it sounds like they know what they're talking about since they give a lot of details. The person says five people have been killed or injured, and they have pictures they say are from the actual scene of the shooting. But a new post from CNN says that forty people have been killed or injured. You refresh the feed and already there are hundreds of new posts, some with pictures and video from people who say they are there. In one of the pictures, you can just make out a little snow on the ground. You've never been to Las Vegas, but it still strikes you as a little weird for early October. A newer post that is already going viral says there is more than one shooter, but when you check back at CNN, they haven't posted anything about it yet. You growl a little in frustration. You just want to know what's really going on, and there are too many posts to keep up with, all saying different things.

By now you are glued to Twitter, as more news rolls in during the course of a few hours. Angst over that quiz at school is now a distant memory. You texted your friends in Vegas to see if they were okay, and luckily, they quickly texted back that they were nowhere near the concert. But that isn't the case for the fifty-eight people who were actually killed that night in October 2017. It takes hours for the news to finally identify the gunman, sixty-four-year-old Stephen Paddock, who opened fire on the concert from the thirty-second floor of the Mandalay Bay hotel. The police identified the shooter after finding him dead from a self-inflicted gunshot wound.

You get up early the next morning and immediately check Twitter. CNN says the police still don't know Paddock's motive. You can't help but wonder who this guy was and why he would do something so horrific. Enter the fake news writers and Twitter trolls. Back on #LasVegas, you see the channel full of posts citing a story from far-right fake news site Gateway Pundit claiming they know the truth.

Another story says Paddock was an anti-Trump liberal. Investigators will discover later that this story originated in a 4chan post in which anonymous users discussed how to pin the shooting on liberals.[1] A third story, this one from Sputnik, a Russian outlet controlled by the government and known to spread fake news, said American media were trying to hide the fact that the shooter had recently converted to Islam. They claimed the FBI had linked Paddock to the Islamic State of Iraq and the Levant terrorist group.[2] There were even some stories identifying the shooter as someone other than Paddock.

These fake articles were so popular that they appeared as "top stories" on Google and Facebook, right alongside real news articles from NBC and CNN.[3] And that was not all. Countless posts on social media, both during and after the shooting, claimed to be from people who were there, had been shot, or had lost relatives. Some of these posts, from fake accounts and users trying to get attention, even included fake pictures.[4]

The Las Vegas shooting is not the only time fake news has spread in the aftermath of disaster. In fact, breaking-news situations are often overrun with false information, fake news, and conspiracy theories that trick people by using many of the same tactics we have talked about in previous chapters. Breaking news often sets off strong emotions and creates a flood of information online, which fake news writers can easily leverage to push out fake stories and cause confusion.

But what is breaking news? Typically, a media outlet labels something breaking news when it has just happened. It is not always a crisis, like a shooting. It can be about politics, the death of someone high-profile, or big developments at important companies. The label is also often used to give an update to an important story that has already been reported, like when a peace agreement between two countries that has been negotiated for months is finally signed.

These days, it can often feel like everything is breaking news. It's not just that so many things are happening, but also partly because some outlets have turned to saying *Breaking News!* more often to attract attention, even when the news item may not warrant it. Fake news websites, which already rely on clickbait headlines, often label something "Breaking News" to get more people clicking on a story. So how do you make sure you are not fooled by fake news during a real breaking-news event?

1. *Stop and breathe.* Fake news moves just as fast as real news. Sometimes it moves even faster, since fake news posters don't have to wait for facts. They can just make stuff up. Breaking-news events can get our blood pumping and our emotions running high, especially as a result of the quick pace. But we are more likely to help spread fake news and inaccuracies about a breaking-news event when we are anxious and feel like we have to do something. So wait, breathe, and then calmly investigate before sharing anything.

2. *Make sure it really is "breaking news."* Sometimes fake news pushers recycle old news stories or create new ones, then label them "breaking news," so make sure the event actually happened. You can do this by checking to see if other news stations (especially ones you've already identified as trustworthy) are reporting on it. One of the first things reporters do when they see breaking news from one media outlet is to check with their own sources to see if they can confirm what is being reported. That is one of the reasons why you will see multiple news outlets cover the same story, even after one breaks the story.

    For example, say you see a story from a news site you are not familiar with claiming a bomb went off in Florida. If it really happened, media outlets from all over will be rushing to cover the story. Wait a minute and then do a quick internet search to see if outlets you know are reputable are reporting on it. If they are not, that might be an indication it is fake news.

3. *Look for news stations closest to the event taking place.* If a breaking-news event is happening in northern Florida, for example, the news outlets that have journalists in that area are probably the best places to get accurate information. Local

reporters on the scene are the most likely to have sources in relevant offices to give them information on what's happening.

4. *Don't trust everything you see on social media.* You know now that social media is a hotbed for fake news. In a breaking-news situation, it's even worse. As people take to social media to share what they know or think about what is happening, fake news writers slip in too, claiming to know what is really going on. Foreign governments—Russia, China, and Iran in particular—deploy bots and trolls to post false information on social media during breaking-news events, to increase confusion and sow divisions on hot-button issues such as race and politics.[5] Racist and extreme political groups, too, often push out fake news and disinformation during and after crisis situations to advance their agenda. For example, after a shooting or attack carried out by a white person, white supremacists often take to social media to spread false information and point the blame at people of color or other minority groups.

Be skeptical of people posting information on social media without citing their sources. If they don't share a link to where they got their information, you don't have any way to verify it. If you see in a social media user's bio that they are a verified journalist, they might be posting information about an event without linking to a news article. That could be because they haven't yet written their article on the event. But when a seemingly random person posts about the event without citing a news article, and they do not appear to be at the actual event, ask yourself how they know what they are saying. Even if they claim to be at the scene of the event, and even if they have pictures, it is possible that they are using old pictures they found online from a similar event.

5. *Don't be discouraged if even your trusted news outlets get the story wrong the first time they report on it.* It can take time for news outlets to put a full picture together. To keep readers updated, they report what they learn during a crisis as it is still actively unfolding, Since that information can quickly change, as they talk to first responders on the scene or others who have inside knowledge of what is happening, stories often change quickly to include that new information.

Additionally, breaking-news stories cannot always provide the relevant context and background on the story. A breaking-news event is a rapidly unfolding situation, so most news coverage during and immediately after will focus on getting the basic facts out first. Sometimes it can take days before the news has the full picture of what happened, who was involved, why it happened, and if something like it has happened before. If it seems like a news outlet you have relied on in the past is changing their story a little, or isn't providing all the context at the beginning of a breaking-news event, it doesn't mean you can't count on them. It just means they are learning new information.

Breaking-news events are one of the times we are most at risk of falling for fake news and passing it to others online. It is worth it to take the time to investigate what is being reported before sharing what we have found.

Exercise:
SORTING THROUGH
BREAKING NEWS

Below are actual tweets that appeared during a real breaking-news event in 2017—Hurricane Harvey. Look at each post and put a check mark next to the ones that look credible. Next, put a star next to each post that might be worth investigating further, along with a note of what you would want to look up to determine if it is a credible source of information. Finally, put an X next to any post you think you should discount completely.

dontpanic 🎭 ⚡ @DontPanicBurns · Aug 26, 2017
So far so good. Fights on tv, noaa radio in the background.
#HurricaneHarvey

Hurricane Local Statement >>>
Tropical Storm Warning >>>
Flash Flood Watch >>>

♡ 1

DarkSyn 🎙️ **#Ω PRU Founder** @Mihero · Aug 26, 2017
Resourceful dog walks away with bag of dog food after **Hurricane** Harvey
huffingtonpost.com/entry/hurrican... **via** @HuffPostWeird

Resourceful Dog Walks Away With Bag Of Dog Food After Hurricane H...
"Must be a Texas dog cause he can survive without help," one person
said.
🔗 huffpost.com

💬 1   ↻ 6   ♡ 5   ⬆️

Nichole Gomez ABC-7 ✔️ @NicholeEGomez · Aug 25, 2017
Some El Paso emergency responders deploy to assist with **Hurricane**
Harvey via KVIA News

ATL NTIC   N7255N

HARVEY HELP

10:05 PM 77°

Some El Paso emergency responders deploy to assist with Hurricane H...
Hundreds of emergency responders are mobilizing across Texas --and
the country-- to help residents in the path of Hurricane Harvey. Some ...
🔗 kvia.com

💬   ↻   ♡ 2   ⬆️

Margaret Browning @Margare06824403 · Aug 25, 2017

Now #FakeNews Wash Post says **Hurricane** H is Cat 4. So sad, scaring the good people of Texas.

John Moffitt
@JohnRMoffitt

#HoustonFlood : #Houston has greedy developers who build expensive homes in a flood plain. Every year we see a lot of cars under water.

Trash Yorlang @StartTrashTalkN · Aug 26, 2017

This is what **Houston flooding** looked like,couldve had a yardsale #Houston #HurricaneHarvery #flooding #hurricane #weatherchannel #yardsale

Screenshot of a tweet posted by
@DontPanicBurns on August 26, 2017

Screenshot of a tweet posted by
@Mihero on August 26, 2017

STAR. The picture from this post looks like it came from a weather app, but it is not clear which one, how old the image might be, or whether it is accurate. The poster does not appear to be from a media outlet and does not claim in the post to have personally taken the picture. The post also does not link to a news article. Because you do not know where the photo came from, you could ask the poster for their source or see if they explain in another post where they got the picture. You could also simply look up the weather report for the area yourself.

CHECK MARK. The post shares an article from an actual media outlet about how one animal was braving the storm. The poster does not make any claim in the post other than what came from the headline. Posting a news article does not mean everything else the poster says on their account is true, but you know that the information in this post comes from an actual news source. If you were unfamiliar with the news outlet, you could do your own research to see if the source of the article is reliable.

X. The post does not link to
the *Washington Post* report it
seems to be citing. You could
do your own research to see if
the newspaper reported what
the account claims, but this
particular post is probably
worth ignoring altogether
because the account makes
a claim that doesn't cite any
sources and calls a reliable
media outlet—the *Washington
Post*—"#FakeNews." Also,
the account does not have a
profile picture and still uses the
alphanumeric username they're
assigned when they create their
profile. Those two things are not
always definitive indicators that
an account might be a bot or a
troll, but they are often signs
that what they post might not be
reliable.

CHECK MARK. The post comes
from an actual reporter who is
sharing news from her media
outlet about the event. The user
is verified, meaning she is who
she says she is. Once again,
posting a news article does not
mean everything else a poster
says on their account is true, but
you know this post comes from
an actual news source. If you
were unfamiliar with the reporter
or her news outlet, you could do
your own research to see if they
are reliable.

Screenshot of tweet posted by John Moffitt on August 27, 2017

Screenshot of tweet by Trash Yorlang on August 26, 2017

X. The picture certainly looks like the results of a hurricane, but it's not clear where the picture came from originally, where it was taken and when, what it is actually of, or why the poster has it. The poster does not appear to be from a media outlet and does not claim to have personally taken the picture. The post does not link to a news article and appears to be intended to support a personal view. You could ask the poster for their source or see if they explain in another post where they got the picture or do a search to see if you can find where they may have gotten the photo. If you are looking for news on the actual event, however, it may be better to ignore this post and look for photos from more reliable sources, like a trusted news outlet.

STAR. The poster implies that they took this picture from their own neighborhood, but it is difficult to verify where the picture really came from. The poster does not appear to be from a media outlet. It is important to remember that even a large-scale event like a hurricane will not affect all areas or people the same way. While the poster may have experienced no flooding in the hurricane, this should not be taken as evidence that the hurricane did not have an impact. The problem with a post like this is that some people might see it and think it is safe to go out when really, their area might not be safe at all. The best thing to do is check in with local, trusted media sources or local emergency response organizations to see what areas have been affected.

CHAPTER 22

CONCLUSION

IN 2017, TWENTY-YEAR-OLD BEST FRIENDS
Rohan Phadte and Ash Bhat noticed some accounts on Twitter
acting strangely. In one of their computer-science classes at the
University of California, Berkeley, they had been given an assignment
to study President Trump's tweets. They had both read a lot about how
Russia had used fake accounts to try to influence US voters during
the presidential election the year before.[1] Some of the Twitter users
they saw commenting on the president's tweets followed some of
the known patterns of the Russian bots they'd studied—pretty new
accounts that only retweeted politically one-sided stuff. They were
sure they'd found fake accounts. But if they could spot fake accounts
themselves, couldn't a computer be programmed to identify the bots
automatically? Phadte and Bhat wondered. The answer, they decided,
was yes.

The key was to help internet users become more informed. The
two students started first by building NewsBot, an app where users
could send in news articles through Facebook Messenger and the
program would analyze them and report back the political leanings

of the source. But they didn't stop there. Next, Phadte and Bhat launched Botcheck.me, a downloadable browser extension for Google Chrome that spots accounts on Twitter that behave like bots. They created the program in just eight weeks, and it had an over 90 percent accuracy rate at identifying bots.[2] Their third project, SurfSafe, was another free browser extension that analyzes text and images to identify if a site claiming to be news is actually trying to mislead you.

It's not political for them; it's about information. "I don't care what someone's political view is, I just want them to be informed," Bhat said in an interview with *Wired* in 2017. "A lot of people may think they're informed while reading very biased sources and having their news very skewed." Every day, Phadte and Bhat try to think of new ways to help people spot fake news because they know the problem isn't going away.

They also know that fake news is not just a government problem or a social-media company problem. It's an all-of-us problem. Each of us has a critical role to play in fighting fake news.

THE PART WHERE IT TAKES ALL OF US

We are living in an amazing time of communication, with more information than we'll ever be able to actually consume in one lifetime. It might feel overwhelming at times, since we know now that fake news pushers are taking advantage of this unprecedented access to try to create confusion and spread false information. But there is good news too. We have more information than ever before to help spot and fight fake news.

We have the benefit of knowing the history of fake news now. Fake news in the age of the pharaoh or the early days of the printing press really wasn't that different from the kind of fake news we encounter today. Although the way it spreads today is faster and easier than when people were writing on papyrus, we know the patterns now. We know the kinds of sensational and divisive stories fake news tries to tell. We know that fake news takes advantage of our emotions to trick us. We know that it plays off things like racism, political division, and conspiracies. We know that it tries to flood us with lies over and over again because the more we hear and see fake news, the more likely we are to fall for it. Every generation of people that has come before us has dealt with the same fake news problem, and every generation has learned from it. So must we. Knowing the history of fake news gives us a road map to follow to combat it.[3]

We might think the simple solution is to trust nothing. That is what fake news pushers want us to do. They want us to think that nothing is true anymore, or that the problem is so insurmountable that it isn't worth our effort. But giving up is the easy way out, and also the dangerous one, because it does not help solve the fake news problem. It ignores the fact that truth still exists and that journalists are out there working hard every day to make sure we know what it is. So it's up to each of us to help fight fake news. We might not all be computer programmers. But, as we've learned in this book, we can all think like an intelligence analyst.

Intelligence analysts consider their biases to make sure they're not discounting the truth simply because they don't agree with it. They take the time to make sure they know where they're getting their information. They see all information as potentially useful, but they first work to verify it before they use it. Intelligence analysts also call out false information when they find it. You can do all these things too, and then help your friends and families learn to do the same.

I often think back to my first day at the CIA, when I spotted that quote carved up on the wall: "And ye shall know the truth and the truth will make you free." It took a while before I came to realize just how important that motto was. I learned at the CIA that discovering the truth was not always easy, but it was always worth it. We've seen the history of fake news, and we know how bad the consequences can be if we do not fight back. If freedom is the reward, surely it is worth each of us committing to cut through the noise of fake news to find out what is true or false.

A c k n o w l e d g m e n t s

———————————

My favorite parts of books are the dedication page and the acknowledgments. No matter how terrible or wonderful the pages in between them might be, I will always read the dedication and acknowledgments because I love the concept of starting and ending a book with gratitude. To say that I am delighted to be able to write my own now is an understatement.

First, I wrote this book feeling an enormous weight on my shoulders. That weight was from feeling like I needed to provide something that might be able to put civilization on a positive path as we all figure out how to make sense of rapidly changing events. I know that in summarizing massive historical events and people like I have in this book, there always comes with it the huge risk of unintentionally trivializing or glossing over another culture, country, history, or person's lived experiences. There is so much more to read and learn about each of these events and people. I hope you'll take the time to research them on your own.

To my readers, thank you for picking up this book—whether you bought it, borrowed it, checked it out at the library, or got it as a school assignment. Reading it means you want to seek and defend fact and truth. As a result, our society is already a little bit stronger. As I said, this is an all-of-us problem. I wrote this book for you. (No pressure!)

Thank you to my agent, Caryn Wiseman, who believed in the importance of this book from the beginning. Here is to many more books together.

Thank you to my team at Macmillan. To my editor, Holly West, who saw a proposal with some ideas and knew exactly how to turn it into what this book needed to be. To Starr Baer, my production editor, whose careful stewardship of this book got it here. Karen Sherman, my eagle-eyed copyeditor, fact-checker, and lifesaver. To Morgan Kane, my publicist, for so enthusiastically making sure people knew about this book. To Patrick Collins and Raphael Geroni, who designed the beautiful pages and cover. And to Kim Waymer, my production manager.

I have been lucky in life to have several true friendships that mean the world to me and also have gotten me to this point. So, thank you to Kelly McGannon, whose sweet spirit and friendship has propelled and inspired me over the years. To Arielle, whose unfailing positivity, generosity, and intelligence inspire all of us lucky enough to know her. To my favorite duo, Heather and B, for their unwavering friendship and also for introducing me to the weirdest Christmas movie of all time—but mostly their friendship. To Kirsti Meyer, who ignited my love of all things YA years ago. To Pilita Mallari for reading every book draft I've written, except, funnily enough, this one.

Thank you also to my dear, sweet friend Anne Meyer, who has always believed in me and my voice. I wouldn't be here without your kindness and your love over the years.

Also, all the thanks to my talented friend and fellow author Katie Kennedy, who let me call upon her expertise and experience time and time again throughout the course of writing this book. To my book bestie Jennifer Iacopelli for your boundless support, encouragement, and well-timed gifs. Thank you also to Becky Albertalli, Natalie C. Parker, Marieke Nijkamp, and Mike Mullin, who have all provided support and publishing advice for no other reason than they are just lovely human beings. This community of writers made the solitary act of writing feel like we were in it together.

Thank you to Mudge, Nada Bakos, Sarah Carlson, Tracy Walder, Jeff Asher, and Mark Stout for your guidance and camaraderie navigating life on the outside.

To the women and men of the CIA, my colleagues. I may not be able to name all of you, but I thank you for your continued service to our country.

To journalists who risk so much to bring us the truth from every corner of the world. You do a tough and thankless job sifting through fact and fiction, speaking truth to power, and holding the corrupt accountable—and it's getting tougher every day. Your job is more important than ever before, so thank you.

To my great-great-great-grandpa Cyrus Field, who laid that first transatlantic telegraph cable I wrote about, which connected the world and changed the course of news and communication. The world is a different place because he risked everything he had. I feel like this book was actually a century in the making for our family.

Thank you to my siblings for their love and support. Also, to my dear nieces and nephews, whom I love so much. Remember: I'm your favorite, coolest aunt. To my own aunt and uncle, Diane and George, whose support for my education made this possible and whose lives of service have made this world a better place for so many.

Finally, to my parents, Sue and Roger. I know how lucky I am to have you as my champions in life. The biggest leg-up I've ever been given started at the very beginning when I got you as my parents. Then, when I was just a sick, bedridden kid, you set me on a particular life-changing course when you started reading to me from the encyclopedia and said: "Well, I guess you're going to have to be smart." I am so thrilled that finally, I get to begin and end my very own book with my thanks and endless love for you both. This is entirely because of and for you.

Notes

INTRODUCTION

1. Edson Tandoc, Zheng Wei Lim, & Rich Ling, "Defining 'Fake News': A Typology of Scholarly Definitions," *Digital Journalism* (2017): 1–17.

CHAPTER 1

1. Nick Tingley, "The Autumn of Terror: The Legacy of Jack the Ripper and the Newspapermen Who Made Him," *History Is Now*, September 5, 2014, http://www .historyisnowmagazine.com/blog/2014/9/5 /the-autumn-of-terror-the-legacy-of-jack -the-ripper-and-the-newspapermen-who -made-him.

2. "'Murder at Bucks Row' from the *Illustrated Police News*," British Library, https://www .bl.uk/collection-items/murder-at-bucks-row-from-the-illustrated-police-news.

3. Gregg Jon Jones, "Murder, Media and Mythology: The Impact the Media's Reporting of the Whitechapel Murders had on National Identity, Social Reform and the Myth of Jack the Ripper," *Reinvention: An International Journal of Undergraduate Research*, August 5, 2013, https://warwick .ac.uk/fac/cross_fac/iatl/reinvention/issues /bcur2013specialissue/jones/.

4. Robert F. Haggard, "Jack the Ripper As the Threat of Outcast London," *Essays in History* 35 (2013), http://www.essaysinhistory.com /jack-the-ripper-as-the-threat-of-outcast -london/.

5. *Ibid.*

6. "Press Reports," Casebook: Jack the Ripper, https://www.casebook.org/press _reports/east_london_advertiser/ela880915 .html.

7. Philip Sugden, *The Complete History of Jack the Ripper* (New York: Constable & Robinson Ltd, 2002).

8. "Jack the Ripper," The National Archives, https://www.nationalarchives.gov.uk /museum/item.asp?item_id=39.

9. *Ibid.*

10. *Ibid.*

11. Jason Daley, "Were the Jack the Ripper Letters Fabricated by Journalists?" *Smithsonian* (February 1, 2018), https://www.smithsonianmag.com/smart -news/were-ripper-letters-fabricated -journalists-180968004/.

12. Alexandra Warwick, "The Scene of the Crime: Inventing the Serial Killer," *Social & Legal Studies* 15, no. 4 (*December 2006*): 552–69, https://doi .org/10.1177/0964663906069547.

CHAPTER 2

1. "Pen-ta-ur: The Victory of Ramses II Over the Khita, 1326 BCE," Internet Ancient History Sourcebook, https://sourcebooks .fordham.edu/ancient/1326khita.asp.

2. Joshua J. Mark, "The Battle of Kadesh & the Poem of Pentaur," *Ancient History Encyclopedia* (January 18, 2012), https://www.ancient.eu/ article/147/the-battle-of -kadesh—the-poem-of-pentaur/.

3. Alex Loktionov, "Ramesses II, Victor of Kadesh: A Kindred Spirit of Trump?" *Guardian* (December 5, 2016), https://www .theguardian.com/science/blog/2016/dec /05/ramesses-ii-victor-of-kadesh-a -kindred-spirit-of-trump.

4. "Egyptian Accounts of the Battle of Kadesh." http://www.reshafim.org.il/ad /egypt/kadeshaccounts.htm.

5. Bill Kovach and Tom Rosenstiel, *Blur: How to Know What's True in the Age of Information Overload* (New York: Bloomsbury, 2011).

6. Loktionov, "Ramses II, Victor of Kadesh."

7. James Allan Evans, *The Empress Theodora: Partner of Justinian* (Austin, TX: University of Texas Press, 2002).

8. *Ibid.*

9. Richard Atwater, trans., *Procopius: Secret History* (Ann Arbor, MI: University of Michigan Press, 1961), https://sourcebooks .fordham.edu/basis/procop-anec.asp.

10. "The Secret History" by Procopius, Translated with an Introduction By G.A. Williamson. The first printing of this particular translation was by Penguin Books in 1966.

https://books.google.com/books?id=teuf9i -AJ2wC&pg

11. J.A.S. Evans, "Justinian and the Historian Procopius," *Cambridge University Press* 17, no. 2 (1970): 218–223.

12. Allison C. Meier, "The Talking Statues of Rome," JSTOR Daily, June 18, 2018, https://daily.jstor.org/the-talking-statues-of-rome/.

13. Jeremiah E. Dittmar, "Information Technology and Economic Change: The Impact of The Printing Press," *The Quarterly Journal of Economics* 126, no. 3 (Fall 2011): 1133–1172.

14. Meier, "The Talking Statues of Rome."

15. Etjo Byringh, *Medieval Manuscript Production in the Latin West: Explorations with a Global Database* (Boston: Brill, 2010).

16. Heming Nelson, "A History of Newspaper: Gutenberg's Press Started a Revolution," *Washington Post* (February 11, 1998), https://www.washingtonpost .com/archive/1998/02/11/a-history-of -newspaper-gutenbergs-press-started-a -revolution/2e95875c-313e-4b5c-9807 -8bcb031257ad/?utm_term=.9e7f6000fa03.

CHAPTER 3

1. Sharon Kettering, "Political Pamphlets in Early Seventeenth-Century France: The Propaganda War Between Louis XIII and His Mother, 1619–20," *The Sixteenth Century Journal* 42, no. 4 (2011): 963–80, https://www .jstor.org/stable/23210619.

2. *Ibid.*

3. Stephen Marche, "How We Solved Fake News the First Time," *The New Yorker* (April 23, 2018, https://www.newyorker.com /culture/cultural-comment/how-we-solved -fake-news-the-first-time.

4. Kettering, "Political Pamphlets in Early Seventeenth Century France," 963–80.

5. Una McIlvenna, *Scandal and Reputation at the Court of Catherine de Medici* (New York: Routledge, 2016).

6. *Ibid.*

7. *Ibid.*

8. Antonia Fraser, *Marie Antoinette: The Journey* (New York City: Anchor, 2002).

9. Robert Darnton, *The Forbidden Best-Sellers of Pre-Revolutionary France* (New York: W. W. Norton & Company, 1996).

10. Dena Goodman, ed., *Marie Antoinette: Writings on the Body of a Queen* (New York: Routledge, 2003).

11. Timothy Jenks, "Blackmail, Scandal, and Revolution: London's French Libellistes, 1758–92 (review)," *Histoire sociale/Social History* 41, no. 81 (2008): 280–82.

12. *Ibid.*

13. Claire Marrone, "Women Writing Marie Antoinette: Madam de Stael and George Sand," *Dalhousie French Studies* 94 (Spring 2011): 113–122.

14. Fraser, *Marie Antoinette: The Journey.*

15. Pierre Etienne Auguste Goupil, ed., *Essais Historiques Sur La Vie de Marie-Antoinette D'Autriche, Reine de France (1789)* (Kessinger Publishing, 2010).

16. *Ibid.*

17. Keith Michael Baker, ed., *Readings in Western Civilization: The Old Regine and the French Revolution* (Chicago: University of Chicago Press, 1987).

18. Kenan Malik, "Fake News Has a Long History. Beware the State Being Keeper of 'the Truth,'" *Guardian* (February 10, 2018), https://www.theguardian.com /commentisfree/2018/feb/11/fake-news -long-history-beware-state-involvement.

19. Robert Darnton, "The True History of Fake News," *New York Review of Books* (February 13, 2017), https://www.nybooks.com /daily/2017/02/13/the-true-history-of-fake -news/.

20. Thomas V. DiBacco, "Banned in Boston: America's First Newspaper," *The Wall Street Journal* (September 24, 2015), https:// www.wsj.com/articles/banned-in-boston -americas-first-newspaper-1443139281.

21. Benson John Lossing, *A History of the United States from the Discovery of the Continent to the Present Time* (Toledo: W. E. Bliss, 1875), https://play.google.com/store /books/details?id=TvXNWjL4UVQC&rdid =book-TvXNWjL4UVQC&rdot=1.

22. Daniel C. Hallin, *We Keep America on Top of the World* (London: Routledge, 1994), https:// books.google.com /books?id=m15mwdY35ywC&pg.

CHAPTER 4

1. Carla Mulford, "Benjamin Franklin's Savage Eloquence: Hoaxes from the Press at Passy, 1782." *Proceedings of the American Philosophical Society* 152, no. 4 (2008): 490–530, www.jstor. org/stable/40541605.

2. Patrick J. Kiger, "How Ben Franklin's Viral Political Cartoon United the 13 Colonies," *History*, October 23, 2018, https://www.history. com/news/ben-franklin-join-or-die -cartoon-french-indian-war.

3. Robert G. Parkinson, "Fake News? That's a Very Old Story," *Washington Post* (November 25, 2016), https://www.washingtonpost .com/opinions/fake-news-thats-a-very-old -story/2016/11/25/c8b1f3d4-b330-11e6-8616 -52b15787add0_story.html.

4. Arthur M. Schlesinger, "The Colonial Newspapers and the Stamp Act," *The New England Quarterly* 8, no. 1 (1935): 63–83.

5. Gregory Evans Dowd, *Groundless: Rumors, Legends, and Hoaxes on the Early American Frontier* (Baltimore: Johns Hopkins University Press, 2016).

6. "Editorial Note: Jefferson, Freneau, and the Founding of the *National Gazette*," Founders Online, https://founders.archives .gov/documents/Jefferson/01-20-02-0374 -0001#TSJN-01-20-dg-0008-fn-0004.

7. "Cabinet Meetings. Proposals Concerning the Conduct of the French Minister, [1–23 August 1793]," Founders Online, https:// founders.archives.gov/documents /Hamilton/01-15-02-0125.

8. "An American No. 1, [4 August 1792]," Founders Online, https://founders.archives .gov/documents/Hamilton/01-12-02-0126.

9. "Editorial Note: Jefferson, Freneau, and the Founding of the *National Gazette*."

10. James W. Cortada, "How New Is 'Fake News'?" OUPblog, March 23, 2017, https://blog.oup.com/2017/03/fake-news- trump-jackson-jefferson/.

11. John Ferling, *Adams vs. Jefferson: The Tumultuous Election of 1800*. (Oxford, England: Oxford University Press, 2004).

12. Sarah Pruitt, "Jefferson & Adams: Founding Frenemies," History Stories, History, updated September 10, 2018, https://www.history.com/ news/jefferson-adams -founding-frenemies.

13. James Thomson Callender, *The History of the United States for 1796; Including a Variety of Interesting Particulars Relative to the Federal Government Previous to that Period* (Philadelphia: Snowden and McCorkle, 1797), https://catalog.hathitrust.org /Record/009259805.

14. History.com Editors, "Alien and Sedition Acts," Topics, History, updated September 13, 2019, https://www.history.com/topics/early -us/alien-and-sedition-acts.

15. *Ibid.*

16. Thomas Jefferson to John Norvell, June 11, 1807, https://www.loc.gov/resource /mtj1.038_0592_0594/?sp=2&st=text.

CHAPTER 5

1. Arthur Hobson Quinn, *Edgar Allan Poe: A Critical Biography* (Baltimore, Maryland: Johns Hopkins University Press, 1998).

2. Philip Potempa, "Edgar Allan Poe's Tragic Life Revealed for Chicago Stage Premier," *Chicago Tribune* (January 9, 2018), https://www.chicagotribune.com/suburbs/post -tribune/lifestyles/ct-ptb-potempa-column -st-0110-20180109-story.html.

3. Harold Beaver, ed., *The Science Fiction of Edgar Allan Poe* (New York: Penguin Books, 1976).

4. Harold H. Scudder, "Poe's 'Balloon Hoax,'" *American Literature* vol. 21, no. 2 (May 1949): 179–90, https://www.jstor.org /stable/2922023?seq=1#page_scan_tab _contents.

5. Jill Lepore, "The Humbug: Edgar Allan Poe and the Economy of Horror," *New Yorker* (April 27, 2009), https://www.newyorker .com/magazine/2009/04/27/the-humbug.

6. *Ibid.*

7. David Ketterer, "Poe's Usage of the Hoax and the Unity of 'Hans Phaall,'" *Criticism* 13, no. 4 (1971): 377–85.

8. Jeffrey Gottfried, Katerina Eva Matsa, and Michael Barthel, "As Jon Stewart steps down, 5 facts about *The Daily Show*," Pew Research Center, August 6, 2015, http://www.pewresearch.org/fact-tank/2015/08/06/5-facts-daily-show/.

9. Sarah Zielinski, "The Great Moon Hoax Was Simply a Sign of Its Time," *Smithsonian* (July 2, 2015), https://www.smithsonianmag.com/smithsonian-institution/great-moon-hoax-was-simply-sign-its-time-180955761/.

10. *Ibid.*

11. History.com Editors, "'The Great Moon Hoax' Is Published in the *New York Sun*," *History*, updated August 21, 2019, https://www.history.com/this-day-in-history/the-great-moon-hoax.

12. Matthew Wills, "How the *Sun* Conned the World With 'The Great Moon Hoax,'" JSTOR Daily, November 7, 2017, https://daily.jstor.org/how-the-sun-conned-the-world-with-the-moon-hoax/.

13. Steven W Ruskin, "A Newly-Discovered Letter of J.F.W. Herschel concerning the 'Great Moon Hoax,'" *Journal for the History of Astronomy* 33, no. 1 (2002): 71–74.

14. *Ibid.*

15. J. B. Legendre, letter to the editor, *Wichita (KN) City Eagle*, February 12, 1874, http://chroniclingamerica.loc.gov/lccn/sn85032573/1874-02-12/ed-1/seq-1/.

16. *Ibid.*

17. Gabe Bullard, "The Heartbreak That May Have Inspired the Telegraph." *National Geographic.* April 26, 2016. https://www.nationalgeographic.com/news/2016/04/160426-samuel-morse-wife-lucretia-telegraph-invention/.

18. Joseph Stromberg, "How Samuel Morse Got His Big Idea," *Smithsonian* (January 6, 2012), https://www.smithsonianmag.com/smithsonian-institution/how-samuel-morse-got-his-big-idea-16403094/.

19. Samuel Finley Breese Morse, *First Telegraphic Message—24 May.* 24 May 1844. Image. https://www.loc.gov/item/mmorse000107.

20. John Steele Gordon, *A Thread Across the Ocean: The Heroic Story of the Transatlantic Cable.* (New York: Bloomsbury Publishing USA, 2002).

21. Edward McKernon, "Fake News and The Public: How the Press Combats Rumor, the Market Rigger, and the Propagandist," *Harper's Magazine* (October 1925), https://harpers.org/archive/1925/10/fake-news-and-the-public/.

22. *Ibid.*

23. *Ibid.*

CHAPTER 6

1. Ben Procter, *William Randolph Hearst: The Early Years, 1863–1910* (New York: Oxford University Press, 1998).

2. Edwin Diamond, *Behind the Times: Inside the New New York Times.* (Chicago: The University of Chicago Press, 1993).

3. Philip Brenner and Peter Eisner, *Cuba Libre: A 500-Year Quest for Independence* (Lanham, MD: Rowman & Littlefield, 2018).

4. Martin J. Manning and Clarence R. Wyatt, *Encyclopedia of Media and Propaganda in Wartime America* (Santa Barbara, CA: ABC-CLIO, 2010).

5. W. Joseph Campbell, *Getting It Wrong: Debunking the Greatest Myths in American Journalism* (University of California Press, 2016).

6. Clifford Krauss, "The World; Remember Yellow Journalism," *New York Times* (February 15, 1998), https://www.nytimes.com/1998/02/15/weekinreview/the-world-remember-yellow-journalism.html.

7. Philip M. Seib, *Campaigns and Conscience: The Ethics of Political Journalism* (London: Greenwood Publishing Group, 1994).

8. Brenner and Eisner, *Cuba Libre.*

9. James M. Lindsay, "TWE Remembers: The Sinking of the USS *Maine*," *The Water's Edge* (blog), Council on Foreign Relations, February 15, 2012, https://www.cfr.org/blog/twe-remembers-sinking-uss-maine.

10. "The World of 1898: The Spanish-American War," Hispanic Reading Room, Library of Congress, https://www.loc.gov/rr/hispanic/1898/intro.html.

11. Brenner and Eisner, *Cuba Libre.*

12. John Canemaker, "The Kid from Hogan's Alley," *The New York Times*, December 17, 1995, https://www.nytimes.com/1995/12/17/books/the-kd-from-hogan-s-alley.html.

13. "The Real Story of 'Fake News,'" Merriam-Webster, https://www.merriam-webster.com/words-at-play/the-real-story-of-fake-news.

14. Adrienne LaFrance, "How the 'Fake News' Crisis of 1896 Explains Trump," *Atlantic* (January 19, 2017), https://www.theatlantic.com/technology/archive/2017/01/the-fake-news-crisis-120-years-ago/513710/.

15. Merrill Fabry, "Here's How the First Fact-Checkers Were Able to Do Their Jobs Before the Internet." *Time*, August 24, 2017, https://time.com/4858683/fact-checking-history/.

16. Frederick Burr Opper, artist, *The fin de siècle newspaper proprietor / F. Opper* (New York: Published by Keppler & Schwarzmann, March 7, 1894), Photograph, https://www.loc.gov/item/2012648704/.

CHAPTER 7

1. William L Shirer, *The Rise and Fall of the Third Reich* (New York: Simon & Schuster, 2011).

2. Jan Grabowski, "German Anti-Jewish Propaganda in the Generalgouvernement, 1939–1945: Inciting Hate through Posters, Films, and Exhibitions," *Holocaust and Genocide Studies* 23, no. 3, (Winter 2009): 381–412.

3. "Nazi Persecution of the Disabled: Murder of the 'Unfit,'" United States Holocaust Memorial Museum, https://www.ushmm.org/information/exhibitions/online-exhibitions/special-focus/nazi-persecution-of-the-disabled.

4. Kenny Fries, "The Nazis' First Victims Were the Disabled." *The New York Times*, September 13, 2017, https://www.nytimes.com/2017/09/13/opinion/nazis-holocaust-disabled.html.

5. Jeff Nesbit, "History Repeats: Propaganda and the Destruction of the Free Press." *U.S. News & World Report* (October 26, 2017), https://www.usnews.com/news/at-the-edge/articles/2017-10-26/trump-propaganda-and-the-destruction-of-the-free-press.

6. Maja Adena, Ruben Enikolopov, Maria Petrova, Veronica Santarosa, Ekaterina Zhuravskaya, "Radio and the Rise of the Nazis in Prewar Germany" (working paper no. 2013-32, Paris School of Economics, 2013), https://halshs.archives-ouvertes.fr/halshs-00858992/document.

7. Karel Margry, "'Theresienstadt' (1944–1945): The Nazi Propaganda Film Depicting the Concentration Camp as Paradise," *Historical Journal of Film, Radio and Television* 12, no. 2 (1992): 145–62, https://www.tandfonline.com/doi/abs/10.1080/01439689200260091.

8. Rick Noack, "The Ugly History of 'Lügenpresse,' a Nazi Slur Shouted at a Trump Rally," *Washington Post* (October 24, 2016), https://www.washingtonpost.com/news/worldviews/wp/2016/10/24/the-ugly-history-of-luegenpresse-a-nazi-slur-shouted-at-a-trump-rally/?utm_term=.ae1e6b322187.

9. Marc Wortman, "The Fake British Radio Show That Helped Defeat the Nazis," *Smithsonian* (February 28, 2017), https://www.smithsonianmag.com/history/fake-british-radio-show-helped-defeat-nazis-180962320/.

10. Dan Norcross, "Cricket on the Radio: TMS, Fake Nazis, and How to Blend Fact and Fiction," *Guardian* (October 25, 2017), https://www.theguardian.com/sport/the-nightwatchman/2017/oct/25/cricket-radio-tms-fake-news-nazis-commentators.

11. Christopher Woody, "Trickery Wins Every Time: Russia Is Using an Old Kind of Military Deception," *Business Insider* (October 12, 2016), https://www.businessinsider.com/russia-using-inflatable-missiles-and-jets-for-deception-2016-10.

12. Michael J. Donovan, "Strategic Deception: Operation Fortitude," U.S. Army War College. (2002), https://apps.dtic.mil/dtic/tr/fulltext/u2/a404434.pdf.

13. *Ibid.*

14. Sven Stillich, "Donald Versus Hitler: Walt Disney and the Art of WWII Propaganda." *Spiegel Online*, August 10, 2009. https://www.spiegel.de/international/germany/donald-versus-hitler-walt-disney-and-the-art-of-wwii-propaganda-a-641547.html.

15. Walt Disney Studios, *All Together*. 1941. https://archive.org/details/AllTogether.

16. Joachim Neander and Randal Marlin, "Media and Propaganda: The Northcliffe Press and the Corpse Factory Story of World War I," *Global Media Journal: Canadian Edition* 3, no. 2 (2010): pp. 67–82.

17. David Clarke, "The Corpse Factory and the Birth of Fake News," News, BBC, February 17, 2017, https://www.bbc.com/news/entertainment-arts-38995205.

CHAPTER 8

1. Cheryl Mullenbach, *Double Victory: How African American Women Broke Race and Gender Barriers to Help Win World War II* (Chicago: Chicago Review Press, 2013).

2. Federal Bureau of Investigation, "Eleanor Clubs," file 100-11347, https://www-tc.pbs .org/wgbh/americanexperience/media/filer _public/8d/f4/8df452a2-3db8-43d6-b6a0 -75396604961c/eleanor_fbi_eleanor _clubs_2.pdf.

3. Doris Kearns Goodwin, *Franklin & Eleanor Roosevelt: The Home Front in World War II.* (New York: Simon and Schuster, 2008).

4. Howard W. Odum, *Race and Rumors of Race: The American South in the Early Forties*, ed. Bryant Simon (Baltimore: Johns Hopkins University Press, 1997).

5. Craig Timberg and Drew Harwell, "We Studied Thousands of Anonymous Posts About the Parkland Attack—and Found a Conspiracy in the Making," *Washington Post* (February 27, 2018), https://www.washingtonpost.com/business/ economy/we-studied-thousands-of- anonymous-posts-about-the-parkland- attack—and-found-a-conspiracy-in-the- making/2018/02/27/04a856be-1b20-11e8 -b2d9-08e748f892c0_story.html.

6. Odum, *Race and Rumors of Race.*

7. *Ibid.*

8. Jelani Cobb, "Fake News in 1942," March 31, 2017, in *The New Yorker Radio Hour*, produced by David Remnick, podcast, https://www.wnyc.org/story/fake -news-1942/.

9. Federal Bureau of Investigation, "Eleanor Roosevelt Club of Negro Women, Jackson, Tennessee," file 100-1535, https://www-tc .pbs.org/wgbh/americanexperience/media /filer_public/2d/b1/2db1d016-05af-4faa -8332-ac0b5bbffa0b/eleanor_fbi_eleanor _clubs_1.pdf.

10. Claudia Goldin and Claudia Olivetti, "Shocking Labor Supply: A Reassessment of the Role of World War II on Women's Labor Supply," *American Economic Review* 103, no. 3 (2013): 257–62.

11. Joshua Zeitz, "Lessons From the Fake News Pandemic of 1942," *Politico Magazine* (March 12, 2017), https://www.politico.com /magazine/story/2017/03/lessons-from-the -fake-news-pandemic-of-1942-214898.

12. Elizabeth Gillespie McRae, "When White Segregationist Women Hated on Eleanor Roosevelt," The Daily Beast, February 16, 2018, https://www.thedailybeast.com/when -white-segregationist-women-hated-on -eleanor-roosevelt.

13. *Ibid.*

14. Matthew Delmont, "Why African-American Soldiers Saw World War II as a Two-Front Battle," *Smithsonian* (August 24, 2017), https://www.smithsonianmag.com /history/why-african-american-soldiers -saw-world-war-ii-two-front-battle -180964616/.

15. Christina Greene, *Our Separate Ways: Women and the Black Freedom Movement in Durham, North Carolina* (Chapel Hill: The University of North Carolina Press, 2005).

16. Gordon W. Allport and Leo Postman, "An Analysis of Rumor," *Public Opinion Quarterly* 10, no. 4 (1946): 501–17, http://www.jstor.org/stable/2745703.

17. The Mercury Theatre on the Air, "The War of the Worlds," October 30, 1938, radio broadcast, https://www.youtube.com /watch?v=OzC3Fg_rRJM.

18. Martin Chilton, "The War of the Worlds Panic Was a Myth," *Telegraph* (May 6, 2016), https://www.telegraph.co.uk/radio/what-to -listen-to/the-war-of-the-worlds-panic-was -a-myth/.

19. Jefferson Pooley and Michael J. Socolow, "The Myth of the *War of the Worlds* Panic," Slate, October 28, 2013, http://www.slate .com/articles/arts/history/2013/10/orson _welles_war_of_the_worlds_panic_myth _the_infamous_radio_broadcast_did.html.

20. Nina Berman, "The Victims of Fake News," *Columbia Journalism Review* (Fall 2017), https://www.cjr.org/special _report/fake-news-pizzagate-seth-rich -newtown-sandy-hook.php/.

CHAPTER 9

1. Lee McIntyre, *Post-Truth* (Cambridge, MA: The MIT Press, 2018).

2. "Beyond Any Doubt." *Time.* November 30, 1953. Philip Morris Records, https://www.industrydocuments.ucsf.edu/ tobacco/docs/#id=mmkf0164.

3. "A Brief History of Tobacco Statements," *Washington Post* (May 11, 1997), https://www.washingtonpost.com/archive /opinions/1997/05/11/a-brief-history-of -tobacco-statements/f7d5c795-4ff1-46ab -bdf2-7760338c296a/.

4. "Draft of Recommendations for Cigarette Manufacturers." December 22, 1953. http:// www.ttlaonline.com/HKWIS/0296.01.pdf.

5. Tobacco Industry Research Committee, "A Frank Statement to Cigarette Smokers," *New York Times* and other newspapers and periodicals (January 4, 1954), industrydocuments.ucsf.edu /docs/#id=zkph0129

6. Andrew Rowell and Karen Evans-Reeves, "It Was Big Tobacco, not Trump, That Wrote the Post-Truth Rule Book," The Conversation, April 7, 2017, http://theconversation.com /it-was-big-tobacco-not-trump-that-wrote -the-post-truth-rule-book-75782.

7. Tobacco Industry Research Committee, "A Frank Statement."

8. McIntyre, *Post-Truth.*

9. Thun, M J et al. "Excess mortality among cigarette smokers: changes in a 20-year interval." *American Journal of Public Health* vol. 85,9 (1995): 1223-30, doi:10.2105 /ajph.85.9.1223.

10. Philip J. Hilts, "Tobacco Company Was Silent on Hazards," *New York Times* (May 7, 1994), https://www.nytimes.com/1994/05/07 /us/tobacco-company-was-silent-on -hazards.html.

11. Marc Lacey, "Tobacco Industry Accused of Fraud in Lawsuit by U.S." *The New York Times,* September 23, 1999. https://www.nytimes .com/1999/09/23/us/tobacco-industry -accused-of-fraud-in-lawsuit-by-us.html.

12. Civil Action No. 99-2496 (GK) https://www.publichealthlawcenter.org/sites/ default/files/resources/doj-final-opinion.pdf.

13. AJ Wakefield, "Ileal-Lympoid-Nodular Hyperplasia, Non-Specific Colitis, and Pervasive Developmental Disorder in Children," *The Lancet* vol. 351, issue 9103, (February 28, 1998), https://doi.org/10.1016 /S0140-6736(97)11096-0.

14. Julia Belluz, "Research Fraud Catalyzed the Anti-Vaccination Movement. Let's Not Repeat History," Vox, updated March 5, 2019, https://www.vox.com/2018/2/27/17057990 /andrew-wakefield-vaccines-autism-study.

15. Fiebelkorn, Amy Parker et al. "A Comparison of Postelimination Measles Epidemiology in the United States, 2009–2014 Versus 2001–2008." *Journal of the Pediatric Infectious Diseases Society* vol. 6,1 (2017): 40–48. doi:10.1093/jpids/piv080.

16. Kovach and Rosenstiel, *Blur: How To Know What's True.*

17. *Ibid.*

18. Rebecca Woods, "Ghostwatch: The BBC Spoof that Duped a Nation," News, BBC, October 30, 2017, https://www.bbc.com /news/uk-england-41740176.

19. Murray Leeder, "*Ghostwatch* and the Haunting of Media," *Horror Studies* 4, no. 2 (2013).

20. Woods, "Ghostwatch."

21. Ciarán O'Keeffe, "Looking Back: The Ghost in the Living Room." *The British Psychological Society,* vol. 25, 2012. https:// thepsychologist.bps.org.uk/volume-25 /edition-11/looking-back-ghost-living-room.

22. Rebecca Hawkes, "Why Did the World Think The Blair Witch Project Really Happened?" *Telegraph* (July 25, 2016), https://www.telegraph.co.uk/films /2016/07/25/why-did-the-world-think-the -blair-witch-project-really-happened/.

CHAPTER 10

1. Vladislav M. Zubok, "Soviet Intelligence and the Cold War: The "Small" Committee of Information, 1952–53." *The Wilson Center.* Working Paper No. 4. December 1992. https://www.wilsoncenter.org/sites/default /files/ACFB84.pdf.

2. Ashley Deeks, Sabrina McCubbin, and Cody M. Poplin. "Addressing Russian Influence: What Can We Learn From U.S. Cold War Counter-Propaganda Efforts?" *Lawfare,* October 25, 2017. https:// www.lawfareblog.com/addressing-russian -influence-what-can-we-learn-us-cold-war -counter-propaganda-efforts.

3. David Robert Grimes, "Russian Fake News Is Not New: Soviet AIDS Propaganda Cost Countless Lives," *Guardian* (June 14, 2017), https://www.theguardian.com/science /blog/2017/jun/14/russian-fake-news-is -not-new-soviet-aids-propaganda-cost -countless-lives.

4. Ben Popken, "Factory of lies: Russia's disinformation playbook exposed." NBC, November 5, 2018. https://www.nbcnews .com/business/consumer/factory-lies -russia-s-disinformation-playbook -exposed-n910316.

5. "Pneumocystis Pneumonia." *Center for Disease Control.* June 5, 1981. https://www.cdc.gov/mmwr/preview/ mmwrhtml/lmrk077.htm.

6. "HIV and AIDS—United States, 1981–2000," *Morbidity and Mortality Weekly Report,* Centers for Disease Control and Prevention (June 1, 2001), https://www.cdc.gov/mmwr /preview/mmwrhtml/mm5021a2.htm.

7. Thomas Boghardt, "Operation INFEKTION: Soviet Bloc Intelligence and Its AIDS Disinformation Campaign," *Studies in Intelligence* 53, no. 4 (December 2009), https://www.cia.gov/library/center-for -the-study-of-intelligence/csi-publications /csi-studies/studies/vol53no4/pdf/U-%20 Boghardt-AIDS-Made%20in%20the%20USA- 17Dec.pdf.

8. *Ibid.*

9. *Ibid.*

10. "Soviet Disinformation: Allegations of US Misdeeds." Foreign Subversion and Instability Center, Office of Global Issues, Directorate of Intelligence, CIA, March 28, 1986. https://www.cia.gov/library /readingroom/docs/CIA-RDP86T01017 R000100620001-1.pdf.

11. "Soviet Influence Activities: A Report on Active Measures and Propaganda, 1986–87." *U.S. Department of State,* August 1987. https://www.globalsecurity.org/intell/library /reports/1987/soviet-influence-activities -1987.pdf.

12. "Thirty Years of HIV/AIDS: Snapshots of an Epidemic," amfAR, https://www.amfar .org/thirty-years-of-hiv/aids-snapshots-of -an-epidemic/.

13. *Ibid.*

14. Marko Mihkelson, "Disinformation: Russia's Old but Effective Weapon of Influence," *Diplomaatia,* no. 190/191 (June 16, 2017), https://icds.ee/disinformation -russias-old-but-effective-weapon-of -influence/.

15. "Soviet Influence Activities: A Report on Active Measures and Propaganda, 1986–87." *U.S. Department of State,* August 1987. https://www.globalsecurity.org/intell /library/reports/1987/soviet-influence -activities-1987.pdf.

16. Darryl Fears, "Study: Many Blacks Cite AIDS Conspiracy," *Washington Post* (January 25, 2005), http://www.washingtonpost.com /wp-dyn/articles/A33695-2005Jan24.html.

17. H.G. Wells, *World Brain* (Cutchogue, NY: Buccaneer Books, 1994).

18. Gil Press, "A Very Short History of the Internet and the Web," *Forbes* (January 2, 2015), https://www.forbes.com/sites /gilpress/2015/01/02/a-very-short -history-of-the-internet-and-the-web -2/#4b59051f7a4e.

19. Matthew Gray, "Measuring the Growth of the Web: June 1993 to June 1995." *MIT,* 1995. https://www.mit.edu/people/mkgray /growth/.

20. "Total Number of Websites," Internet Live Statistics. https://www.internetlivestats .com/total-number-of-websites/.

21. Kovach and Rosenstiel, *Blur: How To Know What's True.*

22. *Ibid.*

23. McIntyre, Lee. *Post-Truth.* Boston: MIT Press, 2018.

24. Kovach and Rosenstiel, *Blur: How To Know What's True.*

25. Elizabeth Grieco, "U.S. newsroom employment has dropped by a quarter since 2008, with greatest decline at newspapers." Pew Research Center. July 9, 2019. https://www.pewresearch.org/fact- tank/2019/07/09/u-s-newsroom-employment- has-dropped-by-a-quarter-since-2008/.

26. "Newspapers Fact Sheet," Journalism & Media, Pew Research Center, July 9, 2018, http://www.journalism.org/fact-sheet /newspapers/.

27. Katerina Eva Matsa and Jan Lauren Boyles, "America's Shifting Statehouse Press," Journalism & Media, Pew Research Center, July 10, 2014, http://www.journalism .org/2014/07/10/americas-shifting -statehouse-press/.

CHAPTER 11

1. Amina Arraf, "Why Am I Doing This?" *A Gay Girl in Damascus* (blog discontinued), February 21, 2011, https://web.archive .org/web/20110501081136/http:// damascusgaygirl.blogspot.com/2011/02 /why-i-am-doing-this.html.

2. Joshua Keating, "Who First Used the Term Arab Spring," Passport, *Foreign Policy*, November 4, 2011, https://foreignpolicy.com/2011/11/04/who-first-used-the-term-arab-spring/.

3. Liz Sly, "'Gay Girl in Damascus' Blogger Detained," *Washington Post* (June 7, 2011), https://www.washingtonpost.com/world/middle-east/gay-girl-in-damascus-blogger-detained/2011/06/07/AG0TmQLH_story.html.

4. *Ibid.*

5. Liz Sly, "'Gay Girl in Damascus' May Not Be Real." *Washington Post* (June 8, 2011), https://www.washingtonpost.com/world/middle-east/gay-girl-in-damascus-may-not-be-real/2011/06/08/AGZwCYMH_story.html.

6. Uri Friedman, "The Search for 'Gay Girl in Damascus' and a Stolen Photo," *Atlantic* (June 8, 2011), https://www.theatlantic.com/international/archive/2011/06/search-gay-girl-damascus-stolen-photo/351570/.

7. Eyder Peralta and Andy Carvin, "'Gay Girl in Damascus' Turns Out to Be an American Man," *The Two-Way* (blog), NPR, June 12, 2011, https://www.npr.org/sections/thetwo-way/2011/06/13/137139179/gay-girl-in-damascus-apologizes-reveals-she-was-an-american-man.

8. Kevin Young, "How to Hoax Yourself: The Case of A Gay Girl in Damascus," *New Yorker* (November 9, 2017), https://www.newyorker.com/books/page-turner/how-to-hoax-yourself-gay-girl-in-damascus.

9. Seymour, T., D. Frantsvog, and S. Kumar. "History of Search Engines." International Journal of Management & Information Systems (IJMIS), Vol. 15, no. 4, Sept. 2011, pp. 47-58, doi:10.19030/ijmis.v15i4.5799.

10. Greg Botelho and Jacque Wilson. "Thomas Eric Dunca: First Ebola death in U.S." CNN, October 8, 2014. https://www.cnn.com/2014/10/08/health/thomas-eric-duncan-ebola/index.html.

11. David Mikkelson, "Texas Town Quarantined After Family of Five Test Positive for the Ebola Virus." *Snopes*, October 14, 2014.

12. Jestin Coler, "A Former Fake News Creator on Covering Fake News." *Nieman Labs*, May 1, 2017. https://niemanreports.org/articles/a-former-fake-news-creator-on-covering-fake-news/.

13. Laura Sydell, "We Tracked Down a Fake-News Creator in the Suburbs. Here's What We Learned." NPR, November 23, 2016. https://www.npr.org/sections/alltechconsidered/2016/11/23/503146770/npr-finds-the-head-of-a-covert-fake-news-operation-in-the-suburbs.

14. PolitiFact Staff, "PolitiFact's Guide to Fake News Websites and What They Peddle," PunditFact, PolitiFact, April 20, 2017, https://www.politifact.com/punditfact/article/2017/apr/20/politifacts-guide-fake-news-websites-and-what-they/.

15. Joshua Gillin, "Fake News Claims that Walmart Bananas Have HIV Virus Are Fruitless." *PolitiFact*, February 6, 2017. https://www.politifact.com/punditfact/statements/2017/feb/06/cnnews3com/fake-news-claims-walmart-bananas-have-hiv-virus-ar/.

16. "'HIV Virus' Detected in Walmart Bananas After 10 Year Old Boy Contracts the Virus," CNNews3 (site discontinued), https://web.archive.org/web/20160402101931/http://cnnews3.com/hiv-virus-detected-walmart-bananas-10-year-old-boy-contracts-virus.

17. Caitlin Dewey, "What Was Fake on the Internet this Week: HIV Blood in Bananas and SeaWorld Whales in Plastic Bags," *Washington Post* (November 13, 2015), https://www.washingtonpost.com/news/the-intersect/wp/2015/11/13/what-was-fake-on-the-internet-this-week-hiv-blood-in-bananas-and-seaworld-whales-in-plastic-bags/?utm_term=.cde255eb6318.

18. George W. Bush for President (GWBush.com, site discontinued), http://web.archive.org/web/20000301041305/http://www.gwbush.com/.

19. George W. Bush Campaign Headquarters (bushcampaignhq.com, site discontinued), http://web.archive.org/web/19991010032850/http://www.bushcampaignhq.com/.

20. Jeff Mapua, *Understanding Memes And Internet Satire: Critical Thinking About Digital Media.* (New Jersey: Enslow Publishing, LLC, 2018).

21. Terry M. Neal, "Satirical Web Site Poses Political Test," *Washington Post* (November 29, 1999), https://www.washingtonpost.com/wp-srv/WPcap/1999-11/29/002r-112999-idx.html.

22. Ben Collins and Max Toomey, "MartinLutherKing.Org is Owned by Neo-Nazis," The Daily Beast, January 13, 2018, https://www.thedailybeast.com/martinlutherkingorg-is-owned-by-neo-nazis.

CHAPTER 12

1. Marcos Martínez, "Burned to Death Because of a Rumour on WhatsApp," News, BBC, November 12, 2018, https://www.bbc.com/news/world-latin-america-46145986.

2. Patrick J. McDonnell and Cecilia Sanchez, "When Fake News Kills: Lynchings in Mexico Are Linked to Viral Child-Kidnap Rumors," *Los Angeles Times* (September 21, 2018), https://www.latimes.com/world/la-fg-mexico-vigilantes-20180921-story.html.

3. Elizabeth Dwoskin and Annie Gowen, "On WhatsApp, Fake News is Fast—and Can Be Fatal," *Washington Post* (July 23, 2018), https://www.washingtonpost.com/business/economy/on-whatsapp-fake-news-is-fast—and-can-be-fatal/2018/07/23/a2dd7112-8ebf-11e8-bcd5-9d911c784c38_story.html.

4. Simon Kemp, "Digital Trends 2019: Every Single Stat You Need to Know About the Internet." *The Next Web*, January 30, 2019. https://thenextweb.com/contributors/2019/01/30/digital-trends-2019-every-single-stat-you-need-to-know-about-the-internet/.

5. Shearer, Elisa and Elizabeth Grieco. "Americans Are Wary of the Role Social Media Sites Play in Delivering the News." Pew Research Center, October 2, 2019. https://www.journalism.org/2019/10/02/americans-are-wary-of-the-role-social-media-sites-play-in-delivering-the-news/.

6. Darrel M. West, "How to Combat Fake News and Disinformation," Brookings, December 18, 2017, https://www.brookings.edu/research/how-to-combat-fake-news-and-disinformation/.

7. Soroush Vosoughi, Deb Roy, and Sinan Aral. "The Spread of True and False News Online." *Science*, March 9, 2018. Vol. 359, Issue 6380, pp. 1146-1151. DOI: 10.1126/science.aap9559.

8. Paris Martineau, "What Is a Bot?" *WIRED* (November 16, 2018), https://www.wired.com/story/the-know-it-alls-what-is-a-bot/.

9. "Disinformation Warfare: Understanding State-Sponsored Trolls on Twitter and Their Influence on the Web." March 4, 2019. https://arxiv.org/abs/1801.09288.

10. Tim Adams, "The Charge of the Chatbots: How Do You Tell Who's Human Online?", *The Guardian*, November 18, 2018, https://www.theguardian.com/technology/2018/nov/18/how-can-you-tell-who-is-human-online-chatbots.

11. Max Fisher, "Syrian Hackers Claim AP Hack that Tipped Stock Market by $136 Billion. Is It Terrorism?" *Washington Post* (April 23, 2013), https://www.washingtonpost.com/news/worldviews/wp/2013/04/23/syrian-hackers-claim-ap-hack-that-tipped-stock-market-by-136-billion-is-it-terrorism/.

12. David Jackson, "AP Twitter Feed Hacked; No Attack at White House," *USA Today* (April 23, 2013), https://www.usatoday.com/story/theoval/2013/04/23/obama-carney-associated-press-hack-white-house/2106757/.

13. Fisher, "Syrian Hackers Claim AP Hack."

14. Russell Goldman, "Reading Fake News, Pakistani Minister Directs Nuclear Threat at Israel," *New York Times* (December 24, 2016), https://www.nytimes.com/2016/12/24/world/asia/pakistan-israel-khawaja-asif-fake-news-nuclear.html.

15. Ministry of Defense (@Israel_MOD), "reports referred to by the Pakistani Def Min are entirely false," Twitter, December 24, 2016, 6:14 a.m., https://twitter.com/Israel_MOD/status/812662633686069248.

16. Josie Ensor, "MH17: What We Know Two Days After Malaysia Airlines Crash Over Ukraine," *Telegraph* (July 19, 2014), https://www.telegraph.co.uk/news/worldnews/europe/ukraine/10977644/MH17-what-we-know-two-days-after-Malaysia-Airlines-crash-over-Ukraine.html.

17. Terrence McCoy, "Russians Troops Fighting Ukraine? Naw. They're on 'Vacation,'" *Washington Post* (August 28, 2014), https://www.washingtonpost.com/news/morning-mix/wp/2014/08/28/russians-troops-fighting-in-ukraine-naw-just-on-vacation/.

18. Chris Brown, "Moscow Rejects Damning New Report Linking Russian Military Unit to Downing of Flight MH17," World, CBC, May 24, 2018, https://www.cbc.ca/news/world/netherlands-investigation-malaysia-flight17-russia-1.4675756.

19. Eliot Higgins, "SU-25, MH17 and the Problems with Keeping a Story Straight." *Bellingcat*, January 10, 2015. https://www.bellingcat.com/news/uk-and-europe/2015/01/10/su-25-mh17-and-the-problems-with-keeping-a-story-straight/comment-page-4/.

20. Ben Nimmo, "How MH17 Gave Birth to the Modern Russian Spin Machine," Argument, Foreign Policy, September 29, 2016, https://foreignpolicy.com/2016/09/29/how-mh17-gave-birth-to-the-modern-russian-spin-machine-putin-ukraine/.

21. Matthew Field and Mike Wright, "Russian Trolls Sent Thousands of Pro-Leave Messages on Day of Brexit Referendum, Twitter Data Reveals," *Telegraph* (October 17, 2018), https://www.telegraph.co.uk/technology/2018/10/17/russian-iranian-twitter-trolls-sent-10-million-tweets-fake-news/.

22. Fatima Tils, "The Kremlin's Many Versions of the MH17 Story." *Polygraph.info.* May 25, 2018. https://www.polygraph.info/a/kremlins-debunked-mh17-theories/29251216.html.

23. Mike Snider, "Robert Mueller Investigation: What Is a Russian Troll Farm?" *USA Today* (February 16, 2018), https://www.usatoday.com/story/tech/news/2018/02/16/robert-mueller-investigation-what-russian-troll-farm/346159002/.

24. *Ibid.*

25. Cristina Maza, "Russian Propaganda? Moscow Releases Audio Blaming Ukraine for Downing of MH17 Flight That Killed Almost 300," *Newsweek* (September 17, 2018), https://www.newsweek.com/russian-propaganda-moscow-releases-audio-blaming-ukraine-downing-mh17-flight-1124371.

CHAPTER 13

1. Faiz Siddiqui and Susan Svrluga. "N.C. Man Told Police He Went to D.C. Pizzeria with Gun to Investigate Conspiracy Theory." *Washington Post,* December 5, 2016, https://www.washingtonpost.com/news/local/wp/2016/12/04/d-c-police-respond-to-report-of-a-man-with-a-gun-at-comet-ping-pong-restaurant/.

2. Marc Fisher, John Woodrow Cox, and Peter Hermann. "Pizzagate: From Rumor, to Hashtag, to Gunfire in D.C." *Washington Post,* December 6, 2016. https://www.washingtonpost.com/local/pizzagate-from-rumor-to-hashtag-to-gunfire-in-dc/2016/12/06/4c7def50-bbd4-11e6-94ac-3d324840106c_story.html.

3. Amanda Robb, "Anatomy of a Fake News Scandal," *Rolling Stone* (November 16, 2017), https://www.rollingstone.com/politics/politics-news/anatomy-of-a-fake-news-scandal-125877/.

4. *Ibid.*

5. Craig Silverman, "How the Bizarre Conspiracy Theory Behind "Pizzagate" Was Spread," BuzzFeed News, November 4, 2016, https://www.buzzfeed.com/craigsilverman/fever-swamp-election.

6. Fake Twitter account of David Goldberg (@DavidGoldbergNY), https://web.archive.org/web/20161031040006/twitter.com/davidgoldbergny.

7. Robb, "Anatomy of a Fake News Scandal."

8. Gregor Aisch, Jon Huang, and Cecilia Kang, "Dissecting the #PizzaGate Conspiracy Theories," *New York Times* (December 10, 2016), https://www.nytimes.com/interactive/2016/12/10/business/media/pizzagate.html.

9. Robb, "Anatomy of a Fake News Scandal."

10. Cecilia Kang, "Fake News Onslaught Targets Pizzeria as Nest of Child-Trafficking," *New York Times* (November 21, 2016), https://www.nytimes.com/2016/11/21/technology/fact-check-this-pizzeria-is-not-a-child-trafficking-site.html.

11. Kathy Frankovic, "Belief in Conspiracies Largely Depends on Political Identity," *Economist*/YouGov Poll, YouGov, December 27, 2016, https://today.yougov.com/topics/politics/articles-reports/2016/12/27/belief-conspiracies-largely-depends-political-iden.

12. Paul Kane, "Hillary Clinton Attacks 'Fake News' in Post-Election Appearance on Capitol Hill," *Washington Post* (December 8, 2016), https://www.washingtonpost.com/news/powerpost/wp/2016/12/08/hillary-clinton-attacks-fake-news-in-post-election-appearance-on-capitol-hill/.

13. "Disinformation, 'Fake News' and Influence Campaigns on Twitter," Reports, Knight Foundation, October 4, 2018, https://www.knightfoundation.org/reports/disinformation-fake-news-and-influence-campaigns-on-twitter.

14. Craig Silverman. "This Analysis Shows How Viral Fake Election News Stories Outperformed Real News on Facebook. BuzzFeed News, December 16, 2016, https://www.buzzfeednews.com/article/craigsilverman/viral-fake-election-news-outperformed-real-news-on-facebook#.jepaXOx1m.

15. Dan Evon, "Pope Francis Shocks World, Endorses Donald Trump for President," Fact Checks, Snopes, July 10, 2016, https://www.snopes.com/fact-check/pope-francis-donald-trump-endorsement/.

16. David Emery and Brooke Binkowski, "Did Donald Trump Transport Stranded Troops on His Own Airplane?" Fact Checks, Snopes, October 22, 2016, https://www .snopes.com/fact-check/donald-trumps -marine-airlift/.

17. Hannah Ritchie, "Read All About It: The Biggest Fake News Stories of 2016," Media, CNBC, December 30, 2016, https://www.cnbc.com/2016/12/30/read-all-about-it-the-biggest-fake-news-stories-of-2016.html.

18. *Ibid.*

19. Tess Townsend, "The Bizarre Truth Behind the Biggest Pro-Trump Facebook Hoaxes," *Inc.* (November 21, 2016), http://www.inc.com/tess-townsend/ending-fed-trump-facebook.html.

20. Ritchie, "Read All About It."

21. *Ibid.*

22. *Ibid.*

23. Scott Shane, "From Headline to Photograph, a Fake News Masterpiece," *New York Times* (January 18, 2017), https://www.nytimes.com/2017/01/18/us/fake-news-hillary-clinton-cameron-harris.html.

24. Linda Qiu, "Donald Trump's Baseless Claims About the Election Being 'Rigged,'" Truth-O-Meter, PolitiFact, August 15, 2016, https://www.politifact.com/truth-o-meter /statements/2016/aug/15/donald-trump /donald-trumps-baseless-claims-about -election-being/.

25. "Breaking: 'Tens of Thousands' of Fraudulent Clinton Votes Found in Ohio Warehouse," *Christian Times Newspaper* (site discontinued), https://web.archive .org/web/20161002195543/ http://christiantimesnewspaper.com/breaking -tens-of-thousands-of-fraudulent-clinton -votes-found-in-ohio-warehouse/.

26. "How Does One Create a 'Fake News Masterpiece' and What Happens Next?" *All Things Considered*, NPR, January 22, 2017, https://www.npr.org/2017/01/22/511103621 /how-does-one-create-a-fake-news -masterpiece-and-what-happens-next.

27. https://twitter.com/IIIPoe /status/782240801048760321.

28. Scott, "From Headline to Photograph."

29. *Ibid.*

30. Samanth Subramanian, "Inside the Macedonian Fake-News Complex," *WIRED* (February 15, 2017), https://www.wired.com /2017/02/veles-macedonia-fake-news/.

31. *Ibid.*

32. Emma Jane Kirby, "The City Getting Rich from Fake News," News, BBC, December 5, 2016, https://www.bbc.com/news/ magazine-38168281.

33. "The Fake News Machine: Inside a Town Gearing Up For 2020." CNN. https://money .cnn.com/interactive/media/the-macedonia -story/.

34. Director of National Intelligence, "Intelligence Community Assessment: Assessing Russian Activities and Intentions in Recent US Elections," ICA 2017-01D (January 6, 2017), https://www.dni.gov/files/documents/ ICA_2017_01.pdf.

35. April Glaser, "What We Know About How Russia's Internet Research Agency Meddled in the 2016 Election," Technology, Slate, February 16, 2018, https://slate.com /technology/2018/02/what-we-know-about -the-internet-research-agency-and-how-it -meddled-in-the-2016-election.html.

36. Simon Shuster and Sandra Ifraimova. "A Former Russian Troll Explains How to Spread Fake News." *Time*, February 21, 2018. https://time.com/5168202/russia-troll-internet -research-agency/.

37. Shane, Scott and Sheera Frenkel. "Russian 2016 Influence Operation Targeted African-Americans on Social Media." *New York Times*, December 17, 2018. https://www.nytimes.com/2018/12/17/us/ politics/russia-2016-influence-campaign.html.

38. Fake Twitter account of Missouri News (@MissouriNewsUS), https://web.archive .org/web/20160517025111/twitter.com /missourinewsus.

39. Nicholas Thompson and Issie Lapowsky, "How Russian Trolls Used Meme Warfare to Divide America," *WIRED* (December 17, 2018), https://www.wired.com/story/russia -ira-propaganda-senate-report/.

40. *The Mueller Report*. https://books.google .com/books?id=viyVDwAAQBAJ&lpg.

41. Philip Bump, "Timeline: How Russian Trolls Allegedly Tried to Throw the 2016 Election to Trump," *Washington Post* (February 16, 2018), https://www.washingtonpost.com/ news/politics/wp/2018/02/16/timeline-how-russian-trolls-allegedly-tried-to-throw-the-2016-election-to-trump/.

42. Special Counsel Robert S. Mueller, III, "Report on the Investigation into Russian Interference in the 2016 Presidential Election," U.S. Department of Justice (March 2019), https://www.justice.gov/storage/report.pdf.

43. United States v. Internet Research Agency et al. Indictment (US District Court for the District of Columbia, February, 16, 2018), https://www.justice.gov/file/1035477/download.

44. *Extremist Content and Russian Disinformation Online: Working with Tech to Find Solutions, Before the United States Senate Committee on the Judiciary, Subcommittee on Crime and Terrorism*, 115th Cong. (2017) (testimony of Sean J. Edgett, Acting General Counsel, Twitter, Inc.), https://www.judiciary.senate.gov/imo/media/doc/10-31-17%20Edgett%20Testimony.pdf.

45. Craig Timberg and Tony Romm, "New Report on Russian Disinformation, Prepared for the Senate, Shows the Operation's Scale and Sweep," *Washington Post* (December 17, 2018), https://www.washingtonpost.com/technology/2018/12/16/new-report-russian-disinformation-prepared-senate-shows-operations-scale-sweep/.

46. Twitter Public Policy (@policy), "Update on Twitter's Review of the 2016 US Election," Blog, Twitter, updated January 31, 2018, https://blog.twitter.com/official/en_us/topics/company/2018/2016-election-update.html.

47. United States v. Internet Research Agency et al. Indictment (US District Court for the District of Columbia, February, 16, 2018), https://www.justice.gov/file/1035477/download.

48. Cindy Otis, "The FBI Just Indicted 13 Russians for Conspiring to Interfere With U.S. Political Processes," *Teen Vogue* (February 20, 2018), https://www.teenvogue.com/story/the-fbi-just-indicted-13-russians-for-conspiring-to-interfere-with-us-political-processes.

49. Andrew Guess, Brendan Nyhan, and Jason Reifler, "Selective Exposure to Misinformation: Evidence from the Consumption of Fake News During the 2016 U.S. Presidential Campaign," European Research Council, January 9, 2018, http://www.dartmouth.edu/~nyhan/fake-news-2016.pdf.

50. Benjy Sarlin, "'Fake News' Went Viral in 2016. This Expert Studied Who Clicked," NBC News. January 14, 2018, https://www.nbcnews.com/politics/politics-news/fake-news-went-viral-2016-expert-studied-who-clicked-n836581.

51. Don Reisinger, "Twitter Had a 'Fake News Ecosystem' Around the 2016 Election, Study Says," *Fortune* (October 4, 2018), http://fortune.com/2018/10/04/twitter-2016-election-fake-news/.

52. Trump, Donald J. Trump (@realDonaldTrump), "The FAKE NEWS media (failing @nytimes, @NBCNews, @ABC, @CBS, @CNN) is not my enemy, it is the enemy of the American People!" Twitter, February 17, 2017, 1:48 p.m., https://twitter.com/realDonaldTrump/status/832708293516632065.

53. Donald J. Trump (@realDonaldTrump), "Any negative polls are fake news, just like the CNN, ABC, NBC polls in the election. Sorry, people want border security and extreme vetting," Twitter, February 6, 2017, 4:01 a.m., https://twitter.com/realDonaldTrump/status/828574430800539648.

54. Ian Schwartz, "Trump: 'Don't Believe the Crap You See from These People on Fake News,'" RealClearPolitics, July 24, 2018, https://www.realclearpolitics.com/video/2018/07/24/trump_dont_believe_the_crap_you_see_from_these_people_on_fake_news.html.

55. "Leslie Stahl: Trump Admitted Mission to 'Discredit' Press," CBS News, May 23, 2018, https://www.cbsnews.com/news/lesley-stahl-donald-trump-said-attacking-press-to-discredit-negative-stories/.

56. "Indicators of News Media Trust," Reports, Knight Foundation, September 11, 2018, https://www.knightfoundation.org/reports/indicators-of-news-media-trust.

57. Amy B. Wang, "'Post-Truth' Named 2016 Word of the Year by Oxford Dictionaries," *Washington Post* (November 16, 2016), https://www.washingtonpost.com/news/the-fix/wp/2016/11/16/post-truth-named-2016-word-of-the-year-by-oxford-dictionaries/.

58. Alexandra Jaffe, "Kellyanne Conway: WH Spokesman Gave 'Alternative Facts' on Inauguration Crowd," NBC News, January 22, 2017, https://www.nbcnews.com/storyline/meet-the-press-70-years/wh-spokesman-gave-alternative-facts-inauguration-crowd-n710466.

59. Lauren Etter, "What Happens When the Government Uses Facebook as a Weapon?" *Bloomberg Businessweek* (December 7, 2017), https://www.bloomberg.com/news/features/2017-12-07/how-rodrigo-duterte-turned-facebook-into-a-weapon-with-a-little-help-from-facebook.

60. Alexandra Stevenson, "Soldiers in Facebook's War on Fake News Are Feeling Overrun," *New York Times* (October 9, 2018), https://www.nytimes.com/2018/10/09/business/facebook-philippines-rappler-fake-news.html.

61. Camille Elemia, "Photo Used by Duterte Camp to Hit Critics Taken in Brazil, not PH," Rappler, updated April 3, 2019, https://www.rappler.com/nation/144551-duterte-camp-brazil-photo-rape-victim-critics.

62. Clarissa Batino and Andreo Calonzo, "Philippine Journalist Facing Charges as Duterte Goes After Media," Politics, Bloomberg, November 11, 2018, https://www.bloomberg.com/news/articles/2018-11-12/media-freedom-under-attack-as-duterte-pursues-philippine-critics.

63. Shawn W. Crispin, "Mission Journal: Duterte Leads Tri-Pronged Attack on Press amid Condemnation of Controversial Policies," Blog, Committee to Protect Journalists, July 5, 2018, https://cpj.org/blog/2018/07/mission-journal-duterte-leads-tri-pronged-attack-o.php.

64. Jason Schwartz, "Trump's 'Fake News' Mantra a Hit with Despots," Media, Politico, December 8, 2017, https://www.politico.com/story/2017/12/08/trump-fake-news-despots-287129.

65. Cindy Otis, "The 'Free Press,' Explained: What It Is and How It Works," *Teen Vogue* (May 24, 2018), https://www.teenvogue.com/story/the-free-press-explained-what-it-is-and-how-it-works.

66. Jason Schwartz, "Trump's 'Fake News' Rhetoric Crops Up Around the Globe," Politico, July 31, 2018, https://www.politico.com/story/2018/07/30/trump-media-fake-news-750536.

67. Funke, Daniel and Daniela Flamini. "A Guide to Anti-Misinformation Actions Around the World." *Poynter*. https://www.poynter.org/ifcn/anti-misinformation-actions/.

68. Elana Beiser, "Hundreds of Journalists Jailed Globally Becomes the New Normal," Reports, Committee to Protect Journalists, December 13, 2018, https://cpj.org/reports/2018/12/journalists-jailed-imprisoned-turkey-china-egypt-saudi-arabia.php.

69. Megan Specia, "A Deadly Year for Journalists as Risk Shifts to the West," *New York Times* (October 11, 2018), https://www.nytimes.com/2018/10/11/world/americas/journalists-killed.html.

70. Beiser, "Hundreds of Journalists Jailed Globally."

CHAPTER 14

1. "Fact," Online Etymology Dictionary, https://www.etymonline.com/word/fact#etymonline_v_1064.

2. Amy Mitchell, Jeffrey Gottfried, Michael Barthel, and Nami Sumida, "Distinguishing Between Factual and Opinion Statements in the News," Journalism & Media, Pew Research Center, June 18, 2018, http://www.journalism.org/2018/06/18/distinguishing-between-factual-and-opinion-statements-in-the-news/.

3. Kevin Loker, "Confusion About What's News and What's Opinion Is a Big Problem, But Journalists Can Help Solve It," American Press Institute, September 19, 2018, https://www.americanpressinstitute.org/publications/confusion-about-whats-news-and-whats-opinion-is-a-big-problem-but-journalists-can-help-solve-it/.

4. "Unemployment Rate 2.1 Percent for College Grads, 4.3 Percent for High School Grads in April 2018." *Bureau of Labor Statistics*, May 10, 2018. https://www.bls.gov/opub/ted/2018/unemployment-rate-2-1-percent-for-college-grads-4-3-percent-for-high-school-grads-in-april-2018.htm?view_full.

5. Caille Millner, "Many of the Products Millennials Are Killing Deserve to Die," *San Francisco Chronicle* (December 4, 2018), https://www.sfchronicle.com/opinion/article/Many-of-the-products-Millennials-are-killing-13442886.php.

CHAPTER 15

1. Julie Beck, "This Article Won't Change Your Mind," *Atlantic* (March 13, 2017), https://www.theatlantic.com/science/archive/2017/03/this-article-wont-change-your-mind/519093/.

2. Shana Lebowitz and Allana Akhtar, "60 Cognitive Biases That Screw Up Everything We Do," *Business Insider*, updated October 15, 2019, https://www.businessinsider.com/cognitive-biases-2015-10.

3. Keise Izuma, "What Happens to the Brain During Cognitive Dissonance?" *Scientific American* (November 1, 2015), https://

www.scientificamerican.com/article/what
-happens-to-the-brain-during-cognitive
-dissonance1/.

4. Drew Westen, *The Political Brain: The Role of
Emotion in Deciding the Fate of the Nation* (New
York: PublicAffairs, 2007).

5. Julie Beck, "The Christmas the Aliens
Didn't Come," *Atlantic* (December 18, 2015),
https://www.theatlantic.com/health/archive
/2015/12/the-christmas-the-aliens-didnt
-come/421122/.

6. Vaughan Bell, "Prophecy Fail," Technology,
Slate, May 20, 2011, https://slate.com/
technology/2011/05/apocalypse-2011-what
-happens-to-a-doomsday-cult-when-the
-world-doesn-t-end.html.

7. Leon Festinger, Henry Riecken, and Stanley
Schachter, *When Prophecy Fails: A Social
and Psychological Study of a Modern Group
That Predicted the Destruction of the World*
(Minneapolis: University of Minnesota
Press, 1956).

8. Summer Allen and Jeremy Adam Smith,
"How Happy Brains Respond to Negative
Things," *Greater Good Magazine*, March 17, 2016,
https://greatergood.berkeley.edu/article/item/
how_happy_brains_respond_to_negative_
things.

9. Allie Caren, "Why We Often Remember
the Bad Better Than the Good," *Washington
Post* (November 1, 2018), https://www
.washingtonpost.com/science/2018/11/01/why-
we-often-remember-bad-better-than-good/.

10. Hara Estroff Marano, "Our Brain's Negative
Bias," *Psychology Today* (last reviewed June 9,
2016), https://www.psychologytoday.com/us
/articles/200306/our-brains-negative-bias.

11. "Carol Soon Wan Ting and Shawn Goh
Ze Song, "What Lies Beneath the Truth:
A Literature Review on Fake News, False
Information and More," Institute of Policy
Studies, June 30, 2017, https://lkyspp.nus
.edu.sg/docs/default-source/ips/report
_what-lies-beneath-the-truth_a-literature
-review-on-fake-news-false-information
-and-more_300617.pdf.

12. *Ibid.*

13. Alan Cowell, "Oscar Pistorius's Murder
Sentence Is Increased to 15 Years," *New York
Times* (November 24, 2017),
https://www.nytimes.com/2017/11/24/world/
africa/oscar-pistorius-sentence.html.

CHAPTER 16

1. William P. Eveland Jr. and Dhavan V. Shah,
"The Impact of Individual and Interpersonal
Factors on Perceived Media Bias," *Political
Psychology* 24, no. 1 (2003): 101–17, http://www
.jstor.org/stable/3792512.

2. Jack Shafer and Tucker Doherty, "The Media
Bubble Is Worse Than You Think," *Politico
Magazine* (May/June 2017),
https://www.politico.com/magazine
/story/2017/04/25/media-bubble-real
-journalism-jobs-east-coast-215048.

3. Alan D. Abbey, "Balance and Fairness,"
Ethics, Online News Association, https://ethics
.journalists.org/topics/balance-and-fairness/.

4. Glader, Paul. "10 Journalism Brands
Where You Find Real Facts Rather Than Alternative Facts." *Forbes*, February 1, 2017.
https://www.forbes.com/sites/berlinschoolofcr
eativeleadership/2017/02/01/10-journalism
-brands-where-you-will-find-real-facts-rather
-than-alternative-facts/#46d083ae9b5a.

5. Adam Nossiter and Aurelien Breeden, "Fire
Mauls Beloved Notre-Dame Cathedral in Paris,"
New York Times (April 15, 2019), https://www
.nytimes.com/2019/04/15/world/europe/notre
-dame-fire.html.

6. "Frequently Asked Questions," National
Review, https://www.nationalreview.com
/frequently-asked-questions/.

7. Editors of the *Nation*, "Ten Things You Can
Do to Help Progressive Journalism," *Nation*
(April 1, 2010), https://www.thenation.com
/article/ten-things-you-can-do-help
-progressive-journalism/.

8. Mark Landler and Helene Cooper,
"Obama Will Speed Pullout from War in
Afghanistan," *New York Times* (June 22, 2011)
https://www.nytimes.com/2011/06/23/world
/asia/23prexy.html.

9. "Obama Doesn't Thank Petraeus," Fox News,
June 22, 2011, https://nation.foxnews.com
/war-afghanistan/2011/06/22/obama-doesnt
-thank-petraeus.

10. Center for Media and Public Affairs at
George Mason University, "Media Boost
Obama, Bash His Policies," press release, April
27, 2009, https://cmpa.gmu.edu/media-boost
-obama-bash-his-policies/.

11. Daphne Leprince-Ringuet, "Iran Has Its Own Fake News Farms, but They're Complete Amateurs," *WIRED* (UK) (October 25, 2018), https://www.wired.co.uk/article/iran-fake -news.

12. Jeff Stone, "Chinese State Media Bought Twitter Ads to Spread Disinformation About Hong Kong Protests." *Cyberscoop*, August 19, 2019. https://www.cyberscoop.com/chinese -disinformation-hong-kong-protests/.

13. Alex Nowrasteh, "You Say 'Illegal Alien.' I Say 'Undocumented Immigrant.' Who's Right?" *Newsweek* (December 18, 2017), https://www. newsweek.com/you-say-illegal-alien-i-say- undocumented-immigrant-whos-right-750644.

14. *Ibid.*

CHAPTER 17

1. The Media Insight Project, "How Americans Describe Their News Consumption Behaviors," American Press Institute, June 11, 2018, https:// www.americanpressinstitute.org/publications/ reports/survey-research/americans-news- consumption/.

2. Maksym Gabielkov, Arthi Ramachandran, Augustin Chaintreau, Arnaud Legout, "Social Clicks: What and Who Gets Read on Twitter?" *ACM SIGMETRICS / IFIP Performance 2016* (June 2016).

3. *Ibid.*

4. Gregory J. Digirolamo and Douglas L. Hintzman, "First Impressions Are Lasting Impressions: A Primacy Effect in Memory for Repetitions," *Psychonomic Bulletin & Review* 4, no. 1 (March 1997): 121–24.

5. Maria Konnikova, "How Headlines Change the Way We Think," *New Yorker* (December 17, 2014), https://www.newyorker.com/science /maria-konnikova/headlines-change-way -think.

6. Alex Huntley, "Palestinians Recognize Texas as Part of Mexico," The Beaverton, December 6, 2017, https://www.thebeaverton.com/2017/12/ palestinians-recognize-texas-part-mexico/.

7. David Mikkelson, "Did Palestinians Recognize Texas as Part of Mexico?" Fact Checks, Snopes, December 7, 2017, https://www.snopes.com/fact-check/ palestinians-texas-mexico/.

8. Tim Alberta and Zack Stanton, "Senator Kid Rock. Don't Laugh," *Politico Magazine* (July 23, 2017), https://www.politico.com/magazine/ story/2017/07/23/kid-rock-run-senate-serious -michigan-analysis-215408.

9. Hunter Schwarz, "Kid Rock Announces He's Not Actually Running for Senate," Politics, CNN, October 24, 2017, https://www.cnn .com/2017/10/24/politics/kid-rock-announces -hes-not-actually-running-for-senate/index .html.

10. Caroline Wallace, "Obama Did Not Ban the Pledge," FactCheck.org, September 2, 2016, https://www.factcheck.org/2016/09/obama -did-not-ban-the-pledge/.

11. Craig Silverman, "Here Are 50 of the Biggest Fake News Hits on Facebook From 2016," BuzzFeed News, December 30, 2016, https:// www.buzzfeednews.com/article /craigsilverman/top-fake-news-of-2016# .cdnQrVqyv.

12. R. Hobbus, "President Trump Orders the Execution of Five Turkeys Pardoned by Obama," Real News Right Now, January 24, 2017, http://realnewsrightnow.com/2017/01 /president-trump-orders-execution-five -turkeys-pardoned-obama/.

13. Kim LaCapria, "Did President Trump Reverse President Obama's Turkey Pardons?" Fact Checks, Snopes, January 25, 2017, https:// www.snopes.com/fact-check/trump-turkey- pardons-reversed/.

14. Sarah Emerson, "Whitehouse.com, Your Favorite 90s Porn Site, Is Now Protesting the Trump Presidency," Motherboard, Vice, August 25, 2017. https://www.vice.com/en_us/article/ wjj4vx/whitehousecom-your-favorite-90s- porn-site-is-now-protesting-the-trump- presidency.

15. "Marco Chacon Meant His Fake Election News to Be Satire—but People Took It as Fact," Day 6, CBC Radio, November 25, 2016, https://www.cbc.ca/radio/day6/episode-313- montreal-worship-ban-protecting-syrian- schoolsjamaican-bobsleds-fake-news-and -more-1.3863764/marco-chacon-meant-his -fake-election-news-to-be-satire-but-people- took-it-as-fact-1.3863769.

16. Eugene Kiely and Lori Robertson. "How to Spot Fake News." FactCheck.org, November 18, 2016. https://www.factcheck.org/2016/11 /how-to-spot-fake-news/.

CHAPTER 18

1. Andrew Glass, "Truman Defeats Dewey, Nov. 2, 1948," Politico, November 2, 2018, https://www.politico.com/story/2018/11/02/truman-defeats-dewey-1948-950635.

2. https://www.trumanlibrary.gov/photograph=records/95-187.

3. Harry Enten, "Fake Polls Are a Real Problem," Politics, FiveThirtyEight, August 22, 2017, https://fivethirtyeight.com/features/fake-polls-are-a-real-problem/.

4. Abbas Panjwani, "How to Spot Misleading Poll Figures," Blog, Full Fact, August 3, 2018, https://fullfact.org/blog/2018/aug/how-spot-misleading-poll-figures/.

5. Jorge Buendía, "Fake Polls as Fake News: The Challenge for Mexico's Elections," Mexico Institute, Wilson Center, April 2018, https://www.wilsoncenter.org/sites/default/files/fake_news_as_fake_polls_the_challenge_for_mexicos_elections.pdf.

6. Dan Cassino, "How Today's Political Polling Works." Harvard Business Review (August 1, 2016), https://hbr.org/2016/08/how-todays-political-polling-works.

7. Aja Romano, "Boaty McBoatface and the History of Internet Naming Fiascos," Vox, May 10, 2016, https://www.vox.com/2016/5/10/11609192/boaty-mcboatface-internet-naming-poll-fails.

8. Cohn, Nate. "Exit Polls: Why They So Often Mislead." New York Times (November 4, 2014) https://www.nytimes.com/2014/11/05/upshot/exit-polls-why-they-so-often-mislead.html.

9. Andrew Gelman, "How Can a Poll of Only 1,004 Americans Represent 260 Million People with Only a 3 Percent Margin of Error?" Scientific American (March 15, 2004), https://www.scientificamerican.com/article/howcan-a-poll-of-only-100/.

10. Ibid.

11. "America's Changing Religious Landscape." Gallup. May 12, 2015. https://www.pewforum.org/2015/05/12/americas-changing-religious-landscape/.

12. Burke, Daniel. "Millennials leaving church in droves, study finds." CNN, May 14, 2015. https://www.cnn.com/2015/05/12/living/pew-religion-study/index.html.

13. Delphi Analytica, "Kid Rock Ahead in Hypothetical Matchup with Debbie Stabenow, Large Number of Voters Are Undecided," Medium, July 23, 2017, https://medium.com/@DelphiAnalytica/kid-rock-ahead-in-hypothetical-matchup-with-debbie-stabenow-large-number-of-voters-are-undecided-a982092ea12a.

14. "Most U.S. Teens See Anxiety and Depression as a Major Problem Among Their Peers," Social & Demographic Trends, Pew Research Center, February 14, 2019, https://www.pewsocialtrends.org/2019/02/20/most-u-s-teens-see-anxiety-and-depression-as-a-major-problem-among-their-peers/psdt_02-20-19_teens-00-00/.

15. Enten, "Fake Polls Are a Real Problem."

CHAPTER 19

1. Justin McCurry, "Did North Korea Photoshop Its Hovercraft?" Guardian (March 27, 2013). https://www.theguardian.com/world/2013/mar/27/north-korea-photoshop-hovercraft.

2. Aric Jenkins, "An Image of an NFL Player Burning the U.S. Flag Is Circulating on Social Media—It's Fake," Time (September 29, 2017), http://time.com/4963312/seattle-seahawks-michael-bennett-burning-american-flag-fake/.

3. Erik Wemple, "Hurricane Sandy: NYSE NOT flooded!" Washington Post, October 30, 2012. https://www.washingtonpost.com/blogs/erik-wemple/post/hurricane-sandy-nyse-not-flooded/2012/10/30/37532512-223d-11e2-ac85-e669876c6a24_blog.html.

4. Amanda Holpuch, "Hurricane Sandy Brings Storm of Fake News and Photos to New York." The Guardian, October 30, 2012. https://www.theguardian.com/world/us-news-blog/2012/oct/30/hurricane-sandy-storm-new-york.

5. Cuihua Shen, Mona Kasra, Wenjing Pan, Grace A. Bassett, Yining Malloch, and James F. O'Brien, "Fake Images: The Effects of Source, Intermediary, and Digital Media Literacy on Contextual Assessment of Image Credibility Online," New Media & Society 21, no. 2 (February 1, 2019): 438–63, https://doi.org/10.1177%2F1461444818799526.

6. Jordan Hayne, "How Fake News Can Exploit Pictures to Make People Believe Lies," News, Australian Broadcasting Corporation (ABC), updated November 21, 2018, https://www.abc.net.au/news/2018-11-22/fake-news-image-information-believe-anu/10517346.

7. Geoffrey A. Fowler, "I Fell for Facebook Fake News. Here's Why Millions of You Did, Too," *Washington Post* (October 18, 2018), https://www.washingtonpost.com/technology/2018/10/18/i-fell-facebook-fake-news-heres-why-millions-you-did-too/?utm_term=.51a21b6ace54.

8. Alex Hern, "'Deepfake' Face-Swap Porn Videos Banned by Pornhub and Twitter," *Guardian* (February 7, 2018). https://www.theguardian.com/technology/2018/feb/07/twitter-pornhub-ban-deepfake-ai-face-swap-porn-videos-celebrities-gfycat-reddit.

CHAPTER 20

1. Sapna Maheshwari, "How Fake News Goes Viral: A Case Study," *New York Times* (November 20, 2016), https://www.nytimes.com/2016/11/20/business/media/how-fake-news-spreads.html.

2. https://web.archive.org/web/20161112063335/twitter.com/erictucker.

3. Jason Silverstein, "Who Is George Soros and Why Is He Blamed in So Many Right-Wing Conspiracy Theories?" CBS News, updated October 24, 2018, https://www.cbsnews.com/news/who-is-george-soros-and-why-is-he-blamed-in-every-right-wing-conspiracy-theory/.

4. Donald J. Trump (@realDonaldTrump), "Just had a very open and successful presidential election. Now professional protesters, incited by the media, are protesting. Very unfair!" Twitter, November 10, 2016, 6:19 p.m., https://twitter.com/realDonaldTrump/status/796900183955095552.

5. Maheshwari, "How Fake News Goes Viral."

6. Michael Barthel, Amy Mitchell, and Jesse Holcomb. "Many Americans Believe Fake News Is Sowing Confusion." Pew Research Center, December 15, 2016. https://www.journalism.org/2016/12/15/many-americans-believe-fake-news-is-sowing-confusion/.

7. "Most Popular Social Networks Worldwide as of October 2019, Ranked by Number of Active Users." Statista, November 21, 2019. https://www.statista.com/statistics/272014/global-social-networks-ranked-by-number-of-users/.

8. Kristen Bialik, "14% of Americans Have Changed Their Mind About an Issue Because of Something They Saw on Social Media." Pew Research Center, August 15, 2018. https://www.pewresearch.org/fact-tank/2018/08/15/14-of-americans-have-changed-their-mind-about-an-issue-because-of-something-they-saw-on-social-media/.

9. Barbara Ortutay, "Facebook: Fake Account Removal Doubles in 6 Months to 3B," Associated Press, May 23, 2019, https://apnews.com/d276ebdec5224398b9d70a6424bdee7b.

10. "#BotSpot: How Bot-Makers Decorate Bots." *DFRLab Atlantic Council,* December 29, 2017. https://medium.com/dfrlab/botspot-how-bot-makers-decorate-bots-4d2ae35bdf26.

11. Dan Evon, "Did Melania Trump Steal Her United Nations Speech from Michelle Obama?" Fact Checks, Snopes, September 23, 2017, https://www.snopes.com/fact-check/melania-trump-united-nations-obama/.

12. David Emery, "Melania Trump Copied from Michelle Obama's 2008 Convention Speech." Snopes, July 18, 2016. https://www.snopes.com/news/2016/07/18/melania-trump-michelle-obama/.

13. Dan Evon, "Did Melania Trump Steal Her United Nations Speech from Michelle Obama?" Snopes, September 23, 2017. https://www.snopes.com/fact-check/melania-trump-united-nations-obama.

14. Mahmood Fazal, "Richard Dawkins Told Us What He Thinks About Memes," Vice, May 8, 2018, https://www.vice.com/en_us/article/d35ana/richard-dawkins-told-us-what-he-thinks-about-memes.

15. Billy Baker, "One of the Country's Biggest Publishers of Fake News Says He Did It for Our Own Good," *Boston Globe* (April 7, 2018), https://www.bostonglobe.com/metro/2018/04/07/one-country-biggest-publishers-fake-news-says-did-for-our-own-good/fzIDkkKZf7IbYA9oyGuzhI/story.html.

16. Brian Feldman, "The Fake Donald Trump Quote That Just Won't Die," *New York* (November 4, 2016), http://nymag.com/intelligencer/2016/11/the-fake-donald-trump-quote-that-just-wont-die.html.

17. Kiely, Eugene and Lori Robertson. "How to Spot Fake News." FactCheck.org, November 18, 2016. https://www.factcheck.org/2016/11/how-to-spot-fake-news/.

CHAPTER 21

1. Aja Romano, "Most People Saw the Las Vegas Shooting as a Tragedy. Propagandists Saw an Opportunity," Vox, October 5, 2017, https://www.vox.com/culture/2017/10/5/16400394/las-vegas-shooting-fake-news-propaganda.

2. Kevin Roose, "After Las Vegas Shooting, Fake News Regains Its Megaphone," *New York Times* (October 2, 2017), https://www.nytimes.com/2017/10/02/business/las-vegas-shooting-fake-news.html.

3. Sam Levin, "Facebook and Google Promote Politicized Fake News About Las Vegas Shooter," *Guardian* (October 2, 2017), https://www.theguardian.com/us-news/2017/oct/02/las-vegas-shooting-facebook-google-fake-news-shooter.

4. Broderick, Ryan. "Here Are All The Hoaxes Being Spread About The Las Vegas Shooting." BuzzFeed News, October 2, 2017. https://www.buzzfeednews.com/article/ryanhatesthis/here-are-all-the-hoaxes-being-spread-about-the-las-vegas.

5. Jack Stubbs and Christopher Bing, "Special Report: How Iran Spreads Disinformation Around the World," Reuters, November 30, 2018, https://www.reuters.com/article/us-cyber-iran-specialreport/special-report-how-iran-spreads-disinformation-around-the-world-idUSKCN1NZ1FT.

6. DarkSyn (@Mihero), "Resourceful dog walks away with bag of dog food after Hurricane Harvey. . . ." Twitter, August 26, 2017, 4:59 p.m., https://twitter.com/Mihero/status/901595065222561792.

7. Nichole Gomez ABC-7 (@NicholeEGomez), "Some El Paso emergency responders deploy to assist with Hurricane Harvey via KVIA News," Twitter, August 25, 2017, 4:59 p.m., https://twitter.com/NicholeEGomez/status/901232696902418433.

8. Margaret Browning (@Margare06824403), "Now #FakeNews Wash Post says Hurricane H is Cat 4. So sad, scaring the good people of Texas," Twitter, August 25, 2017, 4:59 p.m., https://twitter.com/Margare06824403/status/901232712400257025.

9. John Moffitt (@JohnRMoffitt), "#HoustonFlood : #Houston has greedy developers who build expensive homes in a flood plain. Every year we see a lot of cars under water," Twitter, August 27, 2017, 4:36 p.m., https://twitter.com/JohnRMoffitt/status/901951460476407810.

10. Trash Yorlang (@StartTrashTalkN), "This is what Houston flooding looked like,couldve had a yardsale #Houston #HurricaneHarvery #flooding #hurricane #weatherchannel #yardsale," Twitter, August 26, 2017, 2:45 p.m., https://twitter.com/StartTrashTalkN/status/901561341223292928.

CHAPTER 22

1. Lauren Smiley, "The College Kids Doing What Twitter Won't," *WIRED* (November 1, 2017), https://www.wired.com/story/the-college-kids-doing-what-twitter-wont/.

2. "Cal Students Develop Way to Expose Fake News Accounts, Bots on Twitter." November 4, 2017. https://sanfrancisco.cbslocal.com/2017/11/04/cal-students-expose-fake-news-accounts-bots-twitter/.

3. Kalev Leetaru, "Why Are We Still Using Century-Old Discredited Theories to Explain the Power of Social Media?" *Forbes* (April 21, 2019), https://www.forbes.com/sites/kalevleetaru/2019/04/21/why-are-we-still-using-century-old-discredited-theories-to-explain-the-power-of-social-media/#77347c5a4d75.